MISSION-BASED MARKETING

NONPROFIT LAW, FINANCE, AND MANAGEMENT SERIES

The Art of Planned Giving: Understanding Donors and the Culture of Giving by Douglas E. White

Beyond Fund Raising: New Strategies for Nonprofit Investment and Innovation by Kay Grace

Charity, Advocacy, and the Law by Bruce R. Hopkins

The Complete Guide to Nonprofit Management by Smith, Bucklin & Associates

Critical Issues in Fund Raising edited by Dwight Burlingame

Developing Affordable Housing: A Practical Guide for Nonprofit Organizations by Bennett L. Hecht

Financial and Accounting Guide for Not-for-Profit Organizations, Fifth Edition by Malvern J. Gross, Jr., Richard F. Larkin, Roger S. Bruttomesso, John J. McNally, Price Waterhouse LLP

Financial Empowerment: More Money for More Mission by Peter C. Brinckerhoff

Financial Management for Nonprofit Organizations by Jo Ann Hankin, Alan Seidner and John Zietlow

Financial Planning for Nonprofit Organizations by Jody Blazek

Fund-Raising: Evaluating and Managing the Fund Development Process by James M. Greenfield

Fund-Raising Fundamentals: A Guide to Annual Giving for Professionals and Volunteers by James M. Greenfield

Fund-Raising Regulation: A State-by-State Handbook of Registration Forms, Requirements, and Procedures by Seth Perlman and Betsy Hills Bush

Grantseeker's Toolkit: A Comprehensive Guide to Finding Funding by Cheryl S. New and James Quick

Innovative Nonprofit Management by Christine Letts, Allen Grossman, and William Ryan

Intermediate Sanctions: Curbing Nonprofit Abuse by Bruce R. Hopkins and D. Benson Tesdahl

International Guide to Nonprofit Law by Lester A. Salamon and Stefan Toepler & · Associates

The Law of Fund-Raising, Second Edition by Bruce R. Hopkins

The Law of Tax-Exempt Healthcare Organizations by Thomas K. Hyatt and Bruce R. Hopkins

The Law of Tax-Exempt Organizations, Sixth Edition by Bruce R. Hopkins

The Legal Answer Book for Nonprofit Organizations by Bruce R. Hopkins

The Legal Answer Book for Nonprofit Organizations, Volume II by Bruce R. Hopkins

A Legal Guide to Starting and Managing a Nonprofit Organization, Second Edition by Bruce R. Hopkins

Managing Affordable Housing: A Practical Guide to Creating Stable Communities by Bennett L. Hecht, Local Initiatives Support Corporation, and James Stockard

Managing Upstream: Creating High-Performance Nonprofit Organizations by Christine W. Letts, William P. Ryan, and Allan Grossman

Mission-Based Management: Leading Your Not-for-Profit Into the 21st Century by Peter C. Brinckerhoff

Mission-Based Marketing: How Your Not-for-Profit Can Succeed in a More Competitive World by Peter C. Brinckerhoff

Nonprofit Boards: Roles, Responsibilities, and Performance by Diane J. Duca

Nonprofit Compensation and Benefits Practices by Applied Research and Development
Institute International, Inc.
The Nonprofit Counsel by Bruce R. Hopkins
The Nonprofit Guide to the Internet by Robbin Zeff
Nonprofit Investment Policies: A Practical Guide to Creation and Implementation by
Robert Fry, Jr.
The Nonprofit Law Dictionary by Bruce R. Hopkins
Nonprofit Employment Law: Compensation, Benefits, and Regulation by David G.
Samuels and Howard Pianko
Nonprofit Litigation: A Practical Guide with Forms and Checklists by Steve Bachmann
The Nonprofit Handbook, Second Edition: Volume I—Management by Tracy Daniel
Connors
The Nonprofit Handbook, Second Edition: Volume II—Fund Raising by Jim Greenfield
The Nonprofit Manager's Resource Dictionary by Ronald A. Landskroner
Nonprofit Organizations' Business Forms: Disk Edition by John Wiley & Sons, Inc.
Partnerships and Joint Ventures Involving Tax-Exempt Organizations by Michael I.
Sanders
Planned Giving: Management, Marketing, and Law by Ronald R. Jordan and Katelyn L.
Quynn
Private Foundations: Tax Law and Compliance by Bruce R. Hopkins and Jody Blazek
Program Related Investments: A Technical Manual for Foundations by Christie I Baxter
Reengineering Your Nonprofit Organization: A Guide to Strategic Transformation by
Alceste T. Pappas
Reinventing the University: Managing and Financing Institutions of Higher Education by
Sandra L. Johnson and Sean C. Rush, Coopers & Lybrand, L.L.P.
*Strategic Communications for Nonprofit Organizations: Seven Steps to Creating a
Successful Plan* by Janel Radtke
Strategic Planning for Nonprofit Organizations: A Practical Guide and Workbook by
Michael Allison and Jude Kaye, Support Center for Nonprofit Management
Streetsmart Financial Basics for Nonprofit Managers by Thomas A. McLaughlin
A Streetsmart Guide to Nonprofit Mergers and Networks by Thomas A. McLaughlin
Successful Marketing Strategies for Nonprofit Organizations by Barry J. McLeish
The Tax Law of Charitable Giving by Bruce R. Hopkins
The Tax Law of Colleges and Universities by Bertrand M. Harding
*Tax Planning and Compliance for Tax-Exempt Organizations: Forms, Checklists,
Procedures, Second Edition* by Jody Blazek
*The Universal Benefits of Volunteering: A Practical Workbook for Nonprofit
Organizations, Volunteers and Corporations* by Walter P. Pidgeon, Jr.
The Volunteer Management Handbook by Tracy Daniel Connors

For my wife and best friend,
Christine Hargroves Brinckerhoff,
In a life filled with blessings,
you are the one for which I am most thankful.

MISSION-BASED MARKETING

How Your Not-for-Profit Can Succeed
in a More Competitive World

Peter C. Brinckerhoff

JOHN WILEY & SONS, INC.
New York • Chichester • Weinheim • Brisbane • Singapore • Toronto

Published by John Wiley & Sons, Inc.

Published simultaneously in Canada.

This publication is designed to provide accurate and authoritative information in regard to the subject matter covered. It is sold with the understanding that the publisher is not engaged in rendering legal, accounting, or other professional services. If legal advice or other expert assistance is required, the services of a competent professional person should be sought.

Library of Congress Cataloging-in-Publication Data:

Brinckerhoff, Peter C., 1952–
    Mission-based marketing : how your not-for-profit can succeed in a
more competitive world / Peter C. Brinckerhoff.
       p.   cm.—(Nonprofit law, finance, and management series)
    Originally published: Dillon, Colo. : Alpine Guild, c1997.
    Includes bibliographical references and index.
    ISBN 0-471-29693-7 (cloth : alk. paper)
    1. Nonprofit organizations—Marketing.   I. Title.   II. Series.
HG5415.B667   1998
658.8—dc21   98-25937
                                          CIP

Printed in the United States of America.
10 9 8 7 6 5 4 3 2 1

Acknowledgments

When you sit down to write your third book, you begin to get the idea that you know what you are doing and can handle the task at hand. You are wrong, or at least I was. Yet again, I have many important people to thank for bringing this project to completion.

The main recipients of my gratitude are the staff and volunteers of the not-for-profits whose examples bring so much life and credibility to the ideas found in the following pages. Any good consultant learns while he or she teaches, and I like to think that all of my training and publications are a way of sharing what I have learned. It is certainly true here.

And again, I need to thank my friend, counselor, editor, and publisher, Bob Follett, for making literary lemonade from writing that I am sure had a sour taste at first reading. Bob has a never-ending optimism coupled with a keen sense of what makes a book truly valuable to a reader. If you find this book readable and practical, thank Bob. I have, but I can't do it enough.

Peter Brinckerhoff

About the Author

Peter Brinckerhoff is an internationally renowned trainer, author, and consultant to not-for-profit organizations. A former board member of local, state, and national not-for-profits, he brings years of experience in the field to his work, and has served on the staff and as executive director of two regional not-for-profits. Since the 1982 founding of his consulting firm, Corporate Alternatives, Mr. Brinckerhoff has helped thousands of organizations become more mission-capable.

Peter's list of national clients include the YMCA of the USA, The National Rural Health Association, The Association of Baptist Foundations, The Lutheran Financial Management Association, The Nonprofit Management Association, National Industries for the Severely Handicapped, the National Association of Schools for Exceptional Children, the American Society of Association Executives, and the National Association for the Deaf.

Peter has over 60 articles published in the not-for-profit press, including *Nonprofit World*, *Contributions*, *Strategic Governance*, *Grantsmanship Center News*, and *Association Management.* He is on the editorial boards of *Strategic Governance and Nonprofit Management Review*, and is a regular contributor to the international *Journal of Nonprofit and Voluntary Sector Marketing.*

Peter is the author of the 1994 and 1996 award-winning books, *Mission-Based Management* and *Financial Empowerment,* published by John Wiley & Sons. His third book, *Mission-Based Marketing* has just been published. *Mission-Based Management* and *Financial Empowerment* are used as texts in undergraduate and graduate programs in not-for-profit management at over 60 colleges and universities.

Peter received his Bachelor of Arts Degree from the University of Pennsylvania and his Master's Degree in Public Health Administration from Tulane University. He lives in Springfield, Illinois with his wife, three children, and a Labrador Retriever.

1. Introduction

OVERVIEW

More competition. A competitive environment. The free market. An open market. Market-based pricing. Managed care. These terms are showing up more and more in the literature of the not-for-profit world. But what do they mean to you, your staff, your board, and the people that your not-for-profit serves? And, more importantly, how does your organization fit, survive, and, yes, prosper in an increasingly competitive environment?

This book will show you how to react, respond, and reshape your organization into one that competes successfully in this new era of not-for-profit management. How? By becoming market-oriented while remaining mission-based. By using the well-established and time-tested methods of marketing to do more mission. By treating everyone who interacts with your organization like valued customers. By developing a team approach to marketing where customer satisfaction is everyone's job. By asking customers what they want and trying your best to give it to them.

In this initial chapter, we will look at why your world is "going competitive" and what the linkage is between competition and marketing. We'll look at who this book is written for (the target audience). I'll show you the benefits of reading this book, and of investing your time with me. Finally, I'll give you a brief preview of each of the remaining chapters of the book so that you will have an overview of everything we will cover.

There is no rocket science in the following pages. But there are scores of solid, practical ideas on how to bring your organization into a competitive frame of mind that will keep it in business in the 21st Century. In the chapters that follow, you will learn why marketing is fundamental to being competitive — and staying in operation. You will view a marketing cycle and see how it can be adapted to your organization. You will learn how to identify and keep close to your customers, and how to identify and keep tabs on your competitors. We'll walk through the key elements of incredible customer service and show you applications for your customers.

Marketing is not a discrete event with a beginning and an end. It is a continuing process, a cycle that becomes a discipline, part of your culture. To develop that culture may take months or even years in your organization, or it may be a very short journey. It will depend on your staff, your board, your funders, your community, but most of all on you, the reader. You will be the one who will have the tools to help the others cross the bridge from your current position to being market-oriented. It's a lot of work, but well worth it for your organization, your community, and to the people you serve.

A. YOU ARE NOW IN A COMPETITIVE WORLD

Throughout the not-for-profit community, the tide is changing. And, like tides, the changes at first are barely noticeable, and more evident on some parts of the shoreline than others. But once the tide changes, the momentum is reversed and the outcome is irreversible. The forces at play are too big, too powerful, too global to resist.

In the not-for profit world, the tide has changed and the trend is inexorably, irreversibly moving toward competition, toward free markets, and away from monopolies and restricted markets. Governments, particularly at the state and local levels, have discovered that competition works in the not-for-profit world, and that freeing up this part of the economy produces lower cost and better services just as in other sectors. And, like other transitions from a restricted market to a free market, it always produces a market shakeout: some organizations don't survive because they cannot adjust and compete. Will your organization be a competitor or a footnote in history?

I need to digress here for a moment. During the 40 years we were spending trillions of dollars fighting and ultimately winning the Cold War to keep the world safe for democracy and capitalism, we prevented our not-for-profit sector from benefiting from the open market. We had one of each kind of human services or arts entity in each community and kept others out by not funding them.

● **FOR EXAMPLE:** Look at how we name our not-for-profits; the Adams County Mental Health Center, Springfield Chamber Orchestra, Denver Association of Retarded Citizens, Sacramento Animal Shelter. In our very names, we declare a geographic monopoly for these groups; and local donors, and then United Ways and other funding entities keep out competition under the excuse of "duplication of service."

When you think about it, this is not only incredible, it is also very patronizing and demeaning to the staff and boards of not-for-profits. It says, "We know you are nice folks, but you aren't very good managers and so you can't play by the same rules the rest of us do (the free market). But we need your services, so we'll protect you."

In fact, in all of the major not-for-profit arenas — the arts, research, the environment, human services, education, religion, and associations — only three areas are completely unfettered by this shackle of restricted markets: religion, private (most often higher) education, and associations. The best example of diverse organizations meeting the diverse needs of the population is churches. With no restrictions on size, location, theology, or services, religion has become a truly diversified "industry," with an order and denomination (or "flavor" as my minister puts it) for everyone. Churches are free to compete, and many choices have evolved. But not in the arts or in most human services where most of the government money is spent. These groups have been protected, and at a high price.

But this protection is eroding as governments, stuck in a perpetual budget crunch, try to find new methods of paying for more social and educational services being demanded by citizens.

Part of this evolution is showing up in the outsourcing or privatizing of traditional government services, such as the operation of prisons or even public schools. As those actions become more and more accepted, government funders have taken another look at how they currently fund the original "outsourcers," not-for-profit groups. The funders have realized that they can get more for less by encouraging competition to enter previously sacrosanct areas and, as long as their standards for quality are high, that this should be a win-win-win situation.

● **FOR EXAMPLE:** In Massachusetts, providers of services to adults with disabilities used to get calls from the state saying, "We are going to send you George (or Nancy or Bob) as a client." Just because the organization was there, as long as they did satisfactory work, they got more people to care for. Not any more. Now the organizations must bid against other not-for-profit providers to demonstrate both their service and financial competitiveness to "receive" the client. In Indiana, for-profit providers of residential services are encouraged to bid against not-for-profits.

● **FOR EXAMPLE:** The federal government, long a bastion of continuing contracts, is now bidding out more and more work, particularly in the human services area. They are looking more at outcomes than at process, and are allowing for-profits and not-for-profits to bid on work that used to be set aside solely for not-for-profits.

● **FOR EXAMPLE:** In Indiana, residential services for people with mental disabilities are now offered by the bidding process, and for-profits as well as not-for-profits can bid on the work. Up until just a few years ago, only not-for-profits were allowed to bid.

● **FOR EXAMPLE:** Ask any development officer of any organization whether the fund-raising arena is more or less competitive, more or less outcome-based, more or less driven by the needs and wants of the funder. Their answer will be a resounding "MORE!" I recently saw an article that noted that the ratio of corporate dollars applied for to those granted went from 1,500:1 in 1985 to 13,000:1 in 1995. Certainly the foundation staff that I know are deluged with applications from types of organizations that they had not even heard of five years ago.

This trend, from a taxpayer's view and a donor's view, is good. We get more services, often of better quality, for less money. But from the viewpoint of your not-for-profit, how does it look? Scary? Exciting? Dangerous? Like an opportunity?

Probably some of each. If your organization is not market-centered, not ready for competition, probably the danger and fear are predominant. By reading this book and applying the ideas and techniques you will find here, you can turn adversity into opportunity, and improve your organization's mission capability.

B. WHO THIS BOOK IS WRITTEN FOR

This book is written for the leaders — management and board members — of not-for-profit organizations of all types. Whether your organization is in human services, environmental action, the arts, education, religion, or an association, this book has something for you.

Your organization needs to be more market-oriented. For many entities, that requires a culture change. Such changes are only initiated at the board and senior management level. And, changes of such importance need to be coached consistently over time to take hold. They need to be coached by board members and senior staff.

But, such cultural change will not be successful unless everyone in the culture adopts the new ideas, the new philosophy. As you will read over and over, marketing and competition are *team* sports, and when one person doesn't play well the entire team loses. It is essential that the key ideas in this book be transmitted to the entire team. As a former staff member, executive director, and board member of local, state, and national not-for-profits, I try to provide ideas for all levels of your organization, not just for the executive director or solely for the board. I believe that a strong marketing effort is put forth by a team — one consisting of line staff, senior management, boards, and volunteers — since the more people that can understand the ideas presented here, the easier and faster it will be to implement them.

The book is designed to give you practical advice on how to move your organization as an entire team toward a market-based philosophy. To help you, I have included dozens of real-world examples (that can be found by looking for the "● FOR EXAMPLE" tag), and specific applications for you to apply, in some cases, the same day you read them (that can be found by looking for the "☞ HANDS-ON" tag). At the end of each chapter, I have added two more areas to help you. First, after the RECAP, there is a brief index of all the "☞ HANDS-ON" contained in the chapter to help you find them more easily when you refer back to the book. To get more immediate use out of the book, there is also a list of "**DISCUSSION QUESTIONS**" that focus on the key points of the chapter. These questions are intended to help you lead a team forum to generate discussion about the important issues raised in the book, and to help decide which ideas you can use right away, which will take some time, and which may not be appropriate for your organization.

C. THE BENEFITS OF READING THIS BOOK

By buying and reading this book, I know that you are making an investment of time and money. So what are the benefits of that investment? What will accrue to your organization? *I guarantee that you will get at least the following benefits from this book:*

➡ An understanding of why marketing is so crucial to being a mission-based organization.

➡ An understanding of why marketing is so important to your continued competitiveness.

➡ An understanding of what the marketing cycle is and how your existing and future services and customers fit into it.

➡ A series of methods to help you and your staff treat everyone like a customer.

➡ A clear understanding of the difference between needs and wants, that is crucial to a competitive organization.

➡ Knowledge about the best ways to develop and conduct surveys and focus groups.

➡ An understanding of how and why to write a marketing plan.

➡ New insights on ways to improve your marketing materials and focus them on your many markets.

➡ An understanding, perhaps for the very first time, of who your markets really are.

➡ A list of ways to provide excellent customer service.

➡ Ideas on how to get all board and staff involved on your marketing team.

By the time you finish reading this book you should have an excellent hands-on understanding of marketing, competition, and your role on the marketing team.

To get the most from this book, or from any management text, I strongly recommend that you read it as a team of board and staff. By team reading, team discussion, and team application, there is a much higher likelihood that the ideas included here will get implemented. That is why I have included the DISCUSSION QUESTIONS at the end of each chapter. Have your staff read the book, and then use the questions to generate a healthy discussion that leads to action.

D. PREVIEW OF THE BOOK

So now you know why you need to read the book, and what benefits will accrue to you because of your investment of time and money. Now let's look at how the book is organized and then at a brief summary of each chapter.

The book is divided into two major areas. The first five chapters are about philosophy. They aim to get you to change your ideas about the intersection of marketing, competition, and your not-for-profit. These chapters contain the big concepts, as well as some hands-on ideas for developing needed change in your organization.

Beginning with Chapter 6, we get into the more technical aspects of marketing and competition, including your markets, your competition, ways to ask, methods of improving your marketing materials, customer service, and developing a marketing plan. These seven chapters are the "how-to" part of the book, where I offer specific ideas to help you embrace the concepts provided in the first five chapters.

There are also three appendices that include samples of a Strengths,

Weaknesses, Opportunities, Threats (SWOT) analysis, a sample survey, and a sample of focus group questions.

Let's look at the chapters in more detail.

Chapter 1: Introduction

This is the chapter you are now reading. It provides an overview of the purpose and contents of the book.

Chapter 2: Marketing: The Competitive Edge

In this chapter, we will review why good, consistent marketing is a competitive edge. We will first look at the six characteristics of not-for-profits that are truly competitive. You will see that competitive organizations consistently meet customers *wants,* not just their *needs.* You will get useful ideas on how to treat everyone (including your funders) like valued customers. We'll also take an initial look at how your organization can be better than your competition. Finally, we'll explore why marketing is truly a team effort and show you some ways to bring everyone in your organization onto that team.

Chapter 3: Moving from a Monopoly to a Market-Driven Organization

You are convinced you must move your organization into a new, more competitive era. But how do you bring the rest of the staff and board along? This chapter will give you some tools to motivate staff and board, and will reiterate the six *mission* benefits of becoming and remaining market-driven and customer-oriented. Also included are suggestions for building a marketing culture for the long term.

Chapter 4: Being Mission-Based *and* Market-Driven

At some point your organization will be faced with a dilemma: follow the mission or follow the market. What do you do? This chapter will deal with ways to decide on the best path for your organization, as well as for your own personal ethics and values. The chapter will cover how to move with the markets but maintain your mission. I'll also show you how to delineate and then use core values to make staying on track easier.

Chapter 5: Being Flexible: Changing with the Market

Flexibility is the key to marketing and competitive success. The wants of your markets will change—in unpredictable ways and not always on your schedule. This chapter will show you why you need to stay flexible. It will provide some examples of the pace of change in the market, show you seven workable methods of becoming a change agent in your organization, and identify the ways that you can retain your organizational flexibility.

Chapter 6: The Marketing Cycle for a Not-For-Profit

The cycle for marketing, like a circle, has no end, and it starts at a place that may surprise you. This chapter will show you in detail the proper sequence for marketing, and will also go through the marketing cycle of competitors. Additionally, we will review the biggest barrier that may stand in your way to becoming a competitive marketer: the marketing disability of most not-for-profit staff.

Chapter 7: Who Are Your Markets?

In order to serve the many markets of your organization, you need to first know who they are. This chapter will take you through the surprising process of market identification, and then will show you how to segment those markets and decide which segments you want to pursue most avidly. Once that is accomplished it will then be time for you to select and focus on target markets. The discussion here will show you how. Finally, we'll make sure that you, your staff, and board all understand why *all* of your markets (even your funders) should be treated like valued customers.

Chapter 8: Who Are Your Competitors?

In addition to identifying your markets, you need to identify who — other than your organization — is going after those markets. This chapter will show you how to identify and continually monitor your competition. Then, we will review ways for you to focus on your core competencies so that you can successfully compete.

Chapter 9: Asking Your Markets What They Want

You need to give your markets what they want, within the constraints of your mission and marketing strategies. But you can't know what they want until you ask them. This chapter will cover asking in detail, including surveys, focus groups, informal asking (and common mistakes), and what to do after you ask. Additionally, you will learn how to ask your customers for key information about your competitors.

Chapter 10: Better Marketing Materials

You have many different markets. It makes little sense to have only one or two pieces of marketing material. It makes even less sense to have those marketing pieces focus on your services rather than on your customers' problems. This chapter will show you some specific ideas on how to improve your marketing material, seven things to include in your material, seven things to *avoid* in your material, and ways to customize your materials for various markets.

Chapter 11: Incredible Customer Service

When you have attracted people to your organization, you need to keep them. Attracting and retaining customers requires top-notch customer service. This chapter will reiterate the three core rules of customer service, show you how to empower all your staff to solve customer's problems *now*, provide you eight ways to do better customer contact, and show you tried and true methods of turning your customers into referral sources.

Chapter 12: The Marketing Planning Process

Like other key functions, marketing should be planned, with strategies, goals, and objectives. This chapter will show you how to develop your marketing team, how to plan your asking, and how to target your marketing, and it will provide an outline that you can use as you develop your organization's marketing plan.

RECAP

In this initial chapter, we discussed the more competitive world that your not-for-profit is now entering. We presented ways to get the most from the remainder of the book and previewed the chapters for you.

There is no question that marketing and competition go hand in hand. If you don't know who your customers are, how can you find out what they want? If you don't know what they want, how can you attract and keep them as customers? And you fail the competitive test without customers!

The challenge for you is to bring your organizational culture into a competitive and market-driven world. A culture with this outlook is critical—essential to your success and to survival. For a variety of valid historical reasons this culture change may not yet have occurred in your organization. This book will help you to lead that change.

2. Marketing: The Competitive Edge

OVERVIEW

You have already read in Chapter 1 about the changing, increasingly competitive world that your not-for-profit organization will be working in for the remainder of your career. If you work for an organization that you consider competitive now, how can you stay ahead of the competition? If, as you look objectively at your organization, you do not see a competitive player, what do you do?

The answer to both questions is: you market. At its most fundamental level, marketing is the competitive edge for both for-profits and not-for-profits, and this chapter will start you on your journey to becoming a mission-based *and* market-driven not-for-profit manager.

Chapter Thumbnail
> ➡ **The Characteristics of a Market-Driven Not-For-Profit**
> ➡ **Meeting Customer Wants**
> ➡ **Treating Everyone Like A Customer**
> ➡ **Being Better Than Your Competition**
> ➡ **A Team Effort**

We'll begin with the six characteristics of market-driven, mission-based organizations. These six characteristics will allow you to look at your organization and perhaps see some potential weak points that you can focus on as you read the remainder of the book. They are drawn from my experience with successful not-for-profits in all parts of the not-for-profit sector.

10

After we lay that groundwork, we will look at the difference between meeting needs and wants. You will see a number of examples of how not-for-profits are working hard to gear their services to wants, not needs. Then, we'll go over tried-and-true methods of treating everyone, including your funders, like valued customers. I will debunk one of the worst marketing maxims ever foisted on us, and show you a much more useful slogan to adopt. Your attitude, and more importantly, your staff attitude toward service recipients as customers is absolutely essential to your organizational success.

Next we'll turn to ways to be better than your competition, and give you a first glimpse of how your competition views you and ways to measure yourself against competitors. Finally, I will show you how to start bringing everyone onto the marketing team. Marketing is everyone's job, not just the executive director's or the public relations manager.

By the time you finish this chapter, you will have an initial understanding of the principles that will be presented in the remainder of the book:

- That good marketers mcct wants, not needs.
- That competitive organizations must market aggressively.
- That every one of the people in every one of your markets deserves and needs to be treated like a customer.
- And that everything everyone does in your organization is marketing — everyone is on the team.

A. THE CHARACTERISTICS OF A MARKET-DRIVEN NOT-FOR-PROFIT

So where do I want you to end up? How do I want your organization to eventually look? What comprises a market-driven, and still mission-based, organization? Let's look at the characteristics of not-for-profits that are successful at this difficult and challenging mix of high priorities. The six characteristics below work together as a comprehensive whole. Don't delude yourself into thinking that if you pick 1, 3, and 5 that you will be okay. You won't. You need to move toward complete implementation of *all* of the six.

Not-for-profits that are successful at marketing:

1. Know Their Markets: They realize that their markets extend beyond just the people that they currently serve. They identify, quantify, and target the markets that they want to serve and can serve well.

2. Treat Everyone Like a Customer: Funders, board, staff, and people that receive services are all thought of and treated like customers. Customer service and rapid response are high priorities.

3. Have Everyone on the Marketing Team: They work to develop the attitude that everyone, every staff person and every volunteer, is crucial to the success of the organization's marketing, its customer service, and its competitive edge.

4. Ask, Ask, Ask, and Then Listen: Successful organizations shape their services to meet customer wants, and they are constantly asking customers to stay in tune with how those wants change and develop.

5. Innovate Constantly: To respond to changing market conditions and customer wants, these organizations are extremely flexible, with staff and board encouraged to take reasonable risks on behalf of the people that they serve.

6. Don't Fear the Competition: These organizations focus on their customers' wants and on providing the best possible service. They spend little time worrying about competition.

How do you feel your organization meets these benchmarks? If you feel pretty good about where you are, great! You will learn some excellent techniques about how to turbocharge your organization in the coming pages. If you feel that you don't measure up as well as you would like, don't despair! All of the characteristics will be addressed in the remainder of the book with hands-on suggestions for you to implement.

B. MEETING CUSTOMER WANTS

As I hope you have noticed, I repeatedly use the term "wants" instead of "needs" when describing the target of your marketing interest. Why have I done that? Because there is a *huge* difference between needs and wants. You may need to rethink your traditional view of working to meet customer's needs. What you must target is their *wants*.

Let me describe the difference between needs and wants. We all have needs: to sleep, eat, breathe, work, socialize. We also have wants: chocolate, new clothes, time with our family, a new job. What is the difference? People *have* needs. People *seek* wants. There is no more fundamental, no more important foundation for successful marketing than those six words: *People have needs, people seek wants.* Let's look at some examples of what I mean, both for wants and needs.

● **FOR EXAMPLE:** If you have ever had a friend, family member, or employee who abused alcohol or drugs to a point of becoming dysfunctional, you know that this person *needed* treatment, often intense and immediate treatment, long before they *wanted* it. In fact, everyone around them, friends, family, employers, neighbors, all knew what was *needed*. But as long as the abuser didn't *want* help, he or she wouldn't seek help. A sad example, but one that is played out every day in nearly every community.

● **FOR EXAMPLE:** We all need water to survive. In the United States most of us get our drinking water from municipal water treatment systems or, in rural areas, from wells. Some systems have "hard" water, some "soft." But nearly all our water is safe to drink, and while the taste varies widely from system to system (as a frequent traveler I can attest to this fact), neither medical nor safety reasons mandate or even suggest that we avoid our tap water.

So why the incredible popularity of bottled water? This product is expensive, unneeded, but yet obviously *wanted* by millions of American consumers, so much so that the product now comes not only in over 20 brands, but in five or six primary sizes and innumerable flavors. It's a case study in *wants* surmounting *needs*.

● **FOR EXAMPLE:** Think for a moment of a chocolate milk shake. Who needs one? Nobody. Who wants one? Millions of us, enough so that every major fast-food chain carries them, and in many flavors and varieties other than chocolate.

● **FOR EXAMPLE:** I may have a need for transportation to school or work. But I decide from many choices which method of transportation I will purchase. Car, truck, van, bus, motorcycle, or even roller-blades. And within those choices are many makes and models. I have a need, but I *buy* what I want.

I'm sure that you can come up with your own examples by the dozens of how people have wants that are not really needs, but that they are willing to pay serious money for. Now, what can you do to meet your customer's wants? How can you be competitive with other providers of services like yours or competitive for each donated or earned dollar?

First, you ask. The biggest mistake people make in this area is saying "I've been in this business 20 years and I know what customers want." Wrong. No one knows what any customer wants until he or she asks. You need to develop a culture of asking, and this cultural shift is so important that we will spend an entire chapter on ways to ask, when to ask, and how to ask.

Second, you listen. Then you try to meet as many wants as you can.

This may mean providing services at new times, in different places, in new settings, in different languages. Let's look at some examples:

● **FOR EXAMPLE:** Churches throughout the United States are developing more and more "family night" activities as well as expanded youth activities, and building the buildings to house them. Particularly popular are open gym times, volleyball and basketball leagues, family aerobics, and other family activities. What wants do these activities meet? They address the want of parents for a safe environment for their kids as well as a common ground for planned family interaction and time. Usually these activities have little if any religious overtone or content other than the location. Church and non-church members are usually welcome. The benefit for the church is straightforward: by meeting a want in the community they get people inside their facilities where inevitably some will take an interest and join the congregation.

● **FOR EXAMPLE:** Museums and zoos are providing classroom "experiences" for elementary, junior high, and high schools. These traveling "road shows" expose students to art, history, archeology, and zoology in their schools. The wants met? Enhancements to the traditional curriculum without the cost (in both time and transportation) of a field trip. The benefits? Often the organizations are paid for this type of work, and some kids get interested enough in the museum or zoo to talk their parents into a visit.

How did these organizations find out what their customers wanted? They asked, they observed, they read aggressively, they watched their competition, as well as observing organizations that were not competing with them, and then they asked again. What they didn't do was assume that they *knew what people wanted or, worse, what people <u>needed</u>.*

This brings up an interesting and important point. It is not unusual for a not-for-profit employee to know quite well what a patient, student, client, or other customer needs. After all, their training and experience prepared them for this. And, they may have a moral and professional responsibility to see that the customer gets what they need. Doesn't this negate the principle that you give people what they want? Not at all: both the want of the customer and the responsibility of the professional can be met.

● **FOR EXAMPLE:** A psychologist has a patient that has been evidencing more and more erratic and sometimes self-abusive be-havior. The standard medications and outpatient therapies are obviously not working, and the psychologist's professional opinion is that the patient *needs* inpatient treatment for weeks if not months. Without the treatment, the patient may become suicidal, or violent toward others. But the patient is an adult and can choose to be admitted or not to be admitted. And, at this point, he doesn't *want* to go into a treatment facility.

What should the psychologist do? All the professional knowledge of *need* is powerless in the face of the ability of the patient to follow his *wants*. But the psychologist does not turn away. She works to convince the patient that he *wants* to go into the facility. She does her best to turn the *need* into a *want*. By doing this, she is using an age-old marketing technique, the one that convinces people that they really want a product or, in this case, a service. It is called *sales!*

Work with your staff to help them to understand that no matter how correct they are about needs, customers have the right to want something. Show them that marketing, turning needs into wants, can lead to *more* mission, not less.

While you are having that discussion with your staff, disabuse them of the old marketing maxim that I think makes no sense. It is this: *"The Customer Is Always Right."*

Wrong. The customer is *not* always right. The maxim is so patently untrue that it amazes me that it still survives. In the example above, the customer didn't want what he needed. He was wrong about his needs. His case is not unique. Customers complain about things that are unfixable, have wants that are unattainable, hold strong opinions that are in direct conflict with the facts. Customers are people. And people make mistakes. So the customer is *not* always right

But, **"The Customer Is Always The Customer."** This new maxim goes to the heart of truly treating people like customers—even when they are wrong. Even when the request is outrageous, rude, incredibly stupid, the customer is still the customer. And customers deserve respect, and our best efforts to fix the problem, meet their wants, make them happy.—within our best abilities.

Adopt this new maxim. Use the example above, or provide your staff a case study from your own field of service.

But wait. Just who is your customer? Is it the people you serve, the people who fund you, who? That's the subject of our next section.

C. TREATING EVERYONE LIKE A CUSTOMER

This is such an important concept that I will dwell on it more than once in this book. Successful and competitive organizations realize that everyone in and out of the organization needs to be thought of as a valued customer (even when they are wrong). This is often tougher for not-for-profits, for a variety of reasons that we should review.

The not-for-profit community is the only one that I am aware of that often thinks of its biggest customer as the *enemy*. Those of you with major funding sources from local, state, or federal governmental sources know what I am talking about: you look at these payers as organizations to do battle with, to lobby with, to argue with. This perspective is, to put it mildly, shortsighted. The people who pay you are customers, and deserve to be treated that way. They may be the customers from hell, but they are still customers.

Now let's look at the other side of the ledger—the people that you serve. If you are like most not-for-profits you don't call these people customers, which is fine. You call them students, patrons, consumers, clients, patients, parishioners, recipients, tenants, the congregation. The labels are fine. However, if the labels are joined to an attitude that doesn't acknowledge that these people are also customers, you've got trouble.

> ☞ **HANDS-ON:** Look at your organizational attitude now. Get out your income and expense statement. Look at the four largest sources of income. Now think of the people at those organizations who you deal with the most. Is your image of them as a customer or as a pain in the neck? Are they an opportunity to serve or a barrier to service, at least in your mind? Now ask your senior staff the same question. If you, like so many organizations, tend toward thinking of your funders as a problem rather than as a person who your organization can help, you're in trouble in a competitive world. Now is the time to change that attitude.

A competitive, market-oriented organization, whether for-profit or not-for-profit, thinks of *everyone* outside the organization, and even of those *inside* the organization, as customers. We'll discuss this at greater length in Chapter 4, after we identify all your markets and their differing wants. Then, I'll show you how to treat every customer with "Incredible Customer Service" in Chapter 11. For now, just remember (and begin to preach to your staff and board) that in a competitive environment *everyone* is a customer, and that those organizations that fail to appreciate this truth will fail. The techniques of marketing will help you tremendously in this effort, but the attitude that funders, staff, board, and the people you serve are really, truly customers has to come first, and it has to be believed, reinforced, and, like so many values, led by example — by you.

D. BEING BETTER THAN YOUR COMPETITION

But what about the other guys? In a noncompetitive environment, you don't need to worry about competition. Either there isn't any or there isn't much and you really are protected by your funders from worrying about the market's whims and changes. No more. Not only do you have to pay attention to your markets, ask what they want, and give it to them, you have to compete for the good graces of your customers with other organizations who are trying to lure them away from you.

Competitors come in all shapes and sizes, provide great and innovative services and awful ones, have lots of money and are broke. Obviously, knowing the competition is a critical component of both marketing and becoming competitive, and we'll spend an entire chapter just on this subject. Right now, I want to make two important points about marketing and your competition.

1. The competitive marketing skills you will learn by reading this book will go a great distance toward helping your organization maximize its effectiveness in a competitive market. You can outresearch, outsell, outproduce, outsmart, and be more responsive than your competition (even really well-run organizations) if you apply what you learn in these pages. On the other hand, if you ignore the marketing part of your job, if you don't ask your markets what they want, if you just decide that what you are doing is fine and that you know what's best for all the people you serve, then even the sloppiest competitor who applies a little marketing smarts is going to eat your lunch. You can be better than your competition if you pay attention to what they are doing, if you innovate, and if you are willing to be flexible as the market changes. Most important, you need to be better than your competition not just in your eyes but *in the eyes of your customers.*

● **FOR EXAMPLE:** Let's assume you are trying to retain your physical therapist staff (which for readers not familiar with the human service arena is a *very* tough job; there are many more therapist positions than there are therapists). You check around and find that your salary is very competitive, and your fringe benefits are great. You thus assume that you are competitive, that you are giving the customers (in this case, the therapists) what they want. And then they leave for a job at a *lower-paying* competitor. Why? Because the competitor has traditionally invested in regular staff training and has the best therapy equipment, which is what your therapists value. Why didn't you know this? Because you didn't ask; you assumed that money was the issue. You were better than your competition on the financial scale, but not on the scale that was important to therapists: training and equipment. You lose.

2. You have to begin to preach to your staff (or if you are already there, reinforce with your staff) the underlying philosophy that you have to *compete*. Many, many not-for-profit line staff, midmanagement, and even senior staff feel that they are professionals and thus it is unseemly, undignified, somehow *dirty*, to compete. That's the director of marketing's job. I just do what I am trained for. If I go after other organization's clients (patients, customers, students, members) I will not only sully my reputation, I will anger all my friends at that organization. Sound familiar?

This was fine and honorable thinking in the past, but deadly in the current environment. Attitudes like that will keep staff from believing that they are on the marketing team, it will keep them from accepting the need for flexibility, accommodation, and rapid change to meet customers' wants, it will impede their thinking of everyone as a customer. And, since marketing is a team sport, it will cause the team to do poorly as a whole.

☞ **HANDS-ON:** For many readers, this will be a tough cultural change. Here is how to start. Talk to staff in groups of eight to ten about the changes in your environment. Demonstrate how your field is becoming more competitive. Show them who your competition is and how the competition can now take customers, clients, away. If you have had customers leave (or not return) recently, use them as case studies. Then ask, "How can our organization respond?" Let the staff come to the realization that marketing and competition, while difficult and perhaps distasteful, is the only way that your organization is going to survive to *continue to do more mission*. Like so many other discussions of change, you must emphasize the mission connection, that marketing is good mission, that competing is good mission. If you focus on mission you will have a much better chance of convincing the skeptics. Repeat the exercise for the whole staff, and as you go through your sessions, note which staff are on board and which are holding back. Encourage the people who are buying in to coach and cajole their hesitant peers. Remember that cultural changes like this take time, and that slow and steady repetition, reminders, and training are the essential tools. In the next chapter I'll provide you with seven specific ideas on how to motivate and bring along your board and staff.

Repeat after me: Competing is not bad. Competing is not immoral.

Competing successfully means you will continue to be there to do good works. Competing means being able to do more mission. In the new, more competitive environment, you have to be willing to compete because you believe in your mission, your skills, and in the quality of your outcomes.

One other point: competition should not be confused with military analogies like "conquest" or "total victory". Being competitive often means getting enough market share, enough of the customers that you can serve the *best,* to keep you financially healthy, constantly innovating, and thus prospering. You do not have to be predatory to be competitive. But you do have to be proud enough of what you and your organization do to *not be ashamed* to tell the customers of another organization how good you are.

> ● **FOR EXAMPLE:** A good demonstration of this is in America's churches. They provide an excellent example of what not-for-profits can do where the free market exists. No United Way or government funder says: "There are too many churches in this community, we have duplication of services." And thus there are lots and lots of spiritual choices, with more springing up every day.
>
> I know a lot of ministers, rabbis, and priests. All of them devoutly believe in their church's or synagogue's theology. Few of them think of themselves as competitive (except against evil), but in truth, all of them are competing to attract and retain members for their congregation. Our church recently completed a major building project, moving into a new sanctuary. In the first weeks that we were in the new facility, we had many more visitors than normal as people came to see the new building. Our minister used the opportunity to give a series of sermons on "What We Believe," detailing the key points of our denomination's value structure. While he never derided other churches, he was performing another age-old marketing ritual — product definition. *"Look everyone, here is what makes us different. We believe in it and we hope you will. If you share our beliefs, come join us."*

Were our minister's words from the heart? Absolutely. Was it sales? Without a doubt. Was the minister moving the mission of the church forward? Yep. You see, marketing does not have to be flackery. Just because you believe something deeply does not prohibit you from selling it, and to deny that you are selling is simply self-delusion. Once you accept marketing as mission promotion, you can study marketing (as you are doing by reading this book) and use the techniques to promote more mission. Once you realize that striving to be the best does not require putting down your competition, you will have made the first big psychological leap toward becoming a mission-based competitor.

But you can't do it alone. You need help, and that comes from your staff, board, and volunteers. Let's look at their impact and how you can get them to move with you toward a market-oriented future.

E. A TEAM EFFORT

Marketing is a team sport. And, since competition is often a win-lose proposition, the people in your organization win or lose together. One of the major mistakes that noncompetitive organizations make (both for- profit and not-for-profit) is to allow any employee to think that his or her job has nothing to do with marketing. These are the organizations where you call with a question and are left on hold for half an hour only to be connected to the wrong person, who says they know nothing about your problem. These are the restaurants who cannot accommodate someone with a special dietary need. These are the airlines where the baggage handlers are rude, or the grocery stores where the staff send you on wild goose chases looking for products.

The truth is: *marketing is everything that everyone in your organization does every day.* It is the way that the phone is answered, the grass is cut, the building maintained, the bills are paid or collected, not just how the services are provided. It is the way that customers' problems are solved, the way inquiries are followed up, the way that the staff interacts with each other.

All staff need to develop a perspective that what they do, and how they do it, affects the whole team, the whole organization, not just the people within their immediate field of vision.

● **FOR EXAMPLE:** For those readers who cling to the idea that the senior management is solely responsible for organizational marketing, consider this: when you interact with a business organization, an airline, hotel, car rental agency, restaurant, quick lube shop, who do you come in contact with? What kind of people are responsible to ensure that you are a well-served, happy customer? The *lowest-paid people in the organization,* that's who. At the airline it's the reservation agent, counter staff, flight attendant. At the hotel it's the desk clerk, housekeeping, restaurant servers. At the car rental agency it's the bus driver, counter staff, check-in staff. At all of these organizations it is the people on the "bottom" of the organizational ladder who make or break your experience with the company. If any one of them messes up, the entire experience takes on a bad taste.

And, in each of these cases, there are people, also in the lowest-paid tier, who *never see customers* but who also affect your satisfaction. For example, at a car rental agency, the people who clean the cars and service them are critical. Get into a dirty car, or have a breakdown on the road, and you will not be happy. At the airline, the baggage handlers, the operations staff, the aircraft service crews all go about their work anonymously, but have enormous impact on customer satisfaction.

Who are the people in your organization, well below the management level, who have the most impact on customer satisfaction?

So it is not just the people who deliver the service, nor is it the top management who are in charge of marketing. Everyone is on the team, everyone has impact.

But even though all your staff should be on the marketing team, some may not want to be. What do you do about them?

☞ **HANDS-ON:** Some of your staff may not get this, or they may not want to. They will fear yet another addition to their job description, a function that they aren't sure that they understand — marketing. Assure them that they are probably doing many of the things that they need to do already. Are they polite and helpful to the people you serve? Do they try to solve their problems? Are they making suggestions to you about what they hear from customers? Are they watching what other organizations like yours are doing and bringing the ideas to the table? Are they continuing to read and learn about innovations in your field? All of these things are part of the marketing continuum.

The question is: do your staff know, understand, *believe* that their actions affect the entire organization? If they do, then the way that they do their job, their attitude and commitment, will carry them. If they don't, no amount of marketing technique and training will help.

● **FOR EXAMPLE:** My sister is a woman with severe mental retardation who lives in a small group home in northwest Connecticut. When I visit her at home, I look at many things: how is the physical condition of the building, the yard? How well dressed, clean, and healthy do *all* of the residents look (not just my sister)? How helpful are the staff to me, *and* to the residents? And, how do the staff get along with each other? All of these things are going through my mind before, during, and after a visit. A staff person who thinks I will be happy if my sister is neat, well dressed and happy (all of which is important to me) will miss the boat if the rest of the indicators I listed are negative. While the staff may not agree with me that the lawn being mowed matters, it does to me because I believe that maintenance of a property is an indication of organizational commitment to total quality. What *I* want as the customer should be the bottom line.

Remember, the customer perception of quality is what ultimately counts. In Chapter 3 we'll discuss the marketing disability that most not-for-profit staff suffer from, a disability that makes it hard to focus on what the customer wants. Your staff may be ignorant of how customers perceive your organization, or they may feel that, since no one has complained, customers are happy. Another big mistake.

☞ **HANDS-ON:** To get an idea of how customers perceive your organization, try this. Find a good friend who can act as a potential consumer. Arm the friend with a few key questions, such as "what services do you offer? What kind of payment do you accept? What are your fees? Are you handicapped accessible? Do you have references that I can call? Why should I join (come, purchase, etc.)?" Have the friend first call your organization, and carefully record what happens from the most critical viewpoint possible. How many rings did it take before the phone was answered? How long before the caller was connected with someone who knew this basic information? If the caller was promised a call back, or was told information would be sent in the mail, were they ever called, did the material ever arrive and, did it answer the questions? Was there follow-up? Ask your friend, "Based solely on this interaction, would you pursue using our services further?"

Now, phase two. Have the friend come to your organization, asking the same questions, perhaps overlaying it with being a bit difficult, or asking unusual questions. Again, debrief the friend to find out the result of the visit. Was the information given in person and over the phone the same? What did you think of the part(s) of the facility you saw? How were you greeted? With a smile and a welcoming word, or as if you were interrupting something *really* important (like the receptionist's coffee break)?

If you want, add questions that target a new market that you are after. For instance, if most of your clientele is paid for by Medicaid and you want to move toward people who are covered by private insurance, have your friend say that he or she is a "covered life." Try to have the friend pose a little different question, and see how your people respond. Think about what happens when asking a fast-food clerk for a special order (hamburger, rare, no ketchup, double mustard, two pickles).

Finally, if your wonderful friend is up to it, have him or her present the experiences (good or bad) to your management team or marketing committee in person. Have the friend explain his or her perspective on the interaction. This is a scary but valuable exercise. You and your staff will learn a lot, and you will gain important insight as to how things look on the other side of the admission desk or entryway. It will also reinforce the fact that everyone in the organization must be on the marketing team, all the time.

What about boards? Are they on the team? Of course. Boards are representatives of the community to your organization, and they are also ambassadors back to the community. How they act and interact is important, both at board meetings and elsewhere.

● **FOR EXAMPLE:** Good friends of ours recently began looking for a new church. Their current church had grown too big for them, and they focused on smaller, more intimate congregations. Denomination was not as important to them as how much opportunity there was to get to know the people, to work on church activities, to sing in a good choir, and to have group discussions rather than lectures in Sunday school classes. Over lunch, I asked the couple which churches they were considering, and they rattled off four or five that they had visited, and two or three more that were on their list. I suggested one more church that was in the geographic area of their search, and got an immediate and vehement response: "No way, their board of elders is the most divisive, political group we have seen. We know three couples there and they talk about the divisions at the governance level and how much friction and tension there is." That church, despite its small size, active volunteer program, and excellent music ministry, was a nonstarter. Why? Because the board couldn't get its act together.

There is another point to make from this story. Twenty years ago when someone changed churches, they went to another church of the same denomination. A Methodist (Episcopalian, Lutheran, Catholic) was that for life. The large denominations counted on this and many took their "flocks" for granted. In the past two decades, their numbers have shrunk dramatically, with people moving to small, new, often fundamentalist denominations. Why? Because those churches gave people what they *wanted,* and what they wanted wasn't necessarily what the traditionalists at the mainline denominations felt they *needed.*

Team, team, team. Everyone is on the marketing team. The executive director, the receptionist, the janitor, the volunteer. And everyone in between. Make this your mantra. Repeat it until you, your staff, and board instinctively act that way.

RECAP

In this second chapter, we have covered some key preparatory ground. We first looked at the six characteristics of a successful market-driven, mission-based organization. To quickly review, these are:

1. Know Your Markets

2. Treat Everyone Like a Customer

3. Have Everyone on the Marketing Team

4. Ask, Ask, Ask, and Then Listen

5. Innovate Constantly

6. Don't Fear the Competition

We then went over why marketing and all of its components are such a critical edge in the increasingly competitive world you will inhabit. We then pointed out the core truth about marketing: *people have needs, but people seek wants.* Meeting needs is not enough in a competitive world. Finding out what the wants are and meeting them should be your organization's focus from this day forward. We pointed out that you can turn a need into a want, a particularly important skill for some readers.

Next, we looked at ways to change your mindset about some of your markets so that you can develop a culture where everyone is treated like a customer. This includes your funders, which I acknowledge may be difficult for many readers.

We then turned to the issue of being better than your competition, and why "better" is defined by your customers, not just by you. I showed you some examples of how organizations that compete do not have to be predatory, but how all of them have to meet wants by listening to their markets and responding.

Finally, we discussed how marketing is first, last, and always a team activity. Everyone in your organization must be on the team, and be aware that they are part of the team, if you are to compete successfully. In a competitive world, no one can choose to be off the team.

Mission-based organizations can use marketing as the competitive edge. The tools you will find in the rest of this book can help you compete, help you do more mission, more efficiently, more effectively. Do not fear competition. Do not shy away from it. Competition will make your organization a better one. But you must be competitive to survive; you must survive to get better. Good marketing will give you the edge, the time to not just survive but to thrive. You need to move your organization from what may well be its current monopoly — noncompetitive-status (or attitude) — to being market-based. That's not easy, but it needs to begin now. It's the subject of the next chapter.

☞☞ **HANDS-ON REVIEW:**
- **A reality check on your customer attitude**
- **Small group discussion about change and mission**
- **Are your staff on the marketing team?**
- **An external customer service review**

DISCUSSION QUESTIONS FOR CHAPTER 2:

1. How does our staff view marketing? How can we make ourselves more market-driven?

2. Do we have some, all, or any of the characteristics of a market-driven organization? Which ones? How can we improve against this benchmark?

3. Do we meet needs and wants, or just needs? Do staff and board know the difference between needs and wants?

4. Can we really compete? Are we of a mindset to be competitive?

5. What percentage of our staff and board understand that everyone needs to be on the marketing team? How can we improve/maintain that percentage?

3. Moving from a Monopoly to a Market-Driven Organization

OVERVIEW

In the remainder of this book you will learn a great deal about marketing and competitiveness: the techniques you need to make your organization a mission-based competitor. You will learn how to identify your markets, how to size up your competition, how to put out great marketing material, how to identify market wants, and how to develop a marketing plan. But it doesn't end there. You will also have to manage and coach your organization through a truly grueling change, the change from a near or actual monopoly to a market-based organization. Since the change management, in many ways, starts before the marketing techniques are implemented, we'll look at how to start moving your organization now rather than later.

You can have excellent marketing techniques and still not be a market-based organization to your core. And core competence in marketing, believing in your mission while following the markets, is what I'm talking about. In the next two chapters, we'll look at how to make the transition from monopoly to competitor while being true to your mission.

Chapter Thumbnail
- ➡ **Motivating Board and Staff**
- ➡ **The Results of Becoming Market-Driven**
- ➡ **The Results of Staying Service-Driven**
- ➡ **The Never-Ending Marketing Cycle**

In this chapter, we'll start by showing how to make sure that your board, staff, and volunteers are enthusiastically contributing to the transition. You need to motivate them, and I'll show you how. Then, we'll examine the positive results of becoming market-based, as well as some of the possible downsides. You will want to discuss these thoroughly with your board and staff, as well our next topic, the results of staying where you may be now, a service-based organization. There are more bad than good items on this list, and it bears careful examination by everyone in your organization.

Finally, I'll show you why the marketing cycle never really ends; why you never truly satisfy all the market wants; how you can constantly challenge yourself, your staff, and your organization to attain new heights of quality and customer satisfaction. By the time you are through with this chapter, you will be able to start the transition-the one that I believe is crucial to your organization's continued survival and ability to continue providing your important mission.

A. MOTIVATING BOARD AND STAFF

You cannot make this change alone. For some people in your organization (perhaps including you) this will be the first time you have ever encountered, or had to deal with, competition. For others it will be "old hat." For some, there will be an easy transition. For others, there will never be complete acceptance that the "charity" days are long gone and never returning.

But you can do it. Your organization, if well led, can make the transition to a mission-based and market-driven entity. Look around. You have lots of company.

● **FOR EXAMPLE:** Twenty-five years ago, American hospitals had a pretty good deal. In most communities there were a stable number of hospitals, with a slowly growing number of beds. They often shared physicians, and even certain resources. Rarely did hospitals openly compete, certainly never by advertising. In general, a hospital was a predictable entity: a not-for-profit, community-based organization that did a wide range of different inpatient care and was a user of community resources, including donations and volunteer time. If you walked into a primary, secondary, or tertiary care hospital in New York, Des Moines, or Phoenix, you would see basically the same array of services, the same equipment, and the same approximate size.

Today, you get anything but the "same." Over 20 percent of American health care is delivered in for-profit hospitals, when it is delivered *in* the hospital at all. Hospitals have shrunk; many are not even in business. Hospitals have specialized, and focused on particular things that they can do well. They have merged, acquired, and have been acquired to meet the wants of the markets — not only their patients but also their physicians (the classic model of a referrer), the managed care insurers (who are now the key funders), and even some tough-to-recruit staff, such as physical and occupational therapists.

The hospital that you and your family visit now is, by definition, market-driven. I can say that with assurance because the ones that are not market-driven are gone.

Was this an easy transition? No way. But the change was coupled with a huge increase in the business expertise and education of hospital administrators. Dozens, even hundreds, of master's programs in hospital management and administration sprang up all over the country as people worked hard to learn how to manage these multi-million dollar, not-for-profit businesses in a competitive environment.

● **FOR EXAMPLE:** If you are as old as I am, you can remember "the phone company." You received your local and long-distance service from one carrier — in fact, everyone did. You didn't own your phones, the company did. It was the perfect monopoly, until an upstart company named MCI sued AT&T and won. In the mid-1980s long-distance phone service was deregulated, and AT&T was broken up by a federal judge. Local phone services have followed down the deregulation path. The "Baby Bells" have flourished in the new competitive environment, and our telephone service, except at the local level, is less expensive, more efficient, and now carries much more information. Each company has its own strategies, its own array of products and services, and is reacting to its own market's wants.

To appreciate the magnitude of these changes inside AT&T you need to understand that *everyone* in the senior and midmanagement levels at AT&T and the Bell System had spent *all or nearly all* of their careers working for a monopoly. They didn't need to think about marketing. All they had to do was connect people's phones and make sure that service was dependable and reasonably fast. But there had never been an MCI or Sprint or any other of the dozens of small long-distance competitors that there are today.

At AT&T, prior to the breakup, there was no culture of asking, no systems to monitor customer satisfaction, no method of recruiting customers. Why? Because there was no need to have them. Now, think of all the people that the long-distance providers alone have hired just to pester you during dinnertime trying to hawk their wares! Think of the boost to the advertisement market to carry all the television and print ads! Managers of phone companies have adjusted and adjusted quickly. But it wasn't easy, just because they were a for-profit.

● **FOR EXAMPLE:** Speaking of utilities, a similar overhaul is under way in the selling of electric power. Particularly in the northeastern states, different companies now compete to provide you the electricity you use. While the network of wires, cables, transformers, and switches will remain the property of the local utility, the actual power that you use may come from one of a number of sources. One CEO even envisions selling power like cable television, with a fixed rate per month!

Talk about a major change! Utilities *never, ever* had to worry about a customer choosing someone else. If the customer lived in the utility's service area, the choice was to have power or not to have power, but never did the consumer have real *choice!* Again, *nearly all* of the staff on board when the market changed had spent *nearly all* their lives in the comfort and relative safety of a monopoly. Now they would have to adapt or perish. And again, just as in hospitals and telephone communications, there are mergers and acquisitions by the dozen. The market is going through a shakeout. Some organizations — those that learn to adapt to a market-driven philosophy — will flourish, but those that don't will fade away.

All of these examples have themes similar to the dilemma many not-for-profits face: they had a staff and board that had been raised in a monopoly environment, not in the more frantic, more variable competitive arena. Just like you, they had a choice: adapt or die. Just like you, they were faced with the possibilities of merger, of acquiring, or even being acquired.

And there was also one other thing that all of these industries did: get outside help. Hospital administrators hired marketing staff from the for-profit arena. When that did not always work, they set up master's programs in administration to learn from within. The utilities and phone companies relied heavily on consultants and outside hires who understood the realities of a competitive marketplace. They spent a great deal of money retraining employees, focusing on customer service, learning how to solve problems quickly, efficiently, and even *politely*.

The point is this: *you can too*. As you enter the competitive arena, many of your staff will resist the change. They will bemoan the fact that they took their job to serve, not to sell. Many, in fact, sought the shelter of the not-for-profit environment precisely because they did not want to enter the hurly-burly world of business.

However, some of their resistance will not be solely for philosophical reasons. Many staff will correctly assume that they don't know *how* to act competitively. And, like most people, they would rather do nothing than mess up. So they will resist.

☞ **HANDS-ON:** Get your staff and board the help that they need. Specifically:

- Send people to courses on marketing, customer service, quality control, surveying, focus group development, and creating better marketing materials.
- Have an outside marketing consultant come in and provide you with a competitive assessment. Have him or her tell you what you need to improve, and where your strengths and weaknesses are in terms of expertise and readiness.
- Hire from outside of your discipline. Particularly in the marketing area, a fresh set of eyes, a fresh perspective, can be invaluable. Having this new expertise in-house will be vital in the coming economy.

Most of your staff and board, if they feel that they are properly "equipped" to compete, will do just fine. But you have to get them the "equipment."

What else can you do to motivate the staff and board and to get them over the inertia of resistance?

☞ **HANDS-ON:** Try one or more of these ideas:

1. Talk about the reality of competition.
Engage the staff and board early and often in discussions about competition. Show them information about the competitiveness that is occurring in your sector. Target your information as closely as you can to your own discipline, and your income and service array. For example, if you get 25 percent of your income from small donations, you can show your staff and board members information on how many groups in your community have increased their development efforts. If you only get one percent of your income from fund-raising, don't bother making a case for more competition in that arena.

Have senior staff and board read this book, and then use the discussion questions at the end of each chapter to walk them through topics relevant to the issues developed in the book. This will allow you and your management and policy team to more easily coalesce around the reality of increased competition as well as the need for increased marketing efforts.

2. Talk about your mission.
Discuss the people that your organization has helped. If you can, use real names of real individuals to highlight the value of what your organization does. Note that if you don't compete there is a good chance that you will not be around much longer to help those people who depend on you. If you have a much-disparaged competitor, talk about what happens if the people you serve must start going to them because you are no longer around. Use your mission as a tool for reflection on your value and for motivation to try competing.

3. List organizations such as yours that are in trouble or out of business.
If you can, prepare a list of organizations in your area of work who are in financial trouble. National examples are good, but local or state ones are much better at underscoring the potential outcome of not paying attention to the market forces that are shaping the future of your organization.

4. Get them comfortable with the idea of marketing.
Review with them who your markets are, using the chart you will see in Chapter 7. Help them understand that everyone, even your funders, are really your markets. Remind them that, while mission is always first, if there is no money, there is no mission!

Most important, help them see that they are already marketing and have been for many years. This will help remove some of the "change" and "new" labels from the idea. For example, if you have "non-traditional" hours for services designed to meet the needs of two-income families, you are marketing — designing a service distribution to meet the wants of the market. If you already ask about customer satisfaction in any way, you are marketing — testing the wants of your customers. If you have started up a new service, or opened a new location in response to a customer-stated desire, you are marketing — responding to the markets. I'm sure you have some examples with which to allay the fears and concerns of your staff. Use them.

5. Get them comfortable with the idea of competition.
Show them areas where you have competed in the past, including fund-raising, grant applications, United Way funding. Note that, as service recipients become more and more the focus of funding streams and choice is increased, you will need to compete for those recipients in just the way that you have competed for funding in the past.

Go through the exercise of developing a list of competition using the sample tables in Chapter 8. Make sure you emphasize your organization's strengths at some point, or your board and staff will think that you are facing unbeatable competition.

6. Recognize and acknowledge their fears and concerns. Admit your own.
Acknowledge that this is new turf for all of you, and that many staff and board did not come to the organization to take part in the competitive marketplace. Talk about your fears, concerns, and the need for more training and help. Note that change is inevitable and that, while you don't have the power to change the marketplace, you do have the power to shape your own destiny within that market. Discuss your options and your choices, and then look at the result of becoming market-oriented and the fallout that occurs if you stay service-oriented. (See sections B and C for some help in developing these lists.)

7. State clearly and forcefully that you need to move ahead and do it now.
After this discussion is complete, end on a firm, forceful, and assured message: we need to move the organization ahead and get ourselves ready to compete. Look for agreement, and if you sense that it is not there, note that you are regrettably sure that this direction will alienate some members of the staff and board. And, if that discomfort is too severe, you would recommend that they go elsewhere with their time, energy, and skills.

This is a hard part of the discussion for nearly all of us. But it is true. You are embarking on a long and difficult journey through a countryside in which many of your staff and board never thought that they would set foot. Dragging them along against their will is sure to slow everyone down, distracting you from the job at hand which is leading your organization through the change. It is better to make the hard choices now and recommend that people you feel cannot come along and support the new direction get out now. The train is leaving the station. Better to have these folks leave voluntarily now than to have them derail the train later on. Or for you to have to throw them off.

These seven steps, if discussed with empathy, understanding, but a clear sense of where you are going, will bring on most of your staff and board. Is there any other information that you can give these good people that might motivate them? Certainly, and I've made a list below of the results of becoming market-based. Show it to your staff and board and ask if these are outcomes that your organization would like.

B. THE RESULTS OF BECOMING MARKET-DRIVEN

What good things happen if you go through all the work, effort, and discipline to become and remain market-driven? How can you tell if it is worth the investment? There are some real and tangible results from making this change, and the six listed below are the ones I see most often.

1. You will have happier markets — particularly consumers and government funders.
If you ask and listen, ask and listen, ask and listen, and then make a reasonable effort to accommodate the wants people have, they will have a better feeling about you.

First, simply because you asked. That action shows that you care, are more businesslike, and, in the case of a poor historic relationship with your funders, it shows that you want to improve the relationship.

Second, because you take action and try to accommodate them. Happier customers mean more return customers, more referrals, less hassles from funders, more sweep-up funds and pilot project grants, being given a little slack in a crisis. You want happier service customers and happier funders. Marketing can help you get both.

2. Your organization will have a better image in the community.
People will talk about you as a "businesslike charity," one that is using what they perceive as their money (from donations or taxes) in a more efficient, effective manner. You will have a higher visibility in the community, because you will be out there asking all the time. You will gain a reputation as a responsive organization, not one of those not-for-profits that hasn't changed since the Roosevelt administration (Teddy's, not FDR's!). This image will mean more customers, more donations, better morale for the staff and board, easier board recruitment, more designated donations through United Way, and even, if you are lucky, a better press.

3. You will retain your current markets.
If it is not already happening, it will soon: someone will show up to compete with you for your core business. They may, as we discussed earlier, just take the most lucrative funders, donors, families, or service recipients. But come they will. By doing good marketing starting *now,* not after the competition shows up, you will cement the long-term relationship with many of your core markets. And, by competing and being responsive to changing wants when the competition does arrive, you have a much better chance of keeping those customers on board and loyal.

4. Your organization will be more efficient and effective in the provision of services.
By definition, if you are a market-based organization, you are doing things that your markets want, and not things that they don't want. This will allow you to focus more and be more efficient and effective in what you do. You'll get more mission for the money, because you will be putting your money where it has the most impact.

5. You will develop new revenue sources.
Success breeds success. You will find that happy customers will tell others, and this will result in more business, more customers, and new funders. Organizations that are good marketers attract new revenue like a fully pollinating flower attracts bees. Your business skills will be tested deciding which work to take and which not to, and it will be important to stay focused on your core competencies. But I have seen organization after organization reap the financial rewards of marketing by having new and previously untapped sources of funding within 18 to 24 months of kicking off their marketing effort.

6. Your organization can become and remain more financially stable.
As a result of being more focused and effective, and as more funding sources are developed, you can become much more financially stable. Notice that in the five previous points I use the term you "will," where here I use the term "can." Why? Because just having more income doesn't mean you will be more financially stable. More income gives you the means to stability, but you still need to manage those funds well, assuring your growth doesn't outstrip your cash, that your new expenses don't exceed your new income, that you put some money aside for capital improvements and repairs. But good marketing gives you the opportunity to become financially stable. (For a lot more on this subject, see my book *Financial Empowerment.*)

If you do your marketing well, consistently, and with the entire staff and board on the marketing team, these results will accrue to your organization. They are the tangible benefits of all the work and money that you will put into your organizational change. Some are measurable, some are not, but if you are sensitive to them, you will be looking for the rewards in the right places.

C. THE RESULTS OF STAYING SERVICE-DRIVEN

Now the dark side. What happens if you decide that becoming market-driven is not for you? Or if you can't convince your board that changing into a competitor is a mission-based choice? If you stay focused only on your services and not on what your markets want, one or more of the following things are at risk:

1. You risk continuing to provide outdated services.
The most common term for this is "buggy whips." If you are not asking people what they want, you will miss the fact that they no longer want what you provide. They may continue to patronize you, simply because they don't dislike what you do enough to go elsewhere, or because there is nowhere else to go. But if you do not ask, your organization's tendency will be to continue to do what you've done — out of habit or out of tradition. Not marketing, not asking, not responding, or not paying attention to what your competition is doing is much like going through life with blinders on. By being blind to what is changing around you, you will be less efficient, and less effective. We both know that your organization doesn't have enough resources to meet all the severe needs in your community. Why would you want to squander some of those precious resources on something that is no longer wanted, or that is no longer considered quality service?

2. You risk continuing what may well be a poor relationship with your key funders.
Keep fighting with your key funders. Let your staff and board berate them at every turn. Fuss about them whenever you get the chance to your peers (now your competitors?). See what happens. You will continue to use up a lot of your time in anger, frustration, and the feeling that you have been *wronged.* If you try to turn the relationship around to one where you view the funder as a valued customer, you will put your energy into making things go *right.* Not marketing assures that any current bad relationships — with staff, board, funders, or consumers — stay bad. I don't view that status as an enviable one in a competitive marketplace.

3. You risk losing historically loyal customers.

It is good to believe in what you do, or in the service you provide. But when you believe in it so strongly that you ignore suggestions for improvement, and especially when those suggestions come from customers, you can get yourself into real trouble.

The worst thing that can happen to an organization is to lose its core customers, the ones upon which it has depended year in and year out. Your core customers come in two varieties: the people who you serve and the people who pay you. If you don't pay attention to their wants, in a competitive environment, they will abandon you without a second thought.

● **FOR EXAMPLE:** From about 1967 on, our family owned foreign-made cars. My father, the practical engineer, and my mother, the assertive consumer, saw much more value and safety in cars made in Germany, Sweden, or Japan than in their American counterparts. Thus, the only family cars I ever drove were Toyotas, Volkswagens, and Volvos. The first car I bought was a beat-up Volvo that had 48,000 miles when I bought it. I was a loyal, and somewhat snobby, foreign car owner. A core customer.

As my wife and I had children, our transportation needs evolved and we bought our first minivan, the vehicle of the 1980s. It was a Toyota, from the first model year in which they made vans. It had rear-wheel drive. I put 70 pounds of concrete in the luggage area all winter just to have the traction to get up the not very steep hill by our house. It was also on a truck frame, and thus drove "hard." After six years, we were ready for a new van, and I assumed that we would again buy one of the foreign models. After all, I reasoned, the Japanese really listen to their customers, so they would naturally have improved the van.

Not so. Toyota still only made rear-wheel drive vans on truck frames. I walked away. Where to look now? At the American vans? I guess so, I thought with *great* resignation. There were certainly *a lot* of them on the road. Of course, there was a reason for the popularity: they are *great* vehicles. The makers responded to customer wants. I was sold the minute I *sat* in the van.

Not only did Toyota lose a customer, but I learned that American vehicles can be high quality and customer-oriented. We now own two American-made cars.

The moral here is that if you drive away loyal, core customers because you are not paying attention to their wants, they get a chance to sample the wares of your competitor, something that they might never have bothered with before. Then, they may get out of the habit of coming to you, and you stand the real likelihood of losing them forever.

4. You risk a true, and perhaps fatal, financial crisis.
I don't want to paint a doom-and-gloom picture, but this is already happening to organizations that are focused on their services and not on their markets. Not-for-profits in the arts, education, human services, research, and environmental issues are falling by the wayside because they are running out of money. And this is not solely because "funding was cut." More often than not, funding was cut because the organization wasn't doing its job, was poorly marketed, poorly led, poorly managed. Blaming funding cuts is often blaming the symptom, not the underlying disease. If core customers abandon you, if you are inefficient, if you continue your poor customer relationships, it stands to reason that the dollars will slow, or even cease. Don't let this happen.

> ☞ **HANDS-ON:** To underscore this possibility, again look at the top three or four funders on your income and expense statement. Now, what if just one of these funders cut back on your income 30 percent next year, 30 percent the year after, and shut you off completely in the third year? What would happen to your services, your staff, your mission? This is exactly what happens to hospitals that don't perform up to managed care standards. While the hospital may not like the requirements of the funder (the market), it has to become market-driven to stay in business.

You have the power to avoid all of these results. Get on with making the transition to a market-based organization. Don't wait until next fiscal year, or until after summer vacation, or until the budget is completed. Start *now.*

D. THE NEVER-ENDING MARKETING CYCLE

So where does all this lead? When do you get to the promised land of becoming a market-based organization? How do you know when you have arrived? And, when you arrive, can you stop and rest a bit?

Not really. Once you embark on this journey, it becomes a philosophy as crucial to the performance of your charitable purpose as any other part of your mission statement. For example, you may, as an organization, believe in prevention, early intervention, a particular method of education, or in a particular environmental cause. Those beliefs are closely related to your organizational identity; they describe in large part who you are. Now you need to become a market-based organization that also has those same values, one that puts credence not only in your own beliefs but also in the beliefs and wants of your many markets.

How will you know when you have become market-driven? You will know when you can quickly tell me how your five most important funders feel about you, based on survey or focus group data. Or when you can rattle off the four or five most recent adjustments you have made to your service array, or to the delivery of services, based on information gathered from your customers. When I can walk into your organization and you are sure that I will be greeted with courtesy upon my arrival and asked about my experience upon my departure. When your marketing material is targeted, and when you can quickly list your target markets, your key competitors, and your core areas of competence.

But even when you can do all this, you won't have *arrived*. Because there is not an end point in this process. There is always a little further to go, always a market in flux, a new want in development, a new competitor to face. Marketing is not an endpoint. It is a an ongoing process. It is moving ground, constantly reshaping itself in ways that you can't really predict until you are there.

So you never really arrive, but you cannot afford *not* to embark on the journey.

RECAP

Moving your organization from a service-oriented to a market-oriented philosophy is not an overnight task. It takes belief on your part that it is the best strategy for your organization to be able to continue to pursue its mission. But you have to have the staff, board, and volunteers backing you if you are to succeed.

In this chapter, we talked about ways to motivate staff, board, and, yes, even you to make that journey. First, we talked about team development and I gave you seven discussion threads with which to convince any hesitant staff or board that you are going in the right direction. These discussion topics can also help make them more comfortable with policies that they may know are correct but not yet feel are *right*.

To review, these seven ideas were:

1. *Talk to them about the reality of competition.*
2. *Talk about your mission.*
3. *List organizations such as yours who are in trouble or out of business.*
4. *Get them comfortable with the idea of marketing.*

5. *Get them comfortable with the idea of competition.*
6. *Recognize and acknowledge their fears and concerns. Admit your own.*
7. *State clearly and forcefully that you need to move ahead and do it now.*

By using these topics steadily, and with some empathy for the massive change you may be embarking on, you will bring most, but probably not all, of your staff and board along.

We next reviewed the benefits of becoming a market-driven organization. You can use these points in your discussion with board and staff to motivate and convince them that competition is real and marketing is a mission-based strategy. To quickly review, the six results were:

1. *You will have happier markets — particularly consumers and government funders.*
2. *Your organization will have a better image in the community.*
3. *Your will retain your current markets.*
4. *Your organization will be more efficient and effective in the provision of services.*
5. *You will develop new revenue sources.*
6. *Your organization will become and remain more financially stable.*

Next, we turned the tables and looked at what happens if you remain (or worse, become) service-based as an organization — one that worships what you do, not who you do it for. The downsides are many, and we listed the most important four, which were:

1. *You risk continuing to provide outdated services.*
2. *You risk continuing what may well be a poor relationship with your key funders.*
3. *You risk losing historically loyal customers.*
4. *You risk a true, and perhaps fatal, financial crisis.*

Finally, we looked at the never-ending cycle of marketing, noting that your move from being service-driven to being market-driven is really not a move; it is the beginning of a philosophy of action — an endless process that constantly adapts, changes, improves, and adjusts to the changes of the marketplace. In short, you are starting a journey that never ends.

Now you know why you need to make the change to a market-driven not-for-profit. You have learned skills and the techniques to convince your staff and board that it is the right choice. But, even after all of this work and motivation, you still have to face the final challenge, and answer the ultimate question that a responsible not-for-profit manager should ask: can

40

we really be market-driven and mission-based at the same time? Let's see, in the next chapter.

☞ ☞ **HANDS-ON REVIEW:**
- **Training staff in marketing and competitiveness**
- **A list of things to help overcome inertia**
- **What if you lose one of your four biggest funders?**

DISCUSSION QUESTIONS FOR CHAPTER 3:

1. Do our board members feel competition is a real concern? Why or why not?

2. Do all of our staff members feel that competition is a real concern? How can we regularly underscore this issue?

3. Do board and staff feel that marketing is related to mission? How can we do more to make the connection?

4. Can we do the motivating actions suggested in the chapter? How? When?

5. Looking at the benefits of becoming market-driven, if these came true for us, what would it mean to our mission delivery?

4. Being Mission-Based *and* Market-Driven

OVERVIEW

As you read this, you are probably in one of two positions. You are ready to move toward becoming market-driven, convinced that a competitive marketplace is upon you and that the only way for your organization to survive is to listen and respond to the marketplace. Or, you are still hesitating, unsure of whether becoming market-driven is the right thing for your organization at this time, unconvinced that you can bring your board and staff along.

In both cases, you should be asking the penultimate question: can we *really* be both mission-based *and* market-driven? Can my organization be responsive to the whims, trends, and even the folly of the marketplace and still be considered true to our mission? Can we even hold onto our identity, much less our core values, over time?

All of these are important questions, and ones that I want you to carefully consider, even if you are convinced that market-driven operations are the path to the future for your organization. In this chapter, we will discuss these questions and give you some tools with which to wrestle these dilemmas as they come up. Because they will. Today, tomorrow, next week, next year, you will have a market opportunity that pulls you away from your mission. What will you do? Now is the time to set the guidelines.

Chapter Thumbnail
➙ **Which Is Right, the Markets or the Mission?**

42

➡ **Moving with the Markets, Maintaining Your Mission**
➡ **Holding on to Your Core Values**

First, we'll look at which of the two powerful forces is correct, the market or the mission. One is right, but one should be your focus and your guide and I'll show you which is which. Then we'll look at a number of examples of not-for-profits that have moved with the market while maintaining their mission, and use their experiences to guide you as you proceed. You will see how some organizations adapted their mission to the market, and others that bent the market wants to meet their core mission.

Also in this section, we'll review the important ways that you can use your mission to strengthen your market-based efforts, and to keep you on course.

Finally, we'll go beyond the mission, to your core values. Each organization has them and you should be able to list yours and refer to them often as you try to ensure that you don't stray too far from what you believe. Here too, we'll look at some examples of organizations that had to decide whether to accept the market want, or to say no.

A. WHICH IS RIGHT, THE MARKETS OR THE MISSION?

If your organization moves toward the market, if it listens to what the market wants, some day, some week, some month you will be confronted by a market want that conflicts with your mission, your organizational history, or even your personal values. What are you to do? What should be your guide? Which, in such a conflict, is "right" — the market or your mission?

Let me put it as succinctly as I can in three sentences:

1. The market is *always* right.
2. The market is *not always right for you*.
3. The mission should be your organization's ultimate guide.

The market wants what it wants, and there is no denying it, no ignoring it, no trying to make it not so. The people that you serve want what they want, but you can and, in some cases, *should* only give them so much.

And here is the point: *the choice is always yours as an organization.* You can choose not to meet a market want whenever you feel that it is in conflict with your organization's mission or values. And, further, you have to evaluate whether or not such a market move is in conflict with your personal values and ethics.

● **FOR EXAMPLE:** A good friend of mine was the director of patient education for a set of rural health centers in the Southwest. As she did her market surveys, talked to patients and community members, and reviewed data from focus groups, she saw repeatedly that the community was concerned about a rapid rise in teenage pregnancies and in what seemed to be an epidemic of girls dropping out of high school to care for their babies. She brought this information, along with the other identified concerns, to her marketing committee and eventually to the board of directors.

The board decided to expand the organization's already broad educational role in the community by working with the community's public and private schools to offer more effective classes and counseling on pregnancy prevention, to both boys and girls. This supported the organization's mission of primary care prevention, treatment, and community education, and supported its core value that prevention was a priority. This was fine with my friend. The idea was good, it was something that she could do well, and the board had given her the resources she needed.

But the board added one point she could not abide. In working with the teens, the board directed (after a long and acrimonious debate) that *all* options should be discussed — that all choices, including terminating an unwanted pregnancy, should be presented objectively and without endorsement. My friend has very strong personal feelings about abortion, and she stated that she could not endorse, encourage, present, or even develop such a presentation. After a great deal of personal soul-searching, she resigned her position.

Whatever your views on the very controversial subject of abortion, you have to admire her willingness to sacrifice her job to preserve her own sense of morals, ethics, and values. Two key markets, the board and the community, had indicated their wants, so the market had spoken. The board's method of meeting the community's wants was not the only choice, but it was the option that they selected. And my friend thought it through and said, "I cannot, in good conscience, do that."

My point here is that, if you find yourself being drawn into territory where you feel uncomfortable, stop. Talk it through with friends, coworkers, family members, or a spiritual counselor such as a minister, priest, or rabbi. Don't let the market drag you into a place where you no longer feel good about yourself. As a not-for-profit manager, you have to feel good about what you do, you must exude enthusiasm and commitment to the mission to do your job well. It is that selfless, idealistic energy that makes not-for-profit staff special. It's that same enthusiasm and commitment that gets the organization over the hurdles and barriers it confronts. If you feel you are being forced into a position of doing something wrong, even if your competition is doing it, even if the markets are screaming for it, you will lose that edge, that extra effort, that extra sacrifice you are now willing to make to pursue your mission. Don't lose that by following the markets into a dark place. You can say no. Others, in other organizations, will be there to meet the want, and that's fine. You need to do, first and foremost, what you feel is *right*.

That having been said, how do you decide? Look at the three checkpoints below. You can use these to assure yourself that you are not being drawn into a situation that is wrong for you or your organization.

CHECKPOINT 1: *How does this fit with our organizational mission and values?*
CHECKPOINT 2: *How does this meet my personal ethics and values?*
CHECKPOINT 3: *How does this support our organizational strategic plan?*

Notice that the first checkpoint is your mission, the second checkpoint is your personal values, and the third is an organizational capability/strategy check. There is no priority intended, however. You can do them in any order, because, if the answer to any checkpoint is negative, you should not proceed. So if you are more comfortable putting the personal issues first, fine. If you feel that they should be the final checkpoint, that works as well. Just check them all.

☞ **HANDS-ON:** For a new service or even a major service expansion, here is a checklist that you can run through:

- Does it support our mission?
- Does it support or conflict with our organizational values?
- Does it support our strategic plan goals and objectives?
- Does it wind up with net income or net cost? If it is a loss center, can we afford it?
- Is it something we can do well?
- Is it something I can personally support?

If there are other issues that are important to you, add them to the list. Go through the list considering the mission, values, and ethical issues carefully.

The bottom line in this discussion is this: to be effective, you need to move with the markets whenever you can, but you also need to use your mission, your values, and your personal ethical compass to guide you and set appropriate limits.

That having been said, don't let your mission be the excuse to *never* change. Something new or different is not by definition *anti-mission*. If you hear yourself saying, "We've never done it that way," that doesn't mean you shouldn't. *Use* your mission, don't *hide behind it.*

B. MOVING WITH THE MARKETS, MAINTAINING YOUR MISSION

So what are some practical ways to move with the market and still maintain your mission? The most important skill in this area is learning how to say "no" to a good idea, and even to a real need. Even though a market may want you to provide a service, you need to back away if you can't do it well, or if doing the service would jeopardize everything else you are doing. More and more not-for-profits are learning that they cannot be all things to all people, that they cannot solve all the problems in their community, and thus that they need to pick and choose what they do well, what they can afford, and not just chase every dollar out there.

● **FOR EXAMPLE:** How often has your organization faced a dilemma like this: you are awarded a $1 million contract for services. Not often enough, you say? Well, read on. Let's assume that the contract is for one year and is designed to reimburse all your costs, and thus is a breakeven for you. The funder wants you to start the first of next month. You have no start-up expenses and can just open your doors on the first day and start doing business. (Having no start-up costs would be *extremely* unusual, but it makes the example more understandable.) You will bill the funder monthly on the first of the month and they will take 45 days to pay. Is this great or what? Only if you have $125,000 to invest. That's the cost of the contract for the 45 days that you have to operate before the funding kicks in. You are lending the funder $125,000 *interest-free* for the year of the contract — real money that really disappears for that time.

What do you do? The market (the funder and the service recipients) really want this contract to take place. It supports your mission. But it does not support your organizational value of at least breaking even on every piece of work, and does not support your strategic planning goal of not letting your cash on hand drop below 40 days' operating expenses. Since this contract does not recognize the expense of the "loan" to the state, you lose money (the opportunity cost or interest that you can earn on the $125,000 for the year). And the use of that money to finance the contract draws down all your cash reserve.

The market said move. The mission said move. But your values and goals said stop. Frankly, this problem confronts not-for-profits every day. Should you take the money or not? The market says yes. What do you say?

A second challenge in following the market is that you may not realize the problem until you are already deeply involved with the market change. None of us can predict the full outcome of implementation of new methods of service, different payment methods, or new strategies for identifying and meeting community needs.

● **FOR EXAMPLE:** Earlier, we discussed the impact of managed care on heath care providers and even on the human services industry outside of hospitals, nursing homes, and physicians' offices. Managed care puts health care providers into a situation of incentive/risk, pushing them to keep people healthy, to treat them faster, with more outpatient care. It is a payment strategy that is literally sweeping away old concepts in medicine and dramatically changing the relationship between providers, insurers, employers, and patients. It is a market on the move.

Most hospitals and physicians grudgingly accepted managed care, convincing themselves that the quality of care would not suffer too greatly. And they jumped into programs wholesale. The managed care intermediaries looked first at where the greatest savings were to be found, and it was easy to identify hospital inpatient costs as a huge percentage of overall health care expenses, and a place where significant savings could be quickly realized. So admissions were questioned, stays were shortened, and the hospitals and physicians went along.

Until the insurers crossed an invisible "morality" line, one that no one could have foreseen: they started limiting new mothers to 24, even 18, hours in the hospital after the birth of a child. This policy generated a huge number of complaints that were picked up by the media and outraged the public. Money had overcome basic mission, and people were angry. But what could the hospitals and physicians do? They were contractually obligated to follow the managed care intermediary's rules. Yet they felt morally and mission-obligated to do *something*. Some hospitals let mothers stay and didn't charge for the extra day or two. But there is only so much uncompensated care that any hospital can absorb. So the hospital and medical industries lobbied Congress and state legislatures to change the law and set low-end limits that everyone could live with. They met their mission benchmark, the market want of their patients, *and* the market want of the funding intermediary.

Your next challenge is to make sure that when you move with the market, you don't lose your organizational identity. If you move so far afield from the service, group, or community that people identify you with, you can put your organization into a bind, particularly in fund-raising and board recruitment. No one will know who you really are; no one will be able to connect you to a core cause.

● **FOR EXAMPLE:** In the 1980s the Xerox Corporation expanded its product line, trying to lower its reliance on its central product: photocopiers. Its strategy was to move away from thinking of itself as a copier company and move toward the identity of a manufacturer of office machines. Suddenly you could buy Xerox desktop computers, printers, even answering machines. The slogan "Office Xerox" was plastered all over the business press, and ads appeared in general circulation as well as business magazines.

The problem was that the attempted identity change left the consumer behind. People had a strong image of Xerox as a copier manufacturer, not a computer maker. And not only did they think of Xerox as *a* copier maker, they thought of them as *the* copier maker. "To xerox" was and still is a commonly understood verb. By moving away from a core identity, Xerox not only lost a lot of money on products that didn't sell, they confused their customers, some of whom thought that they were abandoning photocopiers completely. At just this time, rival copier firms such as Mita were able to tell people that *they* would be focused on photocopiers for the long haul, but that Xerox was no longer centrally committed to that product line. Xerox lost market share.

Don't follow a market want into either anonymity or far enough afield to fundamentally confuse people, but, again, don't automatically discard any idea that changes your traditional services or service population.

● **FOR EXAMPLE:** A good example of success in such an identity transition is the YMCA (remember, the "M" stands for "Men's"), which moved across gender lines in the 1950s to expand its potential customer base. (I should point out that the age and religious labels have also been surmounted. You don't need to be young or a practicing Christian to use a Y, be on its staff, or volunteer for a board position.)

48

Thus, changing your identity can be okay, but you need to carefully consider how people think of you now and how they will think of you as you change. And, in some cases, it won't matter.

● **FOR EXAMPLE:** Chaddock is a residential school in Quincy, Illinois, that serves children who come from broken or abusive homes, and who have not been able to succeed in a family foster care environment. Its original name was Chaddock College, then it was the Chaddock Methodist Boys School, and it has gone through a series of name and service changes since its incorporation in 1853. It ceased using this last name in 1983 when it admitted girls for the first time. Yet, in 1995 Chaddock received over 100 donations where the check was made out to "Methodist Boys School." It didn't matter that the organization now serves boys and girls, or that it is no longer closely affiliated with the Methodist Church as it was in its early years. It's image, its identity remain fixed in the minds of many people.

Finally, I want to show you a tool with which to maintain your mission while you move with your markets. You don't even have to go to the hardware store to purchase it. It's in your office right now. It's called your mission statement.

USE YOUR MISSION STATEMENT

Successful managers use all the available resources to get the job done. Mission statements are truly our central tool, our most valuable resource. So why don't we use them more? Here are some ways that you can get more use out of your mission, and have it help you keep your organization mission-based, even while you are in the heat of discussions on how to meet the changing wants of your target markets.

1. Have the mission visible — everywhere.

If you don't already, get your mission statement printed up attractively and hand it out to everyone in the organization. Put it on the wall by the reception area as well as in your staff lunchroom. Have a copy on the table in your conference room, and print it first in your strategic plan, annual report, and even in your newsletter. Have it relentlessly around, a constant reminder of what the point is of your organization.

2. Use the mission statement constantly at management, board, and committee meetings.

Now that it's around, you need to put it to use. If you don't, the mission will just become another essentially invisible wall decoration. So, talk it up. In staff meetings when there is a program or policy choice to be decided, ask, "Which one of these choices is more mission-based, or makes us more mission-capable?" Lead by example and show staff that you rely on the mission to help make your decisions, and that you expect them to do the same. Duplicate this action at board and committee meetings. Make sure that everyone in the organization is mission-focused.

3. Use the mission in your decisions about new markets and new services.

Using the checklist detailed earlier in this chapter, use the mission as one of your most important benchmarks in deciding when (or when not) to move toward a new market, provide a new service, or serve a new clientele.

You already have the entire organization invested in the mission. That's why you are all there doing the good works that you do. So use the mission as a tool to help you keep your organization on track. Not only will it help guide you in marketing, but it will get you into the habit of using the mission in all of your major decision-making and at your staff and board meetings. It's a good mission-based habit to get into.

C. HOLDING ON TO YOUR CORE VALUES

We've talked endlessly about mission, mission, mission. Beyond your mission there is a set of core values that guide the way that you do the things that you do. If you are a school, you might put a high value on teaching the students to work in teams, or in strong discipline, or in faculty esprit de corps. As a church, you might strongly value community service, political application of your spiritual beliefs, a literal interpretation of the Bible, or the funding of overseas ministries. As an art museum, you might focus on the avant garde, on traditional masters, on teaching children, or on reaching out through the schools. Your organization may put a high value on teaching people to help themselves or on a certain theory of therapy.

These values take you part of the way from your mission to the implementation of that mission. They give you guidance on the more practical month-to-month and year-to-year implications of how to stay true to your mission.

● **FOR EXAMPLE:** Here are the mission and values of a state child welfare agency:

Mission: The Department of Child Welfare, in partnership with others, will provide services to children and families to protect and advocate on behalf of children and youth who are, or who are at risk of, being abused, neglected, or removed from their families.

VALUES:
- *That children have a right to a safe, secure, permanent living arrangement, preferably with their own family.*
- *That we should act quickly, competently, and profession-ally to protect children, prevent harm, and advocate for their well-being.*
- *That children and families are served best in homelike set-tings in their own community.*
- *That we should recognize the humanity and importance of each individual, and treat them honestly, with fairness, dignity, compassion, and cultural competence.*
- *That we should foster a stable, supportive workplace, which will allow for each employee to grow, develop, and par-ticipate in the fulfillment of the mission.*
- *That we are accountable for the work we do, and thus, must effectively and efficiently utilize all available re-sources to carry out the mission of the department.*

You can see that the values spoke not only to the mission, but also to the staff, the way the mission would be accomplished (not in institutions), and that everyone should be held accountable. This is a good set of values for a public organization.

National Public Radio's Mission and Values Statement reads as follows:

The Mission of National Public Radio is to work in partnership with member stations to create a more informed public — one challenged and invigorated by a deeper understanding and appreciation of events, ideas, and cultures.

The fundamental values that guide our mission are:
- *Reporting with accuracy, thoroughness, and fairness;*
- *Using sound creatively to engage the intelligence, curios-ity, and imagination of listeners;*
- *Encouraging innovation;*
- *Honoring cultural diversity;*
- *Upholding the tradition and prerogatives of public radio as a local medium;*

- *Making the most of advances in audio technology; and*
- *Encouraging the talent, dedication, creativity, and pro-
ductivity of our staff.*

The use of values in your marketing are many. They can help you select a core market to serve, avoid a funder, take a certain tack in your public relations, and focus on certain organizational outcomes.

They can also help you solve the painful puzzle of which to follow — the market or the mission.

● **FOR EXAMPLE:** Local not-for-profit community hospitals throughout the nation are in a terrible moral bind. There are more and more people with no insurance (and few funds) who are presenting themselves at the emergency room door with real (and sometimes life-threatening) injuries or illnesses. If the hospitals let everyone in (regardless of their ability to pay), they will be out of business and of no help to any one. On the other hand, the hospital mission is to help the sick and injured. How can they turn someone away?

This dilemma is exacerbated in small towns where it seems that everyone knows everyone. Thus, the board and staff are well aware, as they set the policy for what is called "uncompensated care," that they may well be taking an action that will result in refusal of service to a friend, neighbor, or relative. How do values help? In most of the hospitals where I have helped board and staff through this moral mire, there was a value of "maintaining fiscal stability," which balanced the "ease the pain and suffering" value.

Often values do keep each other in balance. I have long held that the first rule of not-for-profits is "Mission, mission, and more mission." And that the second, balancing rule is "No money, no mission." The same is true for your organization: you can have "competing" values.

● **FOR EXAMPLE:** In our jurisprudence system we have many values (mostly listed in the Constitution and Bill of Rights), such as the right to an impartial jury of our peers, the right to a fair and speedy trial, the right to face our accusers. In certain situations, though, we violate these values to meet more compelling values, such as the right to life, liberty, and the pursuit of happiness. For example, in the case of an abused child, certain courts have allowed the child to act as a witness against a defendant without actually appearing in the same court as the accused. The value of the child's well-being and mental health takes precedence over the value of the right of the defendant.

52

In all of these examples, the values of the organization (or system) help people to decide which path is right for them. And, in the examples, there was a lot of opportunity to let certain circumstances result in certain interpretations.

> ☞ **HANDS-ON:** If you don't have a set of organizational values, now is the time to develop them. With your board and key staff (and an outside facilitator), look at your mission statement, and then make a list of the key things that set your organization apart, that make your organization special, that you believe in. Print this list up with your mission statement and use it along with your mission in management and policy discussions.

Your values are important guides in solving the moral, ethical, and mission quandaries that inevitably result from change, especially if that change is externally initiated. Formalize your values and use them as the moral and mission compasses that they are.

RECAP

In this chapter, you have learned the methods — and the dangers — of being simultaneously market-driven and mission-based. You have seen the temptations that will tend to draw you into a world that chases money rather than mission, and I hope you now know the techniques to resist that temptation.

First, we went over the crucial question of which is right, the market or the mission. You learned that, at least in my opinion, the market is always right, but that it will not always be right for you to respond to that market in the way that it wants. I showed you that your mission should be your guide, and that, while you need to listen and respond to the market whenever you can, the ultimate limit on your flexibility should be your mission. I also cautioned you not to let your mission be the rationale for rejecting any response to the market. The market wants will mostly be very appropriate for you, and you shouldn't hide behind the mission.

Next, I told you how to move with the markets while maintaining your mission. I showed you some examples of organizations that are doing just that, and gave you some management ideas on how to get more use out of your mission statement to help you reinforce, remind, and refresh the mission every day.

Finally, we turned to the issue that moves past your mission and into your core values. I suggested that you list those values, discuss them, and use them as yet an additional framework within which to operate. We looked at examples of organizations that rejected new market opportunities that conflicted with their core values, and I provided you with a checklist that your staff and board can use to measure your comfort with a new or modified service based on your values.

☞ ☞ **HANDS-ON REVIEW**
  • **A new-service mission checklist**
  • **Developing organizational values**

DISCUSSION QUESTIONS FOR CHAPTER 4:

1. Are we mission-based? How can we be more so?

2. Are we market-driven? Can we improve our response to the markets? How?

3. What are the biggest barriers we face to achieving and maintaining market-driven status?

4. What are our core values? Should we add them to our mission? Who should be involved in setting them?

5. What are our core competencies? What is it that we do really well? Do these things enhance our mission or distract us from it?

5. Being Flexible: Changing with the Market

OVERVIEW

If you use the ideas presented in this book, you should wind up asking all your customers what they want, and asking regularly. If you ask effectively, you, your staff, and board will be constantly confronted with small, medium, and even large changes in the wants of your many markets.

Can you adapt to these changes? Can your staff? Can your board? Is your organization (and the people in it) flexible enough so that it can re-shape itself constantly to meet the changing environment outside your doors? In the old order, in the protected economy, change came slowly and you had lots of second chances. The community, the funders, the people you served, all gave you a break because you were a not-for-profit. No more. You need to adapt, adjust, change, improve, and modify constantly to keep up with (if not ahead of) your competition. There is no point in going through all the marketing rigmarole that fills these pages if you are not going to change based on the information you have gathered.

So, can you change? If you are like most readers, you probably have your doubts. Some of you are concerned about whether or not you can drag your organization kicking and screaming into the 1970s, much less into the 21st century! Others see not only a problem with staff being willing to change, but with the board acquiescing to fund the changes.

Additionally, there hangs over us the common wisdom that "we all resist change." This "wisdom" has been pounded into our heads for so long that we have all accepted it as profound truth, and that "truth" has become the number one excuse of managers who don't want to make the effort. Get over it. Yes, it is tough to overcome inertia but, once you do, and the momentum is in your favor, it gets easier and easier.

Chapter Thumbnail
➡ **The Need for Flexibility**
➡ **Retaining the Capacity for Flexibility**
➡ **Being a Change Agent**
➡ **The Pace of Change in a Competitive Environment**

In this chapter, I'll show you how to overcome that inertia, how to develop and use the momentum needed for constantly changing and improving your organization. First, I'll try to make a strong case for the need for flexibility, providing you with examples that you in turn can use with any staff or board members who are resistant to change. Then, I'll really get your attention by showing you that change in a competitive environment goes at a much faster pace. As I said above, in the old order we could slog along. No more. In the third section I'll provide you with seven ideas on how to be a change agent for your organization, showing you some hands-on ideas for keeping change moving throughout the organization. And finally, we'll go over some important things your organization needs to do to retain its flexibility. As we get older, we get less flexible. I'll show you how to stretch organizationally.

By the end of the chapter you should have a real feel for ways to keep momentum going. You'll need to. Outside your organization, the inertia has already been overcome and the changes you will need to adapt to are occurring right now. They will occur with or without you. As a good friend of mine likes to say, "The train is leaving the station. You are either on it, or you are under it."

A. THE NEED FOR FLEXIBILITY

So what is all this talk about change? Why do we need to be changing all the time? What's wrong with what we're doing now? Change is such a hassle, and there is no guarantee that when we change we're going to be any better. I like things the way they are. If we do good work, people will continue to use us. What choice do they have? We've done just fine doing the things we've been doing. If it's not broken, don't fix it.

Do any of these sound familiar? Have they come from your board? Your staff? From you? Probably. And, you have a choice. You can be flexible and survive to do more mission another day. Or you can be inflexible and not be around very long. In *Mission-Based Management,* I included "organizational flexibility" as one of my nine criteria of organizational success. This was underscored in *Financial Empowerment,* where I noted that retaining the ability to be financially flexible was a key element of empowerment. Today, in a competitive market, flexibility — the capacity to regularly, and on increasingly short notice, adjust your directions, methods, service mix, and size — is essential.

When we discuss change and flexibility, I am not always talking about huge changes, epic conversions such as new buildings, massive changes in program methodology or reimbursement methods. More often we are talking about small, steady, regular improvements in services, adaptations to the changing wants of your markets. Most people see the word *change* as the word:

☹ CHANGE!!!!!!! ☹

It rarely is that dramatic. Nor is seismic change always good. There is a Japanese philosophy of 100 percent improvement — 1 percent at a time. This is the core of what is commonly called Continuous Quality Improvement or CQI. It doesn't focus on wholesale change, discarding all the "old" ways to embrace the "new." In fact, it builds on the best of the old, making steady improvements every day, every week, every month.

There are many, many examples in the not-for-profit sector of incremental flexibility based on changes in market wants. Let's look at a few.

● **FOR EXAMPLE:** Managed care is the current buzzword for many human services providers. It is seen as a momentous change for the way that business is done in the human field, both by funders and by providers. It is not universally welcomed (to understate) and it does require a rethinking of the way services are viewed. Managed care values *outcomes* rather than *process*. It puts incentives and disincentives in place that push efficiency and effectiveness.

But for many, many readers, managed care is what the market, the funder, wants. Looking only at the outcome measure component, this requires that service providers set outcome goals and document the outcomes rather than the process that got them there. In other words, did the patient get well, not did the patient spend 14 days in treatment.

In working with many organizations going through this change, I hear gnashing of teeth and wailing about how awful this is. The conversation often goes like this. I ask, can you document the outcomes that you have had? *Certainly, but we don't keep a record of it now.* How difficult would it be? *Not hard at all.* So really, what is the big deal? *The big deal is that they want us to do in 14 days what we have been doing in 21.* Can you change what the funder wants? *No.* Then figure out how to do what they ask. Look at other organizations who are accomplishing it and emulate them. Or close.

This example points out two things. First, the documentation of outcomes, something the market wanted, was, in fact, easy. Resisting documenting was just that: pure resistance — putting up roadblocks to what the organization *really* didn't want to do: more outcomes in less time. Here is the second lesson. Once the market has made up its mind, for whatever reason, you are simply wasting your time whining about the philosophy or the change. You can't worry about what might have been. You need to deal with what *is*. The train is leaving the station.

● **FOR EXAMPLE:** Many United Ways realized a number of years ago that allowing donors to target where their money went was a competitive advantage for those donations. This was a change, one that reduced the number of dollars that the United Way committees could allocate, which *really* upset some people. It also caused initial accounting headaches, and these were overcome. But the change allowed the United Ways to compete in the donation marketplace. Other local and state fund-raisers, including churches, allow donors to select the programs that they are giving to. Obviously, choice sells. Perhaps there is an application of this idea in your own development office.

● **FOR EXAMPLE:** Local colleges and universities have needed to expand their student body numbers by including part-time students. This means having classes in the evenings and on weekends, which is a major scheduling change. More instructors have to be recruited. Janitorial duties must be reset for late at night. Maintenance activities that once could take all weekend now have to be compressed. But the market for part-time students is not nine-to-five, five days a week, and the successful organizations have accommodated.

● **FOR EXAMPLE:** If there ever was an industry that has many market segments it is the hotel industry. From the Ritz-Carlton to the Motel 6, the range of what people want in lodging is amazing. Marriot Corporation alone has five different "levels" of hotels. Within the industry there is intense competition, and hotel operators are always looking to build both brand loyalty and loyalty to a particular hotel. So, you see small, steady changes that appeal to the target customer: the businessperson during most of the year and families during vacation seasons. There are frequent-stayer programs, premium room upgrades, coffeemakers in the rooms, express checkout, video checkout (that you can do on your room's television set), free newspapers, courtesy transportation to the airport (or to major local attractions), business-only floors, and, of course, pools and exercise rooms. Two recent additions to these customer-pleasing ideas are interesting. At many hotels, you now get a call in your room from the front desk within ten minutes of checking in. You are asked if everything is in order in your room. This accomplishes two things. First, you know the hotel is concerned about your stay and it gives them a quick opportunity to hear any problems from you while they can still fix them, rather than at checkout. Second, it is a checkup that the housekeeping and maintenance people know will be made with every check-in.

The other interesting "perk" is the environmentally correct option of only changing bed linens every three days or when there is a new guest in a room. I see this more and more. It allows you to get clean linens every day if you wish, but allows you to help save the planet while, of course, saving the hotel money. A double winner for them.

All of these small, usually inexpensive changes meet the markets' wants and add value to the stay, making it more likely that a customer will return.

● **FOR EXAMPLE:** Other examples of user-friendly changes instituted by companies that listen to their customers:
- Airlines have *much* healthier food choices, particularly in first and business classes, than they did ten years ago. People are more concerned about their nutrition and health, and more women (who are more nutrition-conscious as a group than men) are traveling for business.
- Nearly every automobile you see now has cup holders, a rare luxury as recently as 1990. Why? Because people love them, and they are relatively inexpensive to design into a vehicle. A large value-added for little cost.
- Computer software is now *much* easier to install and run than two years or three ago, and indeed, when you buy a new computer, most now have preinstalled software. Why? Because people *hated* getting their new hardware home and spending hours installing software, printers, etc., before they could use it. "Plug and play" is the buzzword now. Indeed the software and hardware industry are leaders in constant adjustments and improvements.

- "Free" refills for soft drinks at fast-food restaurants have gone from a competitive edge when Hardee's introduced them in the early 1990s to a standard today. The expectations of the markets have changed. (It is not a loss, by the way, for the industry. They simply raised the prices for their sodas slightly.) But they had to make this change to accommodate a market want.

All of these examples point to the constant adjustment, accommodation, and willingness to be flexible in successful organizations in both the for-profit and not-for-profit sectors. And, this gets me to a crucial point about change.

It's the steady change, the small improvements every day, not the huge makeovers that make the difference. Not only are they more effective, they are easier for staff and board to accommodate.

Put another way:

Incremental change is less painful.
Less pain means less resistance.

Why is this true? Because if you are market-driven, if you are asking, listening, asking, and listening in relentless persistence, then you will hear of a thousand small ways you can make your customers happier for every one major change. If you change 1 percent a day for 100 days, less than one-third of the year, the entire organization will be renewed, but at a pace that your staff can accept, adjust to, and adapt to. Steady change is the secret.

But you need to make those changes within the context of a plan to make sure your improvements and changes are moving you toward your overall organizational goal. Otherwise your 1 percent daily improvements can take you around in circles.

Has your organization already changed while you weren't looking? Of course. You should not think for a moment that you are not changing. You are. And your staff is. And your board is. You have made accommodations to market changes, and you need to feel good about the changes you have made.

☞ **HANDS-ON:** To emphasize how many changes you have made in your organization in the recent past, do this exercise with your staff and/or board members: look at your organization five years ago. If you have pictures, policies, staff lists, board lists, marketing material, audits, and annual reports, use them to make a comparison of then versus now. Specifically look at:

- *Size:* How much income do you have per year now versus five years ago?
- *Programs:* Do you have more programs? Are the ones that you provided in the past different now than then? How?
- *Location:* Have you moved? Have you purchased or sold a building? Have you remodeled or added on?
- *Staff:* How many new people have been added to the staff? How many of those on staff five years ago have left?
- *Board:* What changes in the board have you seen?
- *Policies:* How have your personnel, financial, quality assurance, and other policies and bylaws changed?
- *Funders:* What is your funding mix? Do you get funding from different sources than five years ago? What changes in reporting and accounting? In auditing and oversight?
- *Technology:* Do you use the same computers and software as five years ago? Cell phones? Faxes? Internet access?

As you answer these questions as group you will see that you have changed **a lot**. Talk about these changes. Some were easy, some were painful. But reinforce the fact that your organization has successfully changed in many, many ways and that you can continue to do it in the future.

Feel good about how far you have come, and don't believe that you have been static while the world has moved on. You may very well feel that you have not kept pace adequately. And, it is true that the pace of change is accelerating. But don't for a minute let yourself, your staff, or your board think that you are going to start changing from a standing start. You are already moving. But how do you stay flexible while you are moving?

B. RETAINING THE CAPACITY FOR FLEXIBILITY

All of us are born flexible. As we age, we all lose flexibility. I'm sure you have watched toddlers bend in ways that would put you or me in the hospital. As we get older, we have to work hard on flexibility or it disappears, much to our disadvantage.

Mentally we can get inflexible as well. By not continuing to learn, not continuing to consider new ideas, or new ways of doing work, our mental processes stiffen up just as surely as our muscles, tendons, and joints. When you hear yourself saying (or thinking), "Ah, that new stuff doesn't interest me. We're doing just fine," you should set off all the alarms. Sometimes the "new stuff" *is* questionable, but more often there is progress there to be embraced. Even if all of a new idea, process, or protocol is not completely applicable to your organization, some of it may be, and thus regular study and reading to both stretch your brain and learn something that may be of value to you later is important. Fight mental rigidity.

Organizationally we get inflexible as well. We get invested in our buildings, a syndrome that I call the "edifice complex." When so much of our assets and our mental set are invested in our building, the building becomes the organization. We become product-oriented, and the product is what we do in the building. If we have classrooms, inpatient beds, display space, or even offices, we *have* to fill them — whether or not the market wants what goes into those spaces.

● **FOR EXAMPLE:** I'm sure you can think of any number of not-for-profits that have provided services out of a particular location for years. In many cases the building is deteriorating and the neighborhood has changed, perhaps for the worse, perhaps for the better. But in either case, it is no longer the ideal place from which to reach people. What do most *for-profits* do in this situation? The successful ones move. They realize that if their customers are not going to come into the neighborhood where they are located, there will be no business at all soon. So, even if the sale of a piece of property means taking a loss, an immediate loss with the realistic expectation of meeting customer wants for the long term is a good move.

What do many *not-for-profits* do? Come up with excuses about why they should stay where they are. Again, in the old economy this was fine, because there was not competition for many readers. In the new economy such rigidity is a quick but painful method of organizational suicide.

You need to remain flexible as an organization, and not just in your buildings. You must also be flexible in your programming, your service array, your methods of reaching people, your methods of recruiting, managing, and retaining staff.

But how do you, your staff, and your board attain and maintain that flexibility? I've already shown you some suggestions on being a change agent, and I have some more suggestions in this area.

1. Retain Financial Flexibility.

Earlier, I mentioned the edifice complex, that terrible financial disorder that requires organizations to feed their buildings rather than pay attention to the marketplace. Part of financial flexibility is having cash to make strategic moves with. Part of it is not having all your assets tied up in your buildings. Part of it is making money *(profit)* each year as an organization so that you can reinvest in your mission. Part of it is starting and maintaining an endowment.

But financial flexibility empowers other kinds of flexibility, including risk-taking, which we will cover in a moment. Suffice it to say here that financial decisions need to be looked at not only through the lens of getting enough financial and mission return on investment but also retaining enough flexibility to allow you to deal with changes in the markets as they develop. (There is much, much more on this subject in *Financial Empowerment*.)

☞ **HANDS-ON:** Take out your most recent balance sheet and a calculator. Look at your fixed assets and divide them by your total assets. Are fixed assets more than 75 percent of all your assets? Now, look at your cash and cash equivalents. Do they equal or exceed the expenditures for more than 60 days of operation? If you have too many fixed assets and too little cash, you are hamstrung when it comes to quickly accommodating changes in the market.

2. Use Risk-Taking as a Flexibility Tool.

Social entrepreneurship, taking risk on behalf of the people you serve, is another of the nine characteristics of successful not-for-profits that I examined in *Mission-Based Management*. This important characteristic can be used here to retain flexibility.

One of the things that people don't like about change is that it is a threat: there is danger in the unknown. The Chinese symbol for change has two parts, one meaning "danger," one meaning "opportunity." There is both in any change. The reason people put up the most resistance is from the fear of the unknown.

In going through change, we are taking risk. That means we are almost certainly going to make mistakes. Everyone does. Mistakes by themselves are no big deal. We all learn better from our mistakes than from our successes. But if your culture is one where anyone who makes any mistake is punished (a blame-friendly environment), people will, of course, not want to try anything new. Why? Because there is a higher likelihood of error in doing new things than there is in doing things that are already known and practiced. If error, any error, means getting chewed out, why take the chance?

Are you risk-aversive as an organization? Do you expect 100 percent perfection? While I have nothing against high-quality services, you need to remember: *organizations that have a zero tolerance for error have a zero capacity for innovation.* Innovation, that essential competitive skill, is all about risk and reward. You try something new (a change) and you risk failure. But you also may succeed and then get rewarded.

You need to encourage prudent risk, regular innovation, and trying new things. Once your staff and board get the idea, you will see them stretching more and more. What do I mean by "stretch"? That's my next suggestion.

3. Stretch by Making Regular, Small Changes.

I'm a runner. Before I run, I stretch. Every time. If, for some reason, I forget, I can really tell. You and your organization need to stretch as well, and do it regularly. How? By making small regular changes *and noting them.* Remember the exercise I suggested of listing all the changes that have occurred in staff, board, service, location, and the like? From here on out, not only make the small changes but make note of them, so that people are used to hearing the words, and realizing that not only are things changing but that they are not getting hurt by those changes. What you want to develop is a culture that is constantly refreshing itself, trying new things, and taking on a new "look."

Here are some small changes that you can make without too much trouble or expense. *Don't* do all of them at once! Meter them out over time, so that some change is *always* going on. I've divided the changes into two groups: *Low Impact* and *High Impact.* The first group is generally less expensive and less threatening to staff or board members, the latter more so.

☞ **HANDS-ON:** Try these changes:
Low Impact
➡ *Change your letterhead.* Not now, but when your supply runs out. I'm not talking about changing the logo or the entire look (which may be timely as well) but rather moving the lines, changing the color, etc. I know that this may require a change in business cards, etc., but those can be phased in over time.

➡ *Repaint, repaper, put down new carpet.* Don't ever think that a change of appearance is unimportant. If you have the money, give staff an allowance to buy wall decorations for their offices.

➡ *Upgrade your software.* Most software has regular upgrades. If yours is functional but not completely up-to-date, consider upgrading. It is often not expensive, and you can be more productive after the change.

➡ *Rethink your meeting schedules.* Do you need staff meetings every week? Team meetings every month? Are the location, duration, and content of the meetings appropriate? Ask those who regularly attend and make the changes that they suggest.

➡ *Start with your own environment.* Move your own office furniture, add a plant, remove a picture. Buy a new coffee mug, eat lunch at a different time each day, drive a new route to work. Get used to difference.

High Impact
➡ *Change offices.* Whoa! Here is a big one. Perhaps a change of location will help some people, or be an avenue for better communication, more effective supervision or improved access to your clientele.

➡ *Change titles.* Starting with your own. Perhaps you have been thinking of moving to a corporate model where the executive director has the title of CEO and where people who were directors become vice-presidents. Perhaps now is the time to implement that.

➡ *Reorganize your table of organization.* Not just to do it, but if you have been putting a needed change off, get on with it. Perhaps there will be a major reorganization, perhaps just a few people will be affected.

Please, don't misunderstand me here. I am not urging you just to stir things up. Don't make changes just to make changes. Any of these that you do implement should be done for a reason, and thoughtfully considered before starting. But a pace of regular change keeps the organization stretching, and thus more flexible.

4. Don't Always Call Change "Change."
Change is what it is. And it is inevitable. But if the word "change" really gets in the way, if when you say "change" the staff or board hear "trouble," switch the nomenclature. Use terms such as improvement, adjustment, innovation, refinement, shift, or variation. There is only so much cajoling, training, coaching, and being helpful that you can do when people fear certain words. If that is true in your organization, go around the barrier instead of through it. Use different terminology, and perhaps it will help.

A final note about the retention of flexibility and change agency. Despite all of your efforts, all of your enthusiasm, and spirited advocacy for moving your organization ahead, it is inevitable that some people just won't get it. They will continue to resist, or they will act out in other ways, some passive-aggressive, some morale-killing, some even outright rude.

When you have given your best effort to bringing these people on the team and they have decided, for whatever reason, not to join, it is time for them to leave. Once the organization has made a decision to go in a certain direction, it is up to them, whether they be staff or volunteer, to get with the program and support it or find other things to do in another organization. What happens when a basketball player refuses to run windsprints? Or a cellist refuses to play a certain piece with feeling? He or she is off the team or out of the orchestra. The same is true with your organization.

If you have read *Mission-Based Management,* you know that I am a great believer in participatory, inclusive management, a system where ideas flow from the point of service to the managers, and where decisions are made as close to the point of service as possible. That having been said, I do not in any way support staff insubordination or refusal to follow policy. Decisions still need to be made. And if we have entrusted those decision makers, whether they are the board, executive team, or line workers, to make a decision, it is up to the rest of us to support it. Those who can't need to go elsewhere.

C. BEING A CHANGE AGENT

As a key staff or board member, you need to lead in terms of the changes your organization pursues. You need to develop plans that outline the way your organization is going, and then delineate what needs to happen to get there. You need to set internal policies that support those plans. You must identify issues and discuss them fully, including staff, volunteers, and even the community in those discussions when appropriate.

But when all is said and done, when all the dust settles and the decisions are made, you need to *lead* on the changes you have just initiated, not just tell people to go do them. You must not be just the initiator of change but the facilitator of it. A change agent is someone who helps people through the process, overcoming the barriers to change. To do this, I have found that the following seven steps are essential.

1. Show the Mission Outcome of the Change.

We're back to the mission. People will resist new stuff. We all know it. But if you can show a relationship between the change and doing more and better mission, *some* of the resistance in *some* of your staff and board will be eliminated. Notice that I did not say *all* of the resistance in *all* of the people. But showing the mission connection is a major help.

2. Go Through the Change Together.

Here's the lesson in a nutshell. People will change much more readily *with* you rather than *for* you.

● **FOR EXAMPLE:** Imagine yourself brought into a large room that you have never seen before. The room is an office for ten people and full of furniture. There is no one else there except you and your supervisor who brought you in. The supervisor points to a door on the far side of the room and says, "That is where we're going now. Get there." And then he or she turns the lights out and leaves. You have to negotiate the new terrain in the dark. You decide not to move at all. You don't want to get hurt, and you didn't really get a good look at the location of all the furniture before the lights were turned out. An hour later, your supervisor returns and says, "Why haven't you done what I asked? I showed you what to do!"

When you tell people what to do and then leave them to their own devices, if they have never been there before, they will naturally be concerned about making mistakes. If, however, you are there for them, if you show them how to make the change, they are much more likely to comply, and with much less resistance. Imagine that same supervisor offering to come with you across the dark room and, better yet, bringing a flashlight.

Stay with people through change. Check in. Be available. Do your changing as a team.

3. Talk Regularly about Competition.

I have spent many pages already talking about competition, your place in a competitive world, and the need for continual asking and adjusting. Your staff need to hear the same message in order to lower their resistance and to see the need for change. At the end of this chapter there are specific discussion points on competition and the need for change. Don't, however, have just one session on this. Make it a regular part of staff meetings, board meetings, your newsletter, or other methods of communication with your staff and volunteers.

4. Point Out Changes Outside the Organization.

Stay informed. Read widely. Pay attention to the outside environment, the world in general, and not just your industry. Learn to make connections between the changes in the outside world and your organization. Then share this information with staff. Be a role model for them of life-long learning.

5. Don't Wait for Big Changes to Make Any Changes.

If the only change your organization ever makes is monumental, you won't do it very well, because you won't have practiced much. Don't save up all your changes to "do it all at once." Incremental regular change is much less threatening. Remember the exercise I wanted you to do with your staff so that they would realize how much you had changed? If you did that, people probably said things to you like, "I had no idea we had come this far." Why didn't they notice? Because the changes were incremental. Now, use that low-profile, incremental approach to make your own organizational changes less threatening. If you do have a big change, can you break it down into more steady, small changes? If you can, it will lower anxiety and resistance.

6. Don't Criticize the Past — Look to the Future.

When you announce a change, do it positively, not negatively. Too often I hear people say, "Now we're finally going to get it right," which of course, implies that your people have been doing something *wrong*. Now THAT will foster resistance! Instead of criticizing the past, talk about how this will be even better, do even more mission, help in your continual quest for higher quality. Look forward, not back.

7. Be Patient!

Change takes time. Nearly any change you initiate, from a large one like a modification of your program policies, to a small one such as a change in a reimbursement form, requires a behavioral change on someone's part. And behavioral change takes time, a lot of time. You need to use your coaching skills to keep people on track. You need to be around so that you can catch small mistakes before they become big ones. You need to encourage and cajole and not expect perfection the first time out. Be patient.

These seven elements, when used together, will make for a much easier change process for your organization. And, the more your leadership team, managers, and supervisors practice them, the better.

D. THE PACE OF CHANGE IN A COMPETITIVE ENVIRONMENT

"The hurrieder I go, the behinder I get" is an old saying that speaks well to the feeling we all have at times about the world we live in. No one can possibly keep up with the changes in their profession, work place, in fashion, sports, music, technology, entertainment, politics, and local, national, and international events. So we have a tendency to throw up our hands and say "OVERLOAD!" and find excuses not to pay attention.

In the "old" days, you could get away with that for a number of reasons. Change was slower paced, if you weren't a "cutting-edge" organization people gave you a break, since you were a not-for-profit, and, most importantly, you probably had a relative or virtual monopoly. Thus, it didn't matter how much you accommodated to changes in the "outside" world. You could accommodate at your own more leisurely (more "professional") pace. Remember when attorneys and physicians berated those in their professions who advertised? Unseemly. Unprofessional. Now you go down the road and see huge billboards advertising for law practices, medical groups, clinics, hospitals, and even individual practitioners. And some of those who refused to advertise are out of business, or have been bought out by their competition.

There are two key points I want to make here:

First, the *pace of change*. It is accelerating with the explosion of information available, the speed of communications, and the general pace of our lives. All are more and more intense.

Second, the *competitive environment.* This environment is one that your organization may already be in or may just be entering. But you and your organization cannot avoid it. Imagine you are at a huge airport. You are walking down an immense concourse to your plane. Suddenly you come upon a moving walkway and are forced by the crowd to get on. Your pace has just picked up. Now the walkway speeds up ever so steadily until you are nearly racing. Things go by faster. You have less time to study them before they are behind you. And the end of the walkway comes up very, very fast. That is the transition from noncompetitive to competitive environments and from the slower pace of yesteryear to the rapid pace of today.

So both the pace of change and the competitive environment affect you, as do some cultural shifts that we should touch on.

1. The average attention span is shorter. I have no "hard" data to back this up, just observations. Look at the length of the average television advertisement, the shortening of the average article in newspapers and magazines (or the entirety of *USA Today*), the shorter stories on the evening television news. We are a short-attention-span, and immediate-gratification, society. The point for you? People don't just leave their short attention span behind when they get up from their television. They bring it with them when they seek the services you provide. How many Americans would wait weeks or months for surgery? In England, people are used to it. How many people do you see frustrated at not being the first in line at the check-out counter in the grocery store? I see lots, including myself.

The issue here is that, to be competitive, you need to be as fast, as responsive, as fulfilling as your competition. And, the competition is always looking for ways to speed up their service.

> ● **FOR EXAMPLE:** The rental car industry has long sought to speed people from airplane to car. The bane of any renter is a long line to get a car, and even more, a long line to check the car back in at the airport. You want to get on your way. Hertz, Avis, Budget, and the rest have all experimented with ways to speed up the process. They tried express check-in, where you drop your rental agreement in a box and the company sends you a bill. But some people either didn't trust the company to get it right or they needed their receipt for accounting purposes immediately. So Hertz then implemented a system to accomplish both wants: a fast return and a receipt. When you pull up in a Hertz lot at an airport, a Hertz employee with a handheld computer approaches you, and while you are emptying the car of your belongings, takes your rental agreement, enters the mileage, and then prints out your receipt on a small thermal printer hanging off their belt. The handheld unit is connected by radio and phone lines to the central Hertz computer system, and you are on your way with little or no delay, and no line! What did Avis and Budget do? Imitated the system as fast as they could.

What can you do to accommodate this change in attention span? Value your customer's time. Think through how you can do things more efficiently, more effectively. If you think that your customers don't care, consider your own response to a long wait for service at the restaurant, bank, or other facility.

2. Louder, brighter advertisement and media. This is directly related to number one. If you saw a retrospective on television ads from ten to fifteen years ago, you would be bored silly. The ads were, by comparison to today's machine-gun-style messages, bland and *long* (one whole minute!). Today, you have to nearly grab people by the throat to get their attention. And with the explosion of inexpensive PC-based design and printing software as well as dirt-cheap, high-quality color printers, the spread of really bright, classy-looking material is everywhere. The issue for you in a competitive environment is that your marketing, advertising, and promotion have to look "current," which means constantly updated. If you don't, you won't get people's attention. If you don't get their attention, they won't use your services. "It was boring" — referring to your marketing material or your services — is the ultimate pejorative, and a deadly one in a competitive world.

3. The product cycle is now much shorter. It used to be that the time from the idea to the marketplace was many years. Now the turnaround is much, much faster. Just look at the rapid pace of updated computer hardware and software. They are often literally outdated when they arrive on the shelves. Now, the fact that they are outdated doesn't mean that they are useless, but that fact is not the issue. The perception of not being new is the key. The auto industry did this for years, putting out new cars to replace perfectly good ones. But remember when all the new models came out in the fall? Now they arrive at different points in the year. The television "season" also used to start after Labor Day and go through the spring. Now the season is shorter, has more cancellations and mid-season replacements, and is broken up by more "specials," all in an effort to keep our attention.

The point for you? Just like their attention spans, people bring their focus on the new to your organization. Is what you do *exactly* as it has been for many years? Strike one. Is your pace of change so slow that you would need to gear up now for a service adjustment to meet a market want in two fiscal years? Strikes two and three. People won't wait that long, because your competition won't and then your customers will have choices of places to go other than yours. The admonition from you "We'll be there in a while!" doesn't work any longer.

4. The end of annual cycles. In the old economy, people in the not-for-profit world lived on an annual cycle, usually based on their state's or the federal fiscal year. We had annual budgets. We knew what our year "looked" like well in advance. No more.

● **FOR EXAMPLE:** I have told you that in Massachusetts, when a person with a disability is placed in a community agency, the state lets bids based on the needs of the individual. In telling you about it before, I used it as an example of previously noncompetitive services becoming more and more competitive. In this case you should know that not-for-profits that wish to provide services must respond in *15 days* with a full service plan, and one of the competitive issues is how quickly they can begin providing actual services. This often means that, to be competitive, and to get the work, the staff must drop other things that they are doing to meet the 15-day response clock. This is meeting a customer want in order to be competitive. The example also shows that budgets are not always static and predictable. It also emphasizes that there is a vastly greater emphasis on a relationship, where the government is a customer and the not-for-profit is a vendor that must be responsive to keep its contract.

Your organization must be responsive and reactive to meet customers' wants, even when those customers are the long-disliked major funder.

5. There is much less sympathy for the not-for-profit that can't keep up. I've touched on this a number of times already, but it has impact here as well. Ten years ago, when you had poor service, pitiful marketing, or obsolete buildings people said, "Oh well, they are just a charity. What do you expect?" Now they expect much, much more. People see the funds you use as *theirs*, and often, they have a point. The money may be from tax revenues or it may be from donations, or both. And people want outcomes from their investment in you. So you don't get the break you did before. You need to compete, and more importantly, you need to be seen as competitive, up-to-date, and fully professional by your community.

You are in a rapidly changing, competitive environment. Whether you like it or not. You have to adjust, adapt, and have increasingly rapid responses to keep up. Whether you like it or not. In the next two sections I'll show you how to lead your organization through this constant change and provide you with some ideas on how to keep your organization flexible so that it can respond.

Before we move on, however, I would be derelict if I did not discuss two important points. I have been making the case for new, new, new. To some of you it may read as trendy, trendy, trendy. In some cases, there is a real and valid reason for not constantly reinventing your organization, in *not* having the latest and greatest. Let's look at two such situations:

1. The Case for Stability: In some organizations it is important to have at least the appearance of sameness, of stability. For example, if your organization treats chronically mentally ill individuals, a predictable, comfortable, consistent environment is often important. If you go changing the office decor every six months (as if you could afford it) you could hurt your mission rather than help it. In other cases, donors want to give to the "same" organization as they always have, and a major change in appearance of logo, stationery, etc., could negatively affect that. In both of these cases, the stability of the appearance, or of the program, are important to key market segments. Respect that. Again, I don't advocate change for change's sake. But I do want you to be aware that your organization is being held to an increasingly rigid standard to keep up with the rest of the world.

2. The Belief in Poverty-Chic: "Poverty-Chic" is the still widely held belief that it is unseemly, if not immoral, for not-for-profits to have any appearance of wealth. Another way of putting this is "you can't do well doing good." There is a long, long story behind why this still common belief persists, but it does present real conflict with all of the exhortations that I have just given you about being up-to-date, professional, and responsive. For example, if you are like most of my clients, you have been criticized about your computers. They are too fancy, too expensive for an organization like yours, some say. And the *same* machines get criticized by your accountant or board members for being so out-of-date. You can't win. If you have professional marketing materials, some people assume you have lots of money and don't need donations. If you have new carpet in the lobby, you are seen as frivolous; if you don't, you are hassled for having crummy space.

It seems you can't win. Well, you can, but it takes some time. First, you need to have your board and staff behind you when you "upgrade." By upgrade I mean the carpet, your vehicles, your computers, your office furniture. The staff and board have to agree that this is a good, mission-related investment. You have to have the people inside the organization on your side. Then, you can begin to make the case outside, but at least your staff and board won't be taking shots at you.

It's a slow process to convince our friends and neighbors to let us be part of the rest of society. As long as they continue to treat us as poor brothers and sisters, we will, at least in part, act that way. And that way is not good mission.

RECAP

In this chapter we have covered an important facet of competitive marketing: flexibility. Maintaining flexibility and welcoming positive change are difficult organizational skills. I showed you a number of ways that may help attain and maintain these skills.

First, we looked at the need for flexibility, and I provided you with a number of examples of organizations that were and were not flexible in the face of changing market wants. Second, I showed you some methods of retaining organizational flexibility, including retaining financial flexibility, using risk-taking as a flexibility tool, stretching by making regular small changes, and not always calling change "change." We reviewed the fact that incremental change is less painful and thus often less resisted.

Third, we examined some specific ways for you to be a change agent. To recap quickly, these included:

1. **Show the mission outcome of the change.**
2. **Go through change as a coach.**
3. **Talk regularly about competition.**
4. **Point out changes outside the organization.**
5. **Don't wait for big changes to make any changes.**
6. **Don't criticize the past — look to the future.**
7. **Be patient.**

Finally, we spent some time going over the pace of change in a competitive environment. The pace is picking up and I pointed out that in the "old" days, people would give you a break because you were a not-for-profit, but those days are long gone. You need to keep pace because, as the environment becomes more competitive, people will have more choices and they may just choose to go somewhere else.

There is no substitute for flexibility. Remember the old story about the grasses on the shore during a storm. They are flexible, they bend, and they survive the storm. The strong, inflexible oak can survive many a wind but will eventually meet a storm that will knock it down.

The competitive storm that you are entering is bigger than you are. Market wants change as fast as winds in a swirling gale, and you need to be flexible to remain standing. Finally, flexibility is not something that we naturally get better at with time; we get worse. Both as individuals and organizations we get set in our ways, we have our traditions ("the way we do things here"), and our investments follow certain paths. The older our organization gets, the bigger it becomes, the more difficult it is to change the path. But you must be able to change direction promptly and with a positive attitude if you are to succeed in the markets of tomorrow.

Now that you know how to retain your flexibility, we've really covered most of the preparatory steps of competitive marketing. Now we'll get to the technical stuff, starting with the real markets you are serving.

☞☞ **HANDS-ON REVIEW:**
   • **A review of small changes that have occurred**
   • **A financial flexibility review**
   • **Some ideas to help you "stretch"**

DISCUSSION QUESTIONS FOR CHAPTER 5:

1. How averse are people here to change? Why? Do we as managers lead through change?

2. How much can we morally change with the market? Are there things that we do now that we couldn't have considered five years ago? Why are they okay now?

3. The list in Section C, Being a Change Agent, shows how to retain our flexibility. Can we do these? When?

4. Do we encourage or discourage prudent risk-taking? How?

5. Is the pace of change in our markets accelerating or stable? What can we do to accommodate it? Can we encourage regular, persistent improvements?

6. The Marketing Cycle for a Not-For-Profit

OVERVIEW

Marketing is not an event, it is a process, and one that never ends. Unlike a linear process with a beginning, middle, and end, marketing is cyclical, with familiar steps repeated over and over as the organization regularly responds to changes in the markets, customer wants, competition, and strategic issues.

And, even though it is important to know that the marketing cycle is just that, a cycle that goes around and around, it is even more important to understand the hub on which the cycle spins. That hub is the customer. *First, last, and in between, the marketing cycle for your organization should revolve around the people you serve.* Not around your existing services, not around your current building or staff or board, but around your customers.

Chapter Thumbnail
➡ **The Marketing Cycle That Works**
➡ **The Marketing Disability of Most Not-For- Profits**
➡ **The Marketing Cycle and Competitors**

This chapter will show you how the cycle functions, and why it is important to attend to each part of the cycle in the prescribed order, as well as with regularity. I will cover a marketing process that works. We will then move our discussion to the marketing disability that really impedes most not-for-profits as they try to market. This disability is a long-standing one, one that has been well ingrained in the minds of most not-for-profit staff and board members, and thus will be difficult to dislodge. If it cannot be overcome, however, the organization that you work for may be permanently behind the competitive curve.

In the last section of the chapter, we'll look at the marketing cycle and how it affects some of your for-profit as well as your not-for-profit competitors. You will learn how they view your organization, how they think about competing with you, and, most importantly, how you should view them. In Chapter 8, we'll cover the competition at much more length, but in this chapter we'll limit our discussion to your competition and their reactions to and interactions with your marketing cycle.

By the end of the chapter, you will have an excellent understanding of a marketing cycle that can work for your organization — for existing products and services as well as for start-up ideas. You will know the disability you have to overcome and that knowledge will be the first step in successfully overcoming to it. And finally, you will be able to see the markets through the eyes of your competitors, a key competitive advantage in an increasingly competitive world.

A. THE MARKETING CYCLE THAT WORKS

Most people seem to think that the marketing cycle starts with the product or service. If I know what I am selling, the theory seems to go, then I start from there. I can then decide how to sell, who to sell to, what way to convince them, and how to price. Those beliefs are wrong, wrong, wrong, and wrong again.

Marketing doesn't start with the product, or the service. Marketing starts with the *market:* the people to whom you are trying to sell or to serve. You start by deciding who you are serving, follow that by asking those people what they want, and then respond by giving it to them. That's marketing. If you start with a product or service and back into a market by asking, "How can I sell this wonderful product or service to these people?" you are destined to succeed only for a very short time and then only if you are a superb salesperson.

Marketing (the verb) has to start with the market (the noun) to be effective over the long haul. And, by putting the appropriate marketing activities together in the correct sequence you can change the way your organization thinks of its markets and ultimately the way those markets think of you — for the better! The cycle that we're about to review works for new products and new services, and for honing and improving existing products or services. It works in human services, the arts, education, religion, environmental action, and legal aid. It works, because at its core it is sensitive to people's wants, not their needs, and it puts those wants first.

With no further delay, let's review this marketing cycle. Below you will see the cycle at its purest and simplest, in a generic form that can be used across disciplines. Later we'll apply it in a few **"FOR EXAMPLES."**

The Marketing Cycle of a Not-For-Profit		
1	Define/Redefine the Market.	
2	What Does Your Market Want?	
3	Shape and Reshape Your Product or Service.	
4	Set a Sensible Price.	
5	Promote the Product or Service.	
6	Distribute the Product or Service.	
7	Evaluate, Evaluate, Evaluate.	
8	Return to #1.	

As you can see, the cycle starts with the identification of the target markets, asks about the markets' wants, and then, and only then, devises or revises the product or service you are going to provide. Nowhere in the display do you see the word "need." There's a reason for that, and you should know the answer if you read Chapter 2: needs are different than wants, and people buy wants, not needs.

Let's dissect the cycle and go through it item by item, discussing each point in some detail. Then we'll reassemble the cycle and look at its application in some real-world not-for-profits.

1. Define/Redefine Your Market.

The first question to ask is, who am I serving? Who are the people, the individuals that I am selling to? How many of them are there? Where are they? Are they, as a group, as a market, growing in numbers or waning?

As you approach this question, do not get sucked into what I call "the census trap." You get caught in the census trap when you assume that your market is all the people in a geographic area. It never is. This assumption is an outgrowth of the monopolies that we discussed at length in Chapter 1. Many organizations had (and some still have) cachement areas, areas that were their "territory," their monopoly. In many cases funding for these organizations was based on population (capitated) so that the illusion that an organization worked for everyone in the cachement area was reinforced.

Nothing, of course, could be further from the truth. Your market is not everyone, it is a much, much more defined group of people. If you are a private school, it is the parents of children in the age groups you teach, who are interested in non-public education and who have the resources to send their children to your school. If you are a health department, for health screenings it might be just people who don't have private physicians, or if it is for lead screenings, just people with very small children who live in older homes with lead-based paint. If you are a church, while your dogma may suggest that the world is your market, in reality, you will most likely appeal to people within five to eight miles of your church. Who are looking for a church. Who do not already have a church home. A much smaller number than "everyone" in the community, or even everyone within your five- to eight-mile radius.

The action statement in bold above says to "Define/redefine your market." Defining a market is pretty straightforward: you identify who you are going to serve. But what do I mean by redefining? It is an important term, because for most readers it will be the more common task. Redefining your market(s) means to periodically go back and look at your markets, assuring yourself that they are still there, that they are the ones you want to serve, and that they still have wants you can meet.

For example, if you are a YMCA and one of your markets (for your athletic summer camps) is kids from eight to eighteen, you might re-examine this market and redefine it to be *kids 8 to18 from homes that have incomes over $30,000*, or *kids from public schools* as opposed to private schools, or *kids who played in your regular youth athletic leagues*. This regular redefinition is crucial since conditions change, markets mature, and wants change along with them. Only by regularly reviewing and redefining who it is that you are serving can you accurately ask those whom you hope to serve what they want.

I hope that you get the idea that you need to identify your target markets carefully, developing as detailed a definition, as particular a description of them, as you can. The more accurate and finite your definition of your market, the more accurate your market projections will be, and thus the more accurate your estimates, assumptions, and plans. This technique should be used for all of your markets, so that you can recognize the many, many different markets that you serve. This activity is so important that we will spend the entirety of Chapter 7 solely on this subject.

2. What Does Your Market Want?

Having identified your market(s) as closely and finitely as you can, what is next? Is it to figure out how to sell your product or service to this newly identified group? Is it to blanket them with literature so that they will want what you have to sell? Is it to offer coupons to entice them into your doors the first time? No, not yet.

What is next in the marketing cycle is to figure out what the market wants. How do you do that? You ask! By asking, asking regularly and then, of course, *listening* and *responding,* you will find out what most people want. And remember our discussion in Chapter 2 — people seek wants, so meet those wants and people will seek out your organization.

You can ask formally and informally. You can ask in surveys, in focus groups, in interviews, in one-on-one conversation. You need to ask, and ask, and ask again. Because asking once is not enough, since people's wants change, and change regularly. This is also a critical issue, and we'll spend all of Chapter 9 on asking in all of its variety of ways.

Suffice it to say that you cannot meet the markets' wants if you don't know what those wants are. And, you cannot know what the wants are unless you ask. The biggest mistake you can make in marketing is to say, "I've been in this business 20 years and I *know* what customers want." Wrong. No one knows until they ask.

● **FOR EXAMPLE:** In 1995 Vice President Gore oversaw a widespread reevaluation of the way that the federal government did business. Called Reinventing Government, this effort included customer service surveys in many federal agencies that had never before considered asking. The results were predictable: people wanted a lot of different things than the "experts" anticipated. My favorite story from the effort is that of a senior administrator (with 25 years of service) at the Veteran's Administration who was supremely confident that veterans didn't mind waiting to be seen at the VA hospitals because "they get to sit around and swap war stories." The survey showed, of course, that veterans, like the rest of us, *hate* to wait, and that long waits were their biggest complaint!

Ask, ask, ask, and listen!

3. Shape and Reshape Your Products and Services.

Only now that you know who your target markets are, and only now that you know what they want — only now can you shape (or reshape) your product or service to meet the wants of these markets. This may mean starting from scratch to develop a new product or service, or, more likely, the amendment, adjustment, and improvement of products and services already in place. Remember, not only will you be redefining your markets regularly, but wants change with time. Even within static markets, wants change. As a result, you need to assess and reassess and reassess your services to ensure that they meet the current wants of the markets.

● **FOR EXAMPLE:** The staff of your organization are a market, and one that you should pay close attention to. Let's assume that you are going to survey staff about what kinds of benefits they would like, as a precursor to making changes in your benefits package. What a great idea! You are asking the market what they want! The survey asks each respondent to rate each of 20 potential benefits on a scale of one to ten. You collect the information and make the changes, trying your best to fit the benefits package to the wants of the staff. Now, go five years into the future. Assume the unlikely, that every staff person that took the previous benefits survey is still there, and no new staff have come on board. You repeat the survey. Would the answers be the same? Of course not. People's wants change as they age, and everyone in the market is five years older. Let's change the assumption. What if you have had normal turn-over in the five-year interval since the first survey? If you readminister the identical survey, would the answers be the same? No, because the market has changed in composition. In both cases, you would need to change the benefits package to continue being market-sensitive.

You cannot reasonably meet *every* want of *every* market. For example, if one potential customer for counseling services says that she can only come in between midnight and eight in the morning, it is probably not reasonable or cost-efficient to have a counselor on-site overnight just for that one customer. However, the information is important, because it may point out a previously hidden market — those who work second-shift jobs and are ready to seek services at night rather than during traditional hours. Is there enough of a market to support a reshaping of your services to accommodate this want?

You need to be sensitive to regular changes in market wants by making adjustments in the way you provide your services. However, you need to cushion your desire to meet every customer's want fully with prudent business assessments and financial planning to ensure that you meet the wants you can afford to and defer on those that you cannot do either efficiently, effectively, or with a high degree of quality.

4. Set a Sensible Price.

A sensible price is one that: *first,* recovers all of your costs of providing a service or manufacturing a product; *second,* adds a profit to that price, and *third,* meets the realities of the market. The first and second parts increase the price. The third part usually reduces it.

Let me focus you for a moment on the first part: full cost recovery. I know far too many organizations that are convinced that they must under-price their competition at any cost; that cost is all that motivates a customer. Thus, they often juggle their costs around so that their sales price appears to be one that assures full cost recovery but really doesn't. In this way they feel that they are assured of getting the work, of locking in the customer. What they are *really* doing is ensuring that each time they provide the service they *lose* money.

It is crucial in price setting to remember that people don't buy based on price — they buy based on *value.* Price is a variable component of value. For some people price is 99 percent of value, for others just a small amount. If price was the only issue, there would be no luxury products or services, no first-class seats on airlines, no Ritz-Carlton hotels, no limousines clogging up the streets in our big cities. If price was everything, we would send all of our correspondence by mail. Federal Express would be shut down in a day. So would Gucci, Saks, and most of the stores on Fifth Avenue in New York, or Rodeo Drive in Beverly Hills.

So don't just think about price. Think about value. Do people highly value your service or the way that you deliver it? If so, they will be willing to consider paying more for it. If they don't value your services, then even a lower price may not bring them on as customers.

● **FOR EXAMPLE:** An organization that I work with provides interpretive tours of historic districts in its city. The organization is devoted to historic preservation and uses its net revenues to fund historic preservation efforts. The problem was that its tours were too popular. The organization only had so many really good tour guide/interpreters and it knew that it could not train more very quickly. So, to reduce demand the organization raised the price. By *doubling* it. The rationale was that if more excellent guides could not be trained (and they couldn't in the short, two-year term), the organization would only do what it could do excellently. And, by raising prices, it would reduce demand naturally, instead of making people mad by having groups too large, or by turning people away completely.

It was a gutsy action, and one that most not-for-profits would not be comfortable taking. Other organizations would have rationalized that since their costs had not risen, their prices should not. They would assume that their status as a not-for-profit did not enable them to make a profit, and would not react to the market demand. But this group did, and with very, very unpredictable results.

Demand went up. Way up. It doubled in the first six months. Why? Because people assumed that a tour that cost a lot would be good-and thus desirable. The tours *were* good and got rave reviews. But the increase in price did not decrease demand. So what did the organization do? It limited the size of tours, set up a reservation system including advanced payment (so that it got to use people's money early), but did not do more tours per day than it could do well. Yes, that disappointed people, but five years later the tours are still sold out five months in advance, and, as another benefit, donations from tourists are way up, again based on the perceived value of the service and the quality of the organization.

Don't ever assume that price is everything. Recover your costs, add a profit, and then listen to the markets. This is another really important issue, and I have included a complete chapter on the subject in my book *Financial Empowerment*.

5. Promote the Product or Service.

By now you know your market, you know what they want, you know what you are providing, and you know the price. Great. But does your market know about you? Do they know that you are in business, that you have this wonderful product or service that is shaped to meet their wants? They will know because of your promotion. Promotion is cold calls, warm calls, direct mail, advertising, word of mouth, in-person sales, referrals, and public information.

Don't just shotgun your information. Carefully gauge how and what you tell your markets. Track how they find you, and use only those methods that work. Experiment with new ones, but drop them if they are not delivering for you. A great example of this trial and error is the explosion in homepages on the World Wide Web that has occurred since 1995. Will they result in more business? For some organizations, yes; for some, no. The Web offers access to huge markets, but are they the people you want to seek? For example, if you serve mostly homeless or poor people, it is a fairly safe bet to assume that they do not have access to a computer. Choose another marketing method.

You need to promote to customers, to people that you serve. You also need to promote to people who send you customers; your referral sources. For a rehabilitation hospital this might be neurologists, for an ex-offender program it might be court adjudicators, for a wildlife preserve it might be travel agents or local hotels and restaurants. You need referral sources, and you need to give them information that helps them understand what you do and why they should send people to you.

Here again is a very important issue. You need excellent marketing materials, and you need to put them in the right hands at the right time. Better marketing materials will be our entire focus in Chapter 10.

6. Distribute The Product or Service.

It may be easier for you to think of distribution as service delivery with the following context: *who* delivers, *when* is it delivered, *where* is it delivered, and *how* is it delivered. Remember that all of these weigh heavily on market satisfaction.

A simple example is day care. If the *who* is not people who relate well to children (and parents); if the *when* is not at hours that meet parents' work schedules; if the *where* is not in an accessible location perceived as open, airy, pleasing, and safe, and if the *how* is not beneficial to the children, then the services will not be patronized well enough to do the community any good.

By asking your customers what they want you will learn a great deal about how they want the services provided. This cycle of asking and providing is yet another case of constant refinement. If there is a change in the wants for delivery, try to meet it sensibly if you can. For example, to return to the day care example, if your community's largest employer (a factory) suddenly went to a second or even a third shift, you might need to rethink the hours that you provide services. But if only one or two families out of 100 need the extended hours, you might offer them in-home sitting rather than keeping the entire facility open all night.

Just because the *what* of your services is excellent doesn't mean that you don't have to pay attention to the *who, where, when,* and *how.* They are also part of the marketing mix and the constant cycle of asking and adjustment.

7. Evaluate, Evaluate, Evaluate.

As you have already seen over and over, the markets and their wants change constantly. You need to be evaluating the effectiveness of your efforts as well. Customer satisfaction surveys are one way, as are regular interviews with funders, service recipients, staff, and board members. But you also need to be watching competitors and tracking where your customers come from. All of these evaluation tools are important. In later chapters, we'll cover how to choose and segment markets, follow the competition, and ask customers what they want, but the essential thing here is to remember that evaluation and improvement are critical parts of the competitive marketing cycle.

Now let's look at two applications of this cycle in real not-for-profits. This should illustrate more fully the applications of the marketing cycle and its usefulness to you and to your organization in your marketing efforts.

● **FOR EXAMPLE:** A symphony wanted to expand its offerings to the local community, but found through surveys of ticket purchasers (particularly season ticket holders) that the number of full symphony concerts were really all that the community could afford. The survey did produce some interesting comments (read: *wants*) from customers. They wanted concerts closer to downtown, and they wanted more intimate music, where they could be closer to the musicians. These comments resulted from the performance hall being a huge auditorium at a local university, ten miles from the center of the city. People also noted that they would like to come earlier than the traditional 8:15 PM start. The symphony already had a chamber orchestra, but it played to small audiences at this admittedly too large auditorium. The board and staff identified their market: new ticket holders with children, as well as those who had responded to the survey. They had asked what this market wanted and the answer was clear — more small intimate concerts closer to downtown, starting earlier. They took an existing service, chamber orchestra concerts, and adapted this service to meet these wants. They changed the distribution — the where and the when.

The next season they held four chamber orchestra concerts in a historic church (with excellent acoustics) in the downtown area. They started on Friday at 7:00 PM rather than Saturday at 8:15. The concert-goers in the first pews could be close enough to the performers to read the music as it was played!

The price was also lower than at the large auditorium (the symphony's costs were down due to less musicians to pay and lower rental fees) and the concerts were promoted heavily through music teachers in the public schools ("Get your parents to take you to a concert"). The result was an immediate success with each concert a sellout. The next season the organization provided eight such concerts and they not only sold out but allowed the symphony to retire a burdensome debt.

The lesson? Even adapting existing services can be a winner when you ask your markets and listen to them.

● **FOR EXAMPLE:** The donations to a thrift store were down. And, the thrift store needed a continuing supply of quality donated goods to meet the constant demand from customers. (As an aside, thrift stores are excellent examples of organizations that work for two *widely* dif-

ferent markets: the donors of the goods and the purchasers of the
goods.) The thrift store already had collection boxes, and would ar-
range to pick up goods if called. But still it wasn't enough. They
decided to administer a survey in the local community, and found
that what people wanted most was to simply get rid of excess "stuff",
but only when they were (a. cleaning out their garage, attic, or base-
ment, or (b. having a garage sale. A garage sale? It made sense, and
the organization moved to adapt its existing pick-up service to meet
the wants of the customer. Staff watched the papers and, every morning, people went to houses that advertised garage sales. They talked
to the homeowners and left leaflets noting that instead of the owners
packing up and retaining the household goods that remained after the
sale, the thrift shop would stop by, do the packing, and take some,
most, or all of the leftovers.

What had they done? Identified the market, asked for wants, adapted
to meet those wants, and changed both their promotion and distribution to
meet those wants. And it worked.

● **FOR EXAMPLE:** A midwest state government department, a
funder of human services that we will call HHS, had decided to change,
yet again, the way that it organized, planned for, and funded the provision of services throughout its state. Over the period of two years,
HHS floated policy papers, researched what was going on in other
similar states, met with legislators, conferred with the direct (not-for-
profit) providers of service, and then announced its sweeping changes.
No longer would providers be funded on grants, but rather funding
would be based on outcomes and on the number of people served (a
modified managed care approach). The providers who could come
up with the most innovative, cost-effective ways to provide services
and still reach desired outcomes would not only be allowed to provide the services, but would be encouraged to expand to other communities, even if that meant pushing out current, in-place
organizations.

What response did the providers give to these changes? About
80 percent screamed that the new system would not work, would hurt
people that were being served, and was unfair to the provider system
as well. About 20 percent quietly tried to figure out how to do what
the funder, the customer, wanted. First, they looked at whether HHS
was still a customer that they wanted, and said yes, it was. Second,
they looked at what HHS wanted: innovation, cost containment, and
outcomes. Third, they asked themselves whether they could reshape

their existing services to meet the wants of HHS and still meet their mission and values. It was not going to be easy, but they decided that they could. Fourth, they looked at their costs and tried to reshape their services along with reducing their costs, again to meet a customer want. They looked at the way they delivered the services, the who, what, where, and when. Finally, they developed a promotion campaign, for the funder, for HHS.

Which agencies were successful here? Did all of the 20 percent of the agencies succeed in making the changes? No. A number felt that they could not do what HHS wanted. And, some of the 80 percent stopped whining and followed the lead of the innovators. Many did not, and three years after the introduction of the new system, over half of those organizations were no longer eligible to provide service to HHS. Why? Because they didn't listen and respond to their market.

Use the marketing cycle to start up new services or adapt your existing ones. In either case, it will help you and your staff become and remain more market-oriented, and thus more competitive.

B. THE MARKETING DISABILITY OF MOST NOT-FOR-PROFITS

You now know that asking, listening, and responding to the wants of your many markets is the core of good marketing. Doesn't sound too hard, right? I agree, and while marketing is certainly work, it is not particularly difficult work, just disciplined work. However, in my years of training and consulting with not-for-profits, I have observed that it seems to be more difficult work for staff than it should be. Staff don't ask, don't listen, or don't respond. Over time, I have come to understand why.

Most not-for-profit staff have a marketing disability. A real and severe disability. One that needs to be addressed and overcome for them to succeed in a competitive environment. Let me explain.

Most staff of not-for-profits come from a service-oriented background. They are curators, teachers, social workers, nurses, ministers, scientists. They are trained to meet people, talk to them, and diagnose their *needs*. Or they are trained to assess a situation, or a community, and discover or reason out its *needs*. They are trained to know with confidence that they are "the professionals." They spent countless hours and lots of money in school learning these diagnostic skills. And, as valuable as those skills are, as necessary as they are in what the organization does, they become a disability as soon as the staff person says: "I know better than those people (the customers) what is *needed*, so I don't need to listen to what they *want*."

Do you see the problem? By focusing on and reacting to their training, not-for-profit staff members negate the key transaction in good marketing: asking customers what they *want* and valuing the answer enough to respond. By centering solely on their own expertise, these staff discount the value of their customers' opinion. Therefore, they don't listen. They often don't even ask! Thus, they *can't* respond to the wants of the customer, and they are *doomed* in a competitive market.

> ☞ **HANDS-ON:** Talk to your staff, particularly your most highly-trained staff about the importance of listening to the wants of the people you serve. Remind them that listening is not an inherited skill, it is a practiced one, and that listening, really listening, is not just waiting their turn to talk! Finally, work with them on how to see things from their customers', their clients', their students' perspectives. The more that they can do that, the more value they will attach to the opinions, the complaints, the concerns, *the wants* of the people that your organization serves — and the more value they will have in helping your organization succeed in a competitive environment.

To overcome this disability you need to constantly remind yourself and your staff that the people that you serve have the right to have wants, and that those wants are important. Your skills as a diagnostician should not be diminished by this attention to wants. In fact, training yourself to listen in a new way may actually enhance your sensitivity to what your service recipients are saying. As a result, you may be able to serve them in new and better ways.

Remember the marketing disability. Too many professionals want to meet needs, not satisfy wants. This disability is with you always, and you need to overcome it if you are to be successful, competitive, and market-sensitive.

C. THE MARKETING CYCLE AND COMPETITORS

You have studied the marketing cycle that I want you to use. You know that it starts with the target markets, asks for wants, and then shapes (and reshapes) both services and products to meet those wants, including market-sensitive pricing, distribution, and promotion.

So where in this mix are your competitors? What about those people who want to take away your customers? How can you adapt and respond to the competition?

As I said in the Overview, your competition is so important that we will spend all of Chapter 8 on just that subject. Here I want to go over the parts of the marketing cycle and examine what your competition is doing. And, by doing that I hope to highlight a key point, and one of the characteristics of a market-driven organization:

DO NOT FEAR THE COMPETITION. LEARN FROM THEM.

Should you pay attention to your competitors? Certainly! Should you respect them? If they deserve respect. You certainly should respect the marketplace and its forces. But should you fear competition? No. If you do excellent work, if you ask your customers what they want and solve their problems, if you focus on customer service, and let the markets lead you, in most situations, competition will not be life-threatening. Competition hones you, making you more efficient, effective, and focused on what you really do well. And that's good, for you, for your organization, and for the people you serve.

So, know your competitor, learn from the good ones, and be aware that new competition can show up at any time, but don't live in fear. Put your energy into constructive avenues. Let's start by seeing how your competition reacts to the marketing cycle.

1. Define/Redefine The Market.

As we have seen, for you this means figuring out who you are going to serve (or who you already serve in a more defined way). For your competition, it means the same thing, but perhaps in a different way. They may look at who you serve and try to take away only the most lucrative segment or only the one closest to them. For example, in the mid-1980s dozens of proprietary substance abuse centers sprang up throughout the nation and took away the high-end customers, the customers who either paid cash or had insurance, from the traditional not-for-profits. This is called "creaming" (as in skimming off the cream) and it happens in a lot of areas. Private schools may take only the best (or richest students), museums seek to focus on kids (since parents will follow), environmental groups aim at people who want to buy "green" products.

☞ **HANDS-ON:** Sit down with your senior staff and ask them this: What do we do better than our main competition? Can we do more of this? How do we know we are better? Can we improve on our best? The idea is to reduce the fear of your competitors.

As I have said over and over, you have competition. Are you doing something for someone that your competition can do as well or better?

Then watch out, because they are watching you! You may need to redefine your market to accommodate to the competition.

2. What Does Your Market Want?

Ask, ask, ask, and listen! You've read that already. But you can also learn from your competition's asking, and play off what they learn.

● **FOR EXAMPLE:** Perhaps ten years ago, McDonald's, Showbiz Pizza, and many other for-profit enterprises started offering birthday parties for kids, where parents could go for a one-stop, full-service party, with favors, activities, food, and supervised play. This idea was the result of careful market research (asking) and focus groups (more asking), and was an immediate hit. Now it seems that everyone but your local gas station offers such services. Including not-for-profits. In our community, the state museum, the local zoo, a not-for-profit nature refuge, the children's museum, and a number of churches have entered this market, some with a great deal of success. They observed an idea, asked their own customers if this was something that they wanted, and adapted the concept to meet their own resources.

While this may seem like a good, cheap way to find out things, do not fall victim to just being a copycat. You cannot always depend on the end product of another's marketing. What if they are making a mistake? What if their core clientele is fundamentally different than yours? Be an aggressive observer, but make sure you do your own research.

Finally in this area, you can be sure that your competition is watching you, asking your customers and perhaps your former employees how you do what you do, how much you charge, what you do well or poorly. Depend on it. Little if anything in business is secret for long.

3. Shape and Reshape Your Product and Service.

Your competition, in observing you, may "steal" your ideas (which, in nearly all cases, are fair game). Then they can improve or adapt them to meet their unique mix of customers and resources. Thus, you may look around one day and find that your best ideas have been improved on, taking away your best customers.

Of course, you can return the favor by doing what we reviewed above: observing, listening to your customers, and providing the best mix of responses to their wants that you can.

● **FOR EXAMPLE:** A few years ago, discount airlines uniformly provided transportation but no food. The idea was to save not only the costs of the food but also labor costs. But customers are used to some food, and surveys showed that they wanted both low cost *and* a meal. Then America West introduced low-cost bagged meals that were handed out *as passengers boarded the plane*. Good idea. Good enough that, not only do most discount carriers now provide such service, but major lines do as well for short flights.

Your competition is watching, experimenting, trying new things. You need to as well. The market's gumbo of ideas, wants, and products and services is never static. Stay flexible and pay attention.

4. Set a Sensible Price.

You've already heard me say that price is not the issue, that value is. That doesn't mean that your competitors won't try to attract customers from you by lowering prices, offering introductory discounts or coupons, or even "low-balling" (where they offer prices below cost to get customers to try them and theoretically to be impressed enough to return).

The danger here for most not-for-profits is that a for-profit competitor probably has deeper pockets, and thus a much greater ability to price lower and for longer than the not-for-profit does. The temptation is to try to match price for price, and that can, in many cases, be deadly. If your competition offers a low price, evaluate it carefully. Does the price include everything that your price does? For example, does an introductory assessment at a competing mental health center for $49 include the same array of services, tests, and record review as yours? Does the lower-cost day care center have the same staff-to-child ratio as yours? Does the "cheaper" tuition at a competing school include all student fees?

Most organizations don't compete solely on price — they compete on a mix of price, quality, availability, service, speed, and comfort. This mix is known as value, as we have already discussed. If your service is truly more valuable to the customer (which you can find out by asking them), people will be willing to pay more. Not necessarily a lot more, but some. Don't get sucked into a price war that you can't win, especially if you can give more value to your customer.

5. Promote the Product or Service.

Here is another part of the mix where you can learn from observation. Watch what your competition does. Particularly if you are being targeted by a for-profit, look at how they let people know that they are there. Do they truly advertise (billboards, in the newspaper, in magazines), do they have handouts, posters in grocery stores, ads on the radio and television? Think about what kind of customer they are trying to appeal to with such advertisements. It may give you a clue about their marketing and business plans. If, for example, the ads for a mental health center note "day care on site," it is pretty clear that they are interested in parents, and more probably in single moms, who may be most in need of such a service while they are using mental health counseling or group therapy services.

As in the caution I included in the service area, don't always assume that every kind of advertising and promotion that your competition uses is automatically for you. It probably isn't. Some of their advertising may be ineffective. Or, with perhaps deeper pockets than you, they may be able to chew you up in a competitive, paid advertising campaign. So pick and choose your places to promote carefully, and don't get drawn into a fight you can't win by your competition.

   ☞ **HANDS-ON:** Get a copy of every one of your marketing and promotional pieces. Look at each one and write down whether it is a broad-based piece or a piece that is targeted to a particular market. If you have more broad-based pieces than targeted, you could be in real trouble if your competition is focused on one small (and usually lucrative) market.

6. Distribute The Product or Service.
Here is the how, where, and by whom part of the equation. Your competitors will, undoubtedly, try new things. They will need to if they plan to draw your customers away from you. Don't be too inflexible to try new things yourself. If what your competition is doing is working, consider if it will work for you. This area, more than any other, goes to the core of becoming and remaining responsive. Watch your competition (they are watching you) and learn from what you see.

   ● **FOR EXAMPLE:** There are more examples here than we have pages to print them on. How about affinity cards, the charge cards that allow you to get frequent flyer miles on a particular airline when you use the card? Many not-for-profits have watched this idea and said: "Why not for us?" Now you can get affinity cards that help many not-for-profits (as of this writing mostly environmental groups). Or first-time visit discounts (mental health centers), money-back guarantees (YMCAs), "free" gifts for membership (public radio and television). All of these concepts come directly from the for-profit sector, from not-for-profits' competitors. All appeal to the customer in special ways. All change the method of service or of enticement.

As I said above, Chapter 8 will be on your competition, and many of these subjects will come up again in more detail. But suffice it to say here that your competition is doing the same basic things that you are. Be observant, open-minded, flexible, and prudent in your responses to their innovations, and you will improve your own set of services, benefit from your competitors' marketing expenses, and, perhaps, remain competitive yourself.

RECAP

In this chapter, I have provided a first exposure to the classic marketing cycle. You need to chisel this sequence into your brain, as you will need it over and over as you go through the endless circle of asking, listening, adjusting, asking, listening, and adjusting.

Let's review it one more time. The marketing cycle is:
1. *Selecting and redefining your markets.*
2. *Finding out what the markets want.*
3. *Developing or amending the product or service to meet the wants.*
4. *Pricing the product or service.*
5. *Promoting the product or servic*e.
6. *Distributing or delivering the product or service.*

Then, we looked at the marketing disability of most not for-profits. Most professionals are trained to diagnose needs, not ask for wants. You need to get over this disability if you are to succeed, and you need to warn your staff about this disability as well. Remember, everyone is on the marketing team, and everyone needs to ask, ask, ask, and then *listen.*

Finally, we looked at the marketing cycle through the filter of your competition, exploring what your competition does at each stage of the cycle and how you can and should react to it. Avoid getting drawn into an escalating promotion or pricing war.

The marketing cycle will work if you follow it consistently. But it is not an event; it is a constant, endless process that will constantly and endlessly result in your improving your services and increasing the satisfaction of your customers. In short, your organization will do more and better mission. So use the process!

☞☞ **HANDS-ON REVIEW:**
- **Talk to your staff about listening to wants**
- **Reducing the fear of the competition**
- **Targeting your marketing pieces**

DISCUSSION QUESTIONS FOR CHAPTER 6:

1. Do we really know who our markets are? For all services and all funders?

2. How do we know what our markets want? When was the last time we asked funders, for example?

3. Do we recover all our costs in our pricing? Plus a profit? Is there a mission reason not to? What is it?

4. Does our promotion just scattershot, or is it targeted, and targeted at a specific target market?

5. Do we suffer from the marketing disability? How can we get staff and board past it?

7. Who Are Your Markets?

OVERVIEW

In Chapter 6, I showed you the marketing cycle that works, and works well, in a wide variety of situations. This cycle allows you to improve your services, make the people that you serve happier, and produce efficiencies and effectiveness that your organization has not seen before. What was the first step in the cycle? Right! *Define/Redefine the Markets*. Good for you! You *were* paying attention! In this chapter we will go into that first step in detail.

Chapter Thumbnail
> ➡ **Market Identification and Quantification**
> ➡ **Market Segmenting**
> ➡ **Focusing on Your Target Markets**
> ➡ **Treating All Your Markets Like Customers**

I'll show you how to define your markets, and who those markets really are. I suspect you will be surprised at some of the markets we list.

Then, I'll show you how to segment your most important markets into smaller parts. This will prove very valuable as you try to focus your efforts on your truly critical markets, and as you differentiate between the markets your organization really wants to serve and those that you would rather not be involved with.

Next, I'll show you some ways to focus on your most important and most desired markets. One of the most important tools in business is the *"80/20 Rule."* I'll explain what it is and how to take advantage of it. I'll also show you ways to use your strategic plan to focus on the most important markets. By using both of these techniques you will be better prepared to make the most out of your necessarily limited marketing funds and time; you can put your efforts where they will do the most good.

Finally, we'll get into detail on a crucial part of the marketing effort: treating each and every one of your markets (even those you may not especially care for) like a valued customer. If you, your staff, and all your volunteers learn this admittedly sometimes difficult skill, you will go a long way in both marketing and competitiveness. I'll show you some specific ideas on how to adapt to this new paradigm.

By the end of this chapter, you will have a thorough understanding of your markets, why they are all important to attend to, and know how to sort through them and then focus on the most important.

A. MARKET IDENTIFICATION AND QUANTIFICATION

What are these different markets we keep referring to? Let's look at a diagram that will help you see the many, many different markets you actually serve. As you look at the diagram, note how many markets there are and keep in mind that this diagram probably does not include all of *your* organization's markets!

THE MARKETS OF A NOT-FOR-PROFIT		
INTERNAL	• Board of Directors • Staff Members	
PAYER	• Government • Membership • Foundations • United Way • Donations • Insurers • User Fees	

SERVICE	• Service A
	  Client Type 1
	  Client Type 2
	  Client Type 3
	  Client Type 4
	• Service B
	  Client Type 1
	  Client Type 2
	  Client Type 3
	  Client Type 4	

Referral Sources	• Many different sources, all with different wants.	

As you can see, you have three different and distinct main categories of markets: internal, payer, and service. Each category is important: you can't provide services without money, you don't need staff or board if you don't have charitable services to provide, you can't get money from payers unless you have staff and board to appropriately spend it. Each category bears further analysis.

NOTE: You can and should develop a form just like this for your organization. Draw one up on a flip chart, or have someone design one on your word processor. You'll have the same internal *markets as here, but you need to be as specific as possible about the* payers, services, *and* referral sources *you have. I'd suggest drawing up the form now, and then having it with you as you read the remainder of the chapter so that you can pencil in your markets as you see examples from other not-for-profits.*

1. INTERNAL MARKETS

There are two of these, board members and staff members. Both are crucial, and both deserve to be treated like markets, utilizing the same marketing process that we discussed in Chapter 6. Both groups deserve to have their wants met, to the extent you can. Unfortunately, most not-for-profits either ignore this issue or drastically underestimate the importance of these markets. They treat their board as a necessary evil, and their staff as a commodity. The management "knows" what the staff want (more money), so they never ask. The management doesn't really care what the board wants as long as they come to meetings and don't ask too many questions.

The downfall of these perceptions is that, in a competitive world, you need excellent board members, and to get and keep them, you need to treat them as a valuable resource. Likewise, you are going to need to attract and retain good staff, and it will be tough: you need good staff more than they need you. And, in a competitive world, good staff have lots of choices.

In the process of becoming market-oriented, and focusing on your external markets, don't forget your internal markets.

2. PAYER MARKETS

These are the people who send you money. You may be offended that I consider these people a market. After all, you are here to do good works. Money is just a vehicle and an unseemly one at that. The people you really need to pay attention to are the people you serve. Right? Partially. In the old days of having a monopoly, you could afford to do this. No more. If, in a competitive market, you ignore the payers and the internal markets and direct your attentions solely to the people you serve, you are on a short road to oblivion. Remember, there are two primary rules of not-for-profits.

Rule One: *Do More Mission.*
Rule Two: *No Money, No Mission.*
Ignore these at your peril.

As you can see, there are many payers, and we should examine their different wants.

➡ **Government.** For many readers, the government (federal, state, county, or city) is a key customer, one that may even form the backbone of your income structure. Too often, unfortunately, not-for-profit managers don't think of these important customers as customers, they consider them the enemy. While that attitude may have worked in the past, you can no longer afford to demonize government payers.

What do government purchasers want? Generally, they want a set of services (carefully defined) provided to a set of people (also carefully defined) in a set period of time, often in a set manner, with no audit exceptions and all paperwork in on time.

If you don't like having government as a key customer, develop a long-range marketing plan that reduces or eliminates them from your income stream. But while they are there, treat them with the respect that all your customers deserve. Ask them what they want and give it to them.

☞ **HANDS-ON:** If your organization has government income, consider this question carefully. When was the last time you asked your government project officer/funder, "How can I make your job easier?" Never? You are not alone, but that kind of question is essential to stabilize and improve relationships with all customers. When you read Chapter 11, "Incredible Customer Service," remember that it applies to this market as well.

Finally, don't fall into the trap of thinking of "government" as all one market, with identical and never-changing wants. You may well get funds from more than one government source, or even from different programs within a single agency or department. Each of these sources and programs have different wants. Each deserves your attention.

➡ **Membership.** Many not-for-profits have a membership, which is an excellent way of developing important linkages with the community and a regular donation base — if, and only if, the membership benefits are worth the fee. Environmental groups, museums, zoos, symphonies, and public broadcasters are all examples of organizations that have built large long-standing membership bases.

What do members want? It depends on the organization and the sales pitch that is used to get the member. PBS members want quality programming, and often get a premium gift and a monthly program guide with their membership renewal. YMCA and YWCA members would not be satisfied just to know that the Y is open. For their fee, they want access to locker rooms, gyms, and pools, and reduced fees on Y programs. Museum members may get reduced admission fees or priority on hard-to-get exhibit tickets.

You need to carefully and regularly assess the benefits that accrue to your members. You might want to make a list of the membership organizations in your community; that's the competition for this kind of funds. Are your members satisfied? You don't know until you ask and, in a competitive world, you can't afford not to know.

➡ **Foundations.** Foundations come in all shapes and sizes. There are huge ones like Ford or Robert Wood Johnson, and hundreds of small local corporate or family foundations spread through nearly every community in the nation. Their interests and funding procedures vary widely, as do the amounts of money awarded each year.

What do foundations want? While the breadth of interests are sweeping, within their areas of interest, most foundations want pretty much the same things: innovative projects that meet their criteria, organizations that can demonstrate strong community support, and projects that can be self-supporting, generally within three years.

Foundation funding is *extremely* competitive and, if you don't carefully research the wants of the foundation, you are wasting your time and theirs. Most foundations give you a good list of their wants right in their funding requirements. If you can, go beyond that and, if the foundation has a staff, talk to a project officer or, better yet, go to meet with them and dig a little deeper into what their "hot buttons" are. Ask what they like to see most and what they like to see least on applications. Then listen and do what they ask!

➡ **United Way**. Some United Ways are looking at not-for-profits as essential mission-based businesses and are funding worthy projects based on merit and community need. And, many are reducing their application requirements to make funding more efficient and less costly to everyone. Most, unfortunately, are not and still provide funds based on how poor the organization is. "If your finances are not precarious, don't apply here. You've got to be broke to deserve our money." This has resulted in many, many of my clients who are financially stable dropping their United Way affiliations. I hope the innovative United Ways will become a trend.

If you are interested in United Way dollars, or get them now, pay attention to changes in funding priorities and methodologies. Talk to people (both staff and volunteers) involved with the organization in your community. Stay on top of any significant changes in wants. These dollars are also increasingly competitive.

➡ **Donations**. Still the bedrock of many small community-based organizations, and certainly the case for all churches, donations (including bequests and corporate funding) are also increasingly competitive. Notwithstanding that, 501(c)(3) organizations that demur from seeking donations ignore one of their key resources: the ability to take tax-deductible gifts.

What do donors want? Again, it depends; lumping all donors together in one market basket is fraught with peril. The wants of annual givers vary widely from people who might want to give you a bequest. Some people want to support one program. Others prioritize giving to an endowment. Some want credit and visibility; most don't. Don't assume. Ask. And, if you are really serious about maximizing your donations, consider obtaining the services of a reputable professional fund-raiser.

➡ **Insurers.** Some readers work for organizations that get funds through insurers. Insurers are, of course, financial intermediaries. As such, they are supposed to be obligated to pay for whatever condition or treatment is prescribed and covered through the insurance policy. However, even though the insurer is supposed to be obligated by the policy of the insured to pay your organization, the speed and ease of that payment (and sometimes even whether the payment is ever received at all) depend in large part on your organization meeting the wants of the insurer. So whether your organization provides health care, home health services, mental health, substance abuse treatment, orthopedic devices, long-term care, or preventive services, meeting the wants of the fiscal intermediary, the insurer, is essential.

What are the insurer's wants? Usually these are heavily centered on process and paperwork. Was the insured medically required to seek services? Were the services preapproved? Does your organization have the right licenses, certifications, and quality assurance? Do your staff? Are the forms complete? All of these are regularly-asked questions. More and more, the question "Are you part of the managed care contract?" is surfacing.

If you are in any part of the human services field, you need to know how to meet the markets' wants. Pay attention to the process, the paperwork, and the fine print. You'll get paid sooner, and more fully.

➡ **User Fees.** These are admissions fees, ticket purchases, tuition, fees for counseling, or other payments received directly from the end user, the person that you serve. Like donations and membership, user fees represent a direct link between your organization and an individual payer who gets benefit from the organization, either in service or self-esteem.

What do users want? They want what they pay for to be *high* quality, *high* value, and to meet their wants. Remember, price is not the issue — value is. If price were the only thing, no one would attend Harvard, Yale, or the University of Chicago. But all three of those institutions, like countless others of high cost, have thousands of applicants on their waiting list. Why? Because of the value of the education they provide.

How do you find out what users want? Again, you ask. And, you try hard not to fall victim to your marketing disability. It is particularly easy here, since you are so often providing services for a fee, and these are services for which you have training and experience. Thus, it is not difficult to fall into the trap of assuming that you know what the customer needs (and you probably do) and ignore what they want (which you don't know until you ask).

All of these markets are important, but later in this chapter, I'll give you some ideas about how to focus on the most important markets, the ones that hold the key to your future.

3. SERVICE MARKETS

Just as in the payer markets, there are many, many service markets. These are the people that you serve, and they can be broken down by age, gender, ethnicity, or the program or programs that they utilize, and in other ways as well. You probably thought that these were the people that you worked for, that this was the market you were serving. It is, but it is only one of several markets. The internal and payer markets are essential as well.

As with the payer markets, it is crucial that you avoid lumping the people you serve together. The more discrete groups that you can identify, the more you can focus your asking and responding to them.

● **FOR EXAMPLE:** A mental health center provided numerous services. As it went through its marketing planning and market identification, it noted many, many markets within each service. Let's look at just one — outpatient counseling. The staff and board identified the following markets within this service:

One-to-one counseling:
>   -Chronically mentally ill
>   -Depression
>   -Post-trauma victims
>   -Veterans
>   -Teens in the high school
>   -Violent offenders

Small support groups:
>   -Grief and mourning
>   -Chronically mentally ill
>   -Veterans with post-traumatic stress syndrome
>   -Violent offenders
>   -AA

Of course, each of these groupings of people have different wants. To assume that all outpatient clients have the same wants would be ludicrous, but I see too many organizations that consider such a lumping appropriate. Don't follow their lead.

Although I cannot do your market analysis for you, I do urge you to break down your services by types of service and types of people. And, I also want to focus in on another critical service market.

➡ **Referral Sources.** We've already noted that your organization, like all others, has a limit on how much time and money it can spend on marketing. Wouldn't it be great to have people (who you don't pay) out there sending you members, clients, students, or parishioners? You can, and you may already. These are called referral sources. These may simply be informal recommendations from happy customers — someone who went to a play at your theater and was impressed, or a parent who loves how his or her child is developing in your preschool. Or they can be formal referrals from another professional, such as a surgeon referring a head trauma patient to a vocational rehabilitation facility, or a minister referring a troubled parishioner to a psychologist or psychiatrist.

What do these referrers want? Be sure to thank them if you are aware of the recommendation. Everyone wants appreciation. For the formal referral sources though, it is a bit more complex. The first thing most referrers want is capacity: for you to have the ability to take the referral immediately and get it off their desk. The second thing they want is quality, which is demonstrated by outcomes, by accreditation, or simply by having the same treatment philosophy that they have. The third thing most referrers want is to find out what happened. Most people want to know the outcomes, and more importantly, they are interested in the personal stories of success that come from interaction with your organization.

These wants are the ones that I see from my travels around the country. But don't depend on my observations. Like any other market, you don't know what they want until you ask. Do you need referrals and recommendations? Absolutely! Find out what your referrers want and give it to them. Remember that, in a very real sense, the recommendations of happy customers are the result of giving those customers what they want. The more you ask, the more you know. The more you know, the more you can respond. The more you respond, the happier your customers will be. The happier they are, the more of these referrals you will get!

All of your markets — internal, payer, and service — deserve attention. Paying close attention to so many diverse groups is not always easy, especially since your organization, like all others, has only so much money and staff time to throw at even this critical activity. So what do you do?

There are two more steps to take control of all this marketing identification. The first is to learn about market segmenting, where you turn the tables and think through who you *want* to serve and compare that to who you currently serve. Then you focus on your targets. I'll show you how to do both, and we'll start with segmenting.

B. MARKET SEGMENTING

We've already begun our discussion of market segmentation in the earlier example of the mental health center that identified in great detail all the different outpatient counseling markets it served. While this kind of differentiation is important, market segmenting in a competitive environment is more complex, and more potentially rewarding than simply breaking down your current markets into the smallest possible divisions.

Market segmenting is the technique of looking at your larger markets in more finite parts, and then deciding which of those parts your organization can, should, and wants to serve. It is a technique that will really focus you on what you do best, and it is relatively easy to learn.

You can view segmenting your markets from several angles. Perhaps you want to look at all the different kinds of people you serve with a particular service. By itself, this listing gives you the ability to focus on different wants, but it also arms you to make some important decisions about the people you serve.

Do we want to continue to focus on this group? Does serving this constituency mesh with our strategic plan, our vision for our future? Is this market segment growing or shrinking, likely to buy more or less of what we are selling? Competitive managers — managers who are responsive to markets and their constant changes — are asking these questions. Unfortunately many not-for-profit managers defer on such tough decisions because they are afraid of offending a traditional constituency by cutting back on a long-standing program, or because staff (or more often board) members resist abandoning a pet program.

> ☞ **HANDS-ON:** As you make lists of your markets and their segments, ask yourself, "Why are we providing this service?" and "Why are we serving this population?" If your immediate answer is solely, "Because we always have," you should stop and assess whether or not you should continue. Think through issues such as: Do you have true expertise with this service or population? Is the service provided elsewhere more efficiently? Is this a core constituency? Is your organization identified primarily with this program or service population? Would reducing or ending this service dramatically affect your fundraising? And, of course, a crucial but not stand-alone indicator: are you making or losing money in this area or with this group? Answers to these and many other questions will help you make your decision, but never just continue to provide a service out of reverence for tradition. Make sure that it makes good mission sense.

Another way to use segmenting is to look at a potential market for a new product or service and to see which areas, which segments, you want to pursue. With this use of segmenting you can pick and choose your target markets more efficiently and effectively.

> ● **FOR EXAMPLE:** An organization in the Pacific Northwest works with individuals with disabilities, finding and creating employment opportunities. The organization was presented with the chance to purchase a car wash, which potentially could provide excellent and steady jobs for its clientele. As it looked at the markets, it didn't fall

into the census trap I discussed earlier; it understood that its market was not the population that lived within fifteen miles but the people *with cars and trucks* that drove by regularly, whether they lived close or not. After making this initial cut, the organization looked at some segments that needed clean vehicles. These can be summarized as follows:

> • *Retail:* People coming in to wash vehicles that they personally own. While this had advantages in terms of community visibility for people with disabilities, it also had the disadvantage of being seasonal, and very dependent on weather and day of the week. Thus the likelihood of steady employment was low.

> • *Pre-sale Cleaning for Auto Dealers:* Dealers need to clean cars prior to showing them. The organization looked at this as a real possibility for steadier work, but found that the liability of having to drive the cars and trucks to their site and the cyclical nature of auto and truck sales were two large barriers.

> • *Cleaning of Fleets:* This market (which can consist of utility, postal, realtor, college and university, government, and other fleets) was a legitimate contender. The contracts would be large, steady, wholesale, and the drivers of the vehicles could simply stop in on a scheduled basis to have their vehicle cleaned.

The result was that the organization moved toward fleet cleaning, but only after trying retail. The initial try at retail was a mission consideration — more positive visibility in the community — but it was overwhelmed by the up-and-down nature of the business, resulting in long idle times for the staff. After this, they moved to the fleet cleaning.

You can use segmenting to affirmatively decide which markets you want to pursue, rather than simply reacting to all comers. But even with segmenting, you will still have many, many markets to monitor. And, as we have already said, only so much time and money is available to spend. You need to focus.

C. FOCUSING ON YOUR TARGET MARKETS

Now you know who your markets are, and you have segmented them to show you where the best market opportunities may lie. But where to focus your efforts? This is important to get the most out of your marketing, and there are two methods to utilize as you try to decide where your target markets lie. Using both is recommended, because by blending the results, you will make the best decision on which markets to target.

1. THE 80/20 RULE. The first assessment method you need to apply comes from the business canon called the "80/20 Rule." This tried and true maxim says that "80 percent of your income comes from 20 percent of your customers." When I first heard this at a business meeting 20 years ago, I thought to myself, "What drivel! How could something so pat and simplistic hold true across industries and businesses that vary so widely?" Perhaps you share my cynicism. Try it. I did, and the rule worked. I regularly apply it for clients that are in the depths of marketing planning to help them focus their efforts on the most financially important of their customers.

☞ **HANDS-ON:** Try this. Take out your income and expense statement for last month. Look at the income side of the ledger for the year to date. Take the total income and multiply it by .8 (80 percent). Then start with the largest customer, add that income to that of the second largest customer, then the third, etc., until your running income total reaches 80 percent of your total income. Now go back and count how many customers that took. If you now look at your entire customer base you will find that the number of customers it took to reach the 80 percent is very, very close to one-fifth, or 20 percent.*

Using the 80/20 Rule for your service markets is sometimes tougher because of the difficulty of coming up with a common denominator of units of service, but it can be applied for most organizations with a little work.

The point of this methodology? Focus on the largest one-fifth of your customers. They produce the bulk of your revenue.

I did not say, however, to ignore the smallest four-fifths. In a competitive environment, customers who are ignored tend to vote with their feet. And I don't think you would like to have 20 percent of your income stream vanish. But this methodology does help you rationalize spending the most time talking to, visiting, and asking your largest customers, both payer and service.

2. THE STRATEGIC PLAN METHOD. Now that you have done the empirical 80/20 approach, look at these same markets from a different point of view, through the lens of your strategic plan and your market research. Ask the question: "Which of these markets do I want to grow?"

---

*Another application of the 80/20 Rule says that 80 percent of your costs come from just 20 percent of your transactions.

"Which parts of my community are the most important in terms of my mission?"

If, for example, you only get $5,000 a year in donations out of $750,000 total income, but your strategic plan calls for raising $200,000 per year in donations in five years, you had better focus on figuring out this market, asking its wants, and attending to them, starting now. If you only looked at the empirical analysis based on percentage of income, you wouldn't spend much time in this area, since it only represents six-tenths of 1 percent of your total income.

Another application of this has to do not with increasing the income from a certain market but with decreasing your dependence on a current large customer. Many not-for-profits are intent upon reducing their dependence on a traditionally large payer, such as the government, United Way, or private donations. In this case, it may make sense to lessen what may have been a day-to-day focus on these markets to a reduced priority. But don't ignore them! They are still large payers and, for the time during which they remain large payers, treat them well.

Once you have done both of these assessments, pick your target markets and focus on them. And here is where you may have the most trouble, at least if your assessment results in a change in priorities. People, following the laws of physics, are governed by inertia. In marketing, that inertia shows up by talking to, helping, selling to, and asking the people you already know, are already familiar with, are already comfortable with — at the cost of not starting out cold in a new but high priority market. Watch yourself to assure that you arc paying attention and dividing your time appropriately, according to both kinds of market analyses.

D. TREATING *ALL* YOUR MARKETS LIKE CUSTOMERS

In Chapter 2, we touched for the first time on this issue. Now that you have seen all the various markets you need to serve, perhaps this issue takes on a slightly different look. Let's go into this a bit deeper.

1. Customers, customers everywhere.

I hope that you and your staff already treat your service recipients as valued customers — greeting them warmly, offering assistance, solving their problems, listening to their concerns. While you may do this personally, it is critical that you and your senior management team both lead in this area and supervise closely by regularly (and unpredictably) wandering around, watching and listening to the interactions of staff and your customers. Unfortunately, just as in the for-profit world, the not-for-profit world is divided into organizations that understand this and organizations that don't.

I am sure that if you and I met and I asked you to give me examples of businesses in your community that were committed to customer service and those that didn't have a clue, that you could give me a list of both immediately. Why? Because people pay attention and remember when they are treated well and when they are not. And, while your not-for-profit, like others, may have been given a break in the past by customers due to the perception that you really weren't a business, that slack has been tightened up, and you are now held to the standard of a proprietary business.

In fact, customer service is an important enough issue for you in your quest for competitiveness that all of Chapter 11 will detail methods to provide "Incredible Customer Service," a level of attention that is rapidly becoming the benchmark for customer interaction throughout the nation. Here, I just want to continue the assault on the first obstacle to overcome: the idea that everyone — funder, staff, board, service consumer — is a customer.

2. Barriers to the customer service mentality.

There are a number of ways that not-for-profit staff fall down in customer service. I want to reiterate them in a slightly different light here to provide you additional insight, and then give you ammunition to convince staff and board members. First, if people are not treated well, most will vote with their feet — they will go somewhere else. Although you have traditionally had total or virtual monopolies on your kind of work and funding in your community, the coming wave of competition does not stop with your funders. Don't let your former status get in the way of dealing with your current condition.

Another barrier to developing a customer service mentality has to do with the marketing disability we discussed earlier. If I know so much more than the people I serve, shouldn't they be simply grateful for my wisdom, my help, my beneficence? Hmmm. Sounds like a lot of doctors that I know. Doctors who don't get the fact that *I* am paying *them,* who make me sit on my heels for hours without apology, who treat me like a kindergartner, who always seem in a rush and don't see the person behind the patient- these are doctors that I no longer consult. Remember, there are customers everywhere.

3. Internal customers.

One result of competition is that your community has or will have more organizations doing what you do. One result of this is that your staff have new options for their employment. They no longer have only one place in the community to ply their trade. There are multiple opportunities.

And to reinforce what I have said for years, you need your good staff more than they need you. Without good staff you cannot do good work.

I don't think anyone can argue that there are a fixed (and limited) number of qualified and engaged board members in any given community, and every organization would like to have them. Thus, if I as a board member want to serve, and I am not getting my wants met in your organization, I can easily resign and go help some other, more customer-oriented organization. An aside here is that many board members want to be associated with "winning" (also called businesslike, customer-oriented) organizations, and the ones that will win in a competitive market are those that market aggressively and serve their customers — all their customers — well.

4. Funder or payer customers.

Now to those pesky funders. This will be the longest stretch for many readers, as an awful lot of you have spent most, if not all, of your careers fighting with your funders rather than thinking of them as customers. Years of this kind of experience and the resulting prejudice and cantankerous interpersonal relationships will be difficult to overcome, what with our egos and pride getting in the way. And, even if you are the first one to stop fighting and start being attentive, the funder will (quite naturally) not trust you, or even be nice to you, for some time. Turning relationships around takes time, so start now.

Many readers are thinking, "But my funders are so unfair! They ask us to do more and more without an increase in funding. They want more paperwork done to account for every nickel, and they want it all done on unreasonable schedules when they themselves are virtually never on time. They are the customer from hell, and they really act more like they *own* us than like a *customer.*" I've heard this basic set of sentiments thousands of times. Here are two points: first, all businesses have customers from hell. Go to any airport during bad weather, and watch the gate agents deal with angry, irrational folks who are mad at the gate agent *personally* because it is snowing. The gate agents don't yell back. They have learned how to deal with these customers. You need to learn to deal with difficult customers, too. Remember the second rule we discussed in Chapter 2. I hope that all your staff are already hearing it from you all the time:

The customer is not *always right. But the customer is* always *the customer.*

All of us, including our customers, are wrong now and then. But that does not mean that the relationship changes because of the error. You are still selling something, and they are still buying. Act that way.

A couple of other notes on funders as customers. If one or more of your funders is from state or local government, and if you are active in your state trade association, you may well be interacting with the same people in two roles: vendor and lobbyist/activist/advocate. Thus one day you work with the state department, wearing the hat of executive director, and ask, "How can I make your job easier?" and the next day you come in the same door as a member of the state association and object to a new regulation, rate, oversight clause, or piece of legislation. This schizophrenia can be trouble. One way to reduce the problem is to clearly and repeatedly identify yourself as a representative of the XYZ *Association,* perhaps even wearing a name tag with their logo on it when you are doing their business. However, even that does not guarantee that the state or local agency staff will differentiate between your differing hats. I am not suggesting that you need to give up lobbying. Just be aware of, and try to minimize, the potential cost.

Second, in many cases, I have seen organizations start to treat their funders like customers and, over the succeeding months, the funders have begun to respond by treating the organization more like a vendor, and less like a slave. In three cases, the funders started to let the not-for-profit be accountable for outcomes, not for process, reducing their paperwork load. In two other cases, the funder changed their funding method to allow the organizations to keep what they earned — the ultimate indicator of the vendor-customer relationship. Here is a case yet again of leading by example, and having people follow your lead.

5. Service customers.

Finally, your service recipients. Why wouldn't you treat them like customers? Because of the not-for-profit marketing disability. You know what they need. It is not a big leap from there to think that you know more than they do and thus devalue them, their ideas, their suggestions, their complaints, their wants. Don't. Each and every person you serve is ultimately a customer, and more and more a customer who can choose not to return. Here, as with the funders, your customers are not always right or reasonable or polite. But they are always customers.

I don't want you to believe that I think this is easy. It's not, particularly at first. But you need to start now to think of all your customers as customers. In Chapter 11 I'll show you a number of tried-and-true techniques to empower your staff to fix problems, deal with complaints, meet customers' wants. But for now, just start thinking of everyone as a customer and start practicing your refrain: "What more can I (we) do for you?"

RECAP

In this chapter, you have, perhaps for the first time, looked at your organization's many and diverse markets. You saw that you have *payer markets, service markets,* and even *internal markets* of board and staff members. Next, we looked at those markets and I gave you some broad generalizations about what each market wants, with the caution that you don't really know what any market wants until you ask. We moved on to market segmentation, and I showed you how to accomplish this task and how to use it to take a more assertive stance in choosing who you want to work for.

With so many markets identified, you need a way to focus your efforts, to target the most important markets. I showed you how to do this important task, with the 80/20 Rule, and by integrating your strategic plan into the marketing mix.

Finally, we turned to the difficult and controversial subject of treating everyone (payers, board, staff, and service recipients) like customers. We covered each group and I hope that I convinced you of the problems you will face if you don't jump on this competitive bandwagon.

In a competitive environment, you have to be aware of who your markets are, and focus on the most important ones. You have to treat each like a customer. You have to ask their wants. Asking and customer service will be the subject of later chapters, but now it is time to move on to the other group identification process that is integral to successful marketing: identifying your competition.

☞☞ **HANDS-ON REVIEW:**
- **Are you treating your funder(s) like a customer?**
- **A market self-assessment**
- **The 80/20 analysis**

DISCUSSION QUESTIONS FOR CHAPTER 7:

1. Let's make a list of all our markets in each of the following categories: funders, internal, service, and referrer.

2. Now, do we want to be in all of these markets, or are we just here because we always have been?

3. Are there markets that we want to prioritize, to target? What are they by the 80/20 Rule? Based on our strategic plan?

4. Do we treat everyone like a customer? How can we be better at it?

8. Who Are Your Competitors?

OVERVIEW

I have said over and over that you are entering an increasingly competitive world, and the facts surrounding that statement are irrefutable. Areas where you didn't compete five years or even five months ago are now open arenas. Things that you feel are secure from outside pressures will not be next year or perhaps even next month.

So, for the first time for many readers, it is important to think of some people and some organizations as competitors. For many readers, anyone outside your own organization has always been "the community" — usually a friendly, welcoming term. In many, even most, cases this will still be true. But, as a not-for-profit manager, you need to learn the often obscure difference between a community member and a competitor, between a colleague and a competitor, between a peer and a partisan. Not an easy, nor, for many readers, a particularly pleasant task. But an essential one if your organization is to compete at all.

Chapter Thumbnail
- ➡ **Identifying Your Competition**
- ➡ **Studying the Competition**
- ➡ **Focusing on Your Core Strengths**

This chapter will show you first how to identify who your competitors are and what they want that you have. We'll look at organizations that are after your clientele, your staff, your funding, your donated dollar. We'll review this competition from the perspectives of funders, the services you provide, the people you serve, and your referral sources.

Then, once we have identified who your competition is, we'll look into what they are doing. I'll show you a number of tried-and-true methods of finding out your competitor's marketing methods, prices, and array of services. You will learn how to learn more about the competition and what makes it different, better (or often worse) than your organization in the eyes of your clientele.

Once these two areas are covered, we'll look at your organization again and review the things that you have learned about yourself by learning about the competition: your core strengths. These core components of your identity are crucial to list and strengthen as you become more competitive. I'll show you how.

By the end of the chapter, you will know who your competition is, how to find out what they are doing, and which areas are your strengths and which are your weaknesses.

A. IDENTIFYING YOUR COMPETITION

Who are those pesky competitors anyway? To figure out who they are, let's review the array of markets that we covered in Chapter 7 and then compare those to your possible competition. You will see that you have competitors for each market, even those you may feel are sacrosanct. We'll start with your internal markets, and then move to payer and service markets. Remember that the categories that I have included are both general and broad: that is, some of the categories that are listed may not be pertinent to your organization, and those that are can undoubtedly be broken into many smaller components by market type and by individual competitor.

As you can see, the internal markets are just as susceptible as the external markets to competition. You may consider the issue of someone from the outside competing for staff no problem for your organization, particularly if you are in a rural area or in a geographic area with no other organization doing what you do. This is probably wrong. For example, if you are a children's museum and the only one for 100 miles in any direction, you cannot assume that no on else will come after your management or line staff: they may very well. Note that in the chart below, I say that the possible competitors for staff are "Organizations hiring people with the same skills as your staff" not "Organizations providing the same services as your staff." There is a big difference.

And, while many people who work in the not-for-profit environment want to stay there and not jump to the for-profit world, there are undoubtedly numerous organizations in your community that are not-for-profit and do good works. As the entire sector becomes more competitive, don't count

INTERNAL Markets	Possible Competitors	How Do You Compete?
Board Members	• Other not-for-profits with board and volunteer positions available. A competitor for the limited board "capital" in any community is the United Way, which can use up thousands of volunteer hours each year. Good organizations want good board members. Don't lose yours.	You ask the board members what they want, treat them as a valued resource, and give them important things to do.
Staff Members	• Other organizations (both for-profit and not-for-profit) that are hiring people with the same skills as your staff.	You treat staff with dignity and respect, involving them in management, budgeting, marketing, and planning. Ask them what they want and give it to them when possible.

on your friend from the United Way board to not "raid" your staff (or your board, for that matter).

Finally, on the subject of staff, while I have long contended that money is not *the* issue for most staff in most organizations, it certainly is *an* issue for every staff in every organization. If your organization is like most not-for-profits, you don't pay your staff what they could get elsewhere in the community, and there may not be a reasonable chance that you can in the near future. But you do need to try to pay a competitive wage, and to do other things that you can to be competitive. Some of those are listed in the table above. More are detailed in the staff management chapter in *Mission-Based Management*. It isn't always about money.

● **FOR EXAMPLE:** Consider this question: Have you ever met an *unhappy* Federal Express delivery person? Neither have I. Second question: Have you ever met an unhappy U. S. Postal Service worker? Me, too. Who gets higher starting salary and benefits? The USPS. The same is true for Disney, Marriott, Lands' End, and many other superb firms, firms that, like all of us, lead with their line staff. Their compensation is fine, but not the best in the industry. To paraphrase J. W. Marriott, Jr., they take care of their people, and their people take care of them.

To be competitive for staff you need to take care of them, and that is not, repeat, not always represented by dollar signs.

Now let's look at your two external markets, starting with the PAYER market. The people that send you money are *certainly* subjects of your competitor's interest. As you review the chart below, remember that your organization will have its own unique set of payers, and the ones you need to pay attention to will be the largest, the ones that have priority in your long-term plan, and the ones that are under the most competitive pressures, *in that order.* Don't wait to treat your target payer markets well until *after* there are competitors in the picture. Start now.

Payer Market	Possible Competitors	How Do You Compete?
Government	Any organization or individual who can qualify for the funding under the government's regulations. More and more government agencies are going to true bidding for all services.	Know your funders' regulations cold. Make sure you meet all their "silly" regulatory and bureaucratic wants. Ask in advance what they want, and be consistent in keeping your promises.
Membership	All other not-for-profits that offer memberships are potential competitors, but mostly within certain fields, such as mental health, environment, the arts, animal rights, etc.	Make sure the benefits of membership are clear and tangible. Ask your members regularly what they want for their membership dollar.
Foundations	Foundation funding is extremely competitive, and the competition comes more and more from organizations that have hired help to appeal to the foundations. Almost all of this competition is not-for-profit organizations; it may or may not be from your town, state, or area of service.	If you are planning to spend a lot of time in the foundation world, read the foundation press, get help from an experienced, successful grantwriter, and stick to the foundations that have an interest in what you do.

Payer Market	*Possible Competitors*	*How Do You Compete?*
United Way	Every other not-for-profit in your community that participates in the United Way, and many new not-for-profits that are starting up and applying to the United Way for funding.	Meet United Way guidelines for funding precisely. If your United Way does community needs assessments, make sure that you participate so that your service area needs are included.
Donations	Any and all not-for-profits who seek and accept charitable contributions. This broad category can be divided into corporate and individual, large and small, regular and bequest.	Focus on the kind of donor most likely to be interested in what you do. State who you are (your mission and values) clearly. Get professional help if you plan to be competitive.
Insurers	Insurers, mostly as a result of managed care pressures, are looking for low cost/high quality providers of human services. No longer limited to just health care, this can include any and all services covered under Medicaid.	Play by all the insurers' rules including their forms, any pre-admission certifications, any licenses and accreditation you may need. Work with the people that you serve to meet the insurers' requirements as well.
User Fees	Any not-for-profit that provides the same type of services that you do and makes the user pay directly through tuition, ticket fees, admission charges, office visit fees, etc.	You need to ask your users what they want, how happy they are with your services and where you can improve — constantly.

As you can see, you have a lot of potential competitors, and in each case I have suggested one or more of the basic components of the marketing cycle: select the target market, find out what they want, and modify (or create) a service to meet the wants.

Next is the set of external markets that you are probably most concerned about, the SERVICE MARKETS. These are subject to competition. And, since the number of people you serve is very often closely tied to the funding you receive, you need to attract and retain your clientele over a long period of time. Beware, though, your competition is doing the same thing. Let's examine the how and why. But before we do, let's start with you doing a little homework.

> ☞ **HANDS-ON:** Make a copy of the table below. If you can enlarge
> the copy to fill an 8 1/2 x 11 sheet of paper, so much the better. Then,
> fill in the table as best you can, either alone or with a team of man-
> agement and line staff. I've provided an example on the next page.

As you do this, remember to be *as specific as possible.*

The Services We Provide	Competitors	Where They Excel	Where We Excel
The People We Serve	**Competitors**	**Where They Excel**	**Where We Excel**

The essential part of using this table is to begin the process of identifying who the competition is, and learning what you do well in that particular market. Additionally, I've divided the chart into two parts: THE SERVICES WE PROVIDE, and THE PEOPLE WE SERVE. This division is intended to focus you on the fact that competitors may come after people first (AARP goes after people over 55 and then focuses on the services that they need) or the service first (an arts organization advertising summer classes). Be thorough, and remember to look at the sample below.

The Services We Provide	Competitors	Where They Excel	Where We Excel
Short-term residential shelter	1. Salvation Army	Capacity	Friendly, accommo-dating staff
Job readiness training	1. Helping Hands 2. Veterans Administration 3. Local Job Corps	? ? ?	Staff with job experience.
Counseling	1. Local Mental Health Association 2. Private psychologists	? ?	Experienced counselors.
The People We Serve	Competitors	Where They Excel	Where We Excel
People who are homeless	1. Salvation Army 2. Helping Hands Homeless Shelter	1. Capacity 2. Capacity, counseling	Sympathetic, non-judgmental.
People with Autism	1. St. Mary's Hospital 2. County DD Association 3. School districts	1. Marketing 2. Array of services 3. Array of services, facilities	High level of training of staff.

As you can see, this agency is just starting its internal analysis and is unsure of where its competition excels. They definitely need to do more research. The things that they feel they excel at are mostly "friendly, experienced staff, sympathy, and training." Fine, but is this what people want?

They need to carefully review and make sure that what they excel at is what people *want*.

Last, but definitely not least, let's examine your all important RE-FERRAL market and see who is competing with you there. Remember that your referral sources are the people who send you clients, students, parishioners, and members. For some readers, you may get referrals solely through word of mouth from currently happy customers. For many, particularly those in human service provision, referrals are a much more formalized part of your organization: a physician refers a patient to your organization for occupational therapy, a social worker refers a teenager to your program for counseling. In these cases it is important to find out the perception of the referral source about your organization and your competition.

If you don't have referral sources in the formal sense, remember this: a happy customer will sing your praises to ten to twenty people over the next year. An unhappy customer will complain about you to 100 people within the next two weeks. Thus, you *do* have referrers, and when we cover customer service you will learn how to keep those referrers happy.

In the following table, you'll see a sample of a referral listing for an organization that provides rehabilitation services to persons with spinal cord and head trauma injuries. It includes headings: OUR REFERRERS, WHAT DO THE REFERRERS WANT?, and WHO DO THEY REFER TO US? This categorization allows the organization to identify groups as well as individuals and focus on both the referrer and the market that they provide. For instance, if Dr. Jones only sends two patients per year, that may not make her a priority for the organization. But, if both of those patients are long-term, high-income patients, perhaps spending some time with Dr. Jones is advisable.

Looking at insurers, you will see that there are significant differences in what the referrers want, and thus differences in which referrers this organization should actively pursue. The same is true for the employers.

Notice that, in this last analysis regarding the employers, the organization doing the analysis has not yet figured out who their competition is to any great extent. They obviously need to complete their inquiries. By using a chart such as this, the organization can be an aggressive market segmenter and choose the markets in which they want to compete, reducing their emphasis on other markets and focusing their limited time and dollars on the market segments that best fit with their strategic plans.

You need to know who your competitors are, but this does not mean simply making a list. You need to look at them through different eyes: your funders, the people you serve, the services you provide, and the people that refer to you. Only by doing these different analyses can you hope to really get a good grasp of where to focus your greatest competitive efforts.

Our Referrers	What Do the Referrers Want?	Who Do They Refer to Us?/Comments	Who Is Our Competition?
Physicians			
Dr. Jones	Quick acceptance of patient, Insurance coverage, Accredited facility	Head Injuries (two 70-day patients last year).	St. Jude's Hanneman Rehab
Dr. Majeski	Insurance coverage, Accredited facility, Specializing in spinal cord	25 occupational rehab patients last year — mostly spinal.	Unknown
Dr. Wheeler	Insurance coverage, Medicaid Certified, Accredited facility	Various patients — mostly inpatient (40 last year).	Unknown
Dr. Foresta	Quick acceptance of patient, Insurance coverage — all types, Accredited facility	Only two patients two years ago but 20 last year, mostly short-term assessment patients.	St. Judes?
Insurers			
Company A	Quick acceptance of patient, Medicare/Medicaid Certified, Accredited facility	20 patients each and every year for the past five years.	Unknown
Company B	Quick acceptance of patient, Medicare/Medicaid Certified, Accredited facility	Just starting to send us longer term. Only reimburse 80% of normal charges. Five patients last year.	Unknown
Company C	Quick acceptance of patient, Medicare/Medicaid Certified, Accredited facility, Managed care capacity	Leader in managed care. Short stays mandatory. 50 patients last year.	Unknown, but talking with three rehab centers about inclusion in managed care network.
Company D	Quick acceptance of patient, Medicare/Medicaid Certified, Accredited facility, Managed Care Capacity	No history. A new player in the community. But covers almost 20% of the community due to three large employers.	Unknown

Our Referrers	What Do the Referrers Want?	Who Do They Refer to Us?/Comments	Who Is Our Competition? Physicians
Insurers (continued)			
Company E	Quick acceptance of patient, Medicare/Medicaid Certified, Accredited facility	Heinous oversight and paperwork. Only 10 patients per year.	Part of new managed care network?
Employers			
Meltdown Utilities	Lowest possible Worker's Comp results, Deal Directly with Insurer, Managed Care Capacity		President is on the board at Hanneman!
Ace Manufacturing	Lowest possible Worker's Comp results, Deal Directly with Insurer, Managed Care Capacity	Five or so injuries per year. Ace is working on risk avoidance, and thus will be sending us less people in the future.	Unknown
Acme Automobiles	Lowest possible Worker's Comp results, Deal Directly with Insurer, Managed Care Capacity	Rapidly growing. Unionized. Sends us 20-30 people per year, but automating quickly.	No preferential arrangement yet.
Cellular Two	Lowest possible Worker's Comp results, Deal Directly with Insurer, Managed Care Capacity	Doubling the size of the workforce every three years. Sent us ten people last year, but all long-term patients.	Unknown.
Microhard Group	Lowest possible Worker's Comp results, Deal Directly with Insurer, Managed Care Capacity	Low accident rate for population.	No admissions in past two years.

B. STUDYING THE COMPETITION

By applying the tools in the previous section, you can develop a list of your competitors and then prioritize the market segments on which to focus your efforts. With that focusing, you still have a list of priority competitors, ones that you need to find out more about. In using the tools I just provided you, you filled in what the competition does well and compared it to what you do well. Your input on those charts was probably preliminary and perhaps based on word of mouth or assumptions. If you are like most readers, it was probably not based on careful analysis.

1. WHAT YOU NEED TO KNOW ABOUT YOUR COMPETITION

You need to find out important information about your competitors that you can then use to become a better competitor yourself. You need to learn the following four core things about your competitors:

➡ *What services do they provide?* Do they compete with you across the board, or only in certain areas? If they are a full-spectrum competitor, you probably need to investigate them more carefully than if they are only competing with you in one area — unless that area is providing your most profitable service.

➡ *What clientele are they seeking?* Do they target the same population that you do? Or, do they just take the most lucrative segment of your population? On the other hand, do your target markets and theirs really overlap? This is also important. If you are targeting people over 60, for example, and the competitor has that age cohort as a secondary or tertiary market, you may not have to worry as much.

➡ *What value do they give to the customer?* Remember, price is not the issue, value is. What does your competitor do that provides value to the customer? An added value at a museum might be a well-designed map or a number of easily accessible benches or rest rooms. An added value for a counseling center might be a particularly friendly receptionist and free coffee in the reception area. Whatever the competition is doing, is it something that you can also provide and provide well — and that is within your mission statement?

➡ *What are their prices?* Is the price truly comparable to yours, or do you (or they) offer more service for the same price? While price is not *the* issue, it is an important issue for many customers. Make sure you do your best to compare apples to apples when looking at price.

Otherwise you may make bad decisions based on the assumption that your price is lower (or higher) than the competition's.

● **FOR EXAMPLE:** I was recently working with two competing not-for-profit organizations who were considering a merger. These organizations provided sheltered employment to people with disabilities. They were reviewing each others' "daily rates" (prices) and one saw that their rate was nearly twice that of their potential partner. They came to me upset, because they feared that this low rate indicated a poor quality of service and they did not want to even consider joining up with a "poor quality organization". I asked them why they felt the service was poor, and their answer was, "Look, our daily rate is $140 and theirs is only $82. They can't give good service for $82." "No," I agreed, "not unless they don't include the same costs in their rate as you do in yours."

And, in the end, we found out that was the case. One daily rate included transportation, meals, and supervision after work. The other organization offered all of these same services but billed them separately. Thus, the comparison of prices with the name "daily rate" was invalid and misleading.

You need to find out about services, target markets, value, and prices. At a minimum. It would also be nice to know about other things, but these are the core issues to look at first. How do you find out? You do a little market research — aimed at your competition.

2. HOW DO YOU RESEARCH YOUR COMPETITION?

Where do you start? What resources do you have? How much time do you spend on this? The answer to all three of these questions is the same: it depends. It depends on how actively you are competing. It depends on whether the competitor is retail (where a lot of information is in the public domain) or wholesale (where prices and services are more difficult to research). It depends on how much time and money you have to spend.

However, you need to start somewhere, so let's look through a list of resources that you can use.

• *The Public Record.* If your competitor is a not-for-profit, it needs to file a report with both the IRS and with your state (either the Attorney General or the Secretary of State each year.) This financial information is available by calling the appropriate agency, or, in many cases, it will be on the Internet. You will learn board names, total income, the organization's mission statement, etc.

If your competitor is a for-profit, you may be able to get information on them through a national database such as Dun & Bradstreet or a local information source, such as the Chamber of Commerce or the Better Business Bureau.

In either case, one of the first steps I would take is to call the competitor, and ask to have information on services and fees sent to you. There is no need to lie and pretend that you are a service recipient. Just ask for written material and have it sent to your home. If you think that they will recognize your name and not send it to you, ask one of your staff to make the same call. If the competitor has a homepage on the World Wide Web (and more do every day), you can often just download the information you seek from the Internet directly (and anonymously).

Common referral sources also usually have sets of information to hand out. For example, a social worker usually will keep information on all the programs he or she may suggest to a client; a minister may have the material from many resources in the community; a teacher may have sets of material on the many available tutoring organizations. (Note: these referral sources should have current copies of your marketing information as well.)

• *Customers.* Your customer base is an excellent source of information. When you do customer surveys, add in some questions on your competition. Ask such questions as: "Have you received this service from other organizations in the community? When? From whom? What did you like best about them? Worst? Why do you utilize our services rather than theirs?"

Between surveys, you can ask customers informally when you see them in your organization. By doing this you will not only often learn important competitive information, but your customers will also feel that you care about their opinion. Don't ever discount the value of informal, regular asking. Your organization needs to have a culture of constantly asking.

• *Board, Staff, and Volunteers.* The more ears and eyes out there, the better. After you make a list of your competitors and prioritize that list for the most pressing investigation, let your board, staff, and volunteers know what kind of information you need, what questions you want answered, and that you would appreciate any help that they can give you in gathering the information. Now, suddenly, instead of just you and your circle of friends and acquaintances, you have 20, 30, 50, or more people gathering information. The likelihood of getting useful information increases dramatically. One important side benefit of asking these people for help is that it reinforces the issue that competition is real and not just some figment of your imagination. Use your resources and, in this case, that means all of the other people inside your organization.

3. WHAT YOUR COMPETITION IS AFTER

What people or things is your competition trying to take away from you? Each group on the list below will have their own sources of information that may be of help to you. Opening up channels of communication early is important, so that you have established trust and access to information. Thus, even though not every one of the items or people on the list below will be a priority for you today, you may need access to information about that area in the future. I am not contending that you should give each area equal priority; just don't completely ignore any of them.

Remember, as you read the list, these categories are those in which competitors are trying to compete with you — for good board members, excellent staff, donations, bid work, volunteers, and direct services. In each, you need to find out how they are competing with you. This will enable you to decide how best to beat them.

☞ **HANDS-ON:** Talk to the following groups about your competition:

• *Board Members.* Ask board members (and friends and neighbors) who are serving or have served on other boards what they like most and least about their board *service.* Don't ask detailed and pointed questions about the other organization — you may not get good information. Focus your questions on the functions of the board that they liked and disliked. If there are board workshops run through your United Way, go to them and learn about the state of the art. You need to make your board service desirable.
• *Staff.* When staff come aboard, ask them what they liked most and least about their previous job. When they leave, ask them in an exit interview what attracted them to their new job (or drove them away from your organization). Read the want ads to check salaries and benefits. Take part in salary surveys run by local or state trade associations to get a handle on competitiveness.
• *Donations.* Be a constant observer of how you are asked for money, and urge your board and staff to do the same. Do you like being asked for money in the supermarket parking lot? By mail? By phone? In person? Within these groupings what approaches do you like and

dislike? Look at the printed material other organizations are handing out. What appeals to you and what doesn't? The field of donations is becoming rapidly more competitive and sophisticated and new innovations pop up all the time.

• *Bid Services.* When you participate in a bidding process, are the other bids, particularly the winning bid, made public? Can you find out who the other bidders were? What did the winning bid offer (assuming that it wasn't your organization)? Try to find out as much about the competition here as you can. I am involved in bidding for a project probably twice a year, and I always ask who else bid, what they offered that was different, and (if I didn't get the work) what was the deciding factor in selecting the other consultant. Sometimes it is something I can't control, such as that the other consultant was from the local community; sometimes it is something I could have done differently, such as the array or sequence of services offered. Sometimes, of course, it comes down to price. But each time I learn, and so can you. Never just walk away from a bidding process. Get as much information as you can.

• *Volunteers.* If your organization uses volunteers (other than the board of directors), then you know how important they are. As with board members and staff, ask your volunteers if they have done similar work for other not-for-profits, what they liked and disliked about their time there, and why they now help you.

☞ **HANDS-ON:** When you talk to your volunteers, use a group session rather than individual meetings. Volunteers tend, for the most part, to be a bit awed by the senior management staff, and putting them in a peer group will not only make them more at ease but also generate more ideas and reactions for you. In addition, it saves you time.

• *Direct Service Ideas.* Here, your antennae need to be out for new services, service innovations, and ways that your competitors are adding value. Your sources here are the customers we discussed above, your staff (again the more ears the better), and, in many cases, the people from whom you buy specialty products or services. Ask these vendors who else they sell to, and learn what you can from them about the organization. For example, if you buy physical therapy equipment from a large vendor, ask them who else in the area is buying similar equipment. They will give you a list of your potential competitors. Don't stop there. When the sales person comes in, ask, "How's business? Any big sales lately?" Suddenly, you find that your most important competitor is replacing all their PT equipment in the next three months. This is important information if you also know that customers value new equipment, or if your staff members want to work with the newest equipment. Ask your vendors as well as your customers.

In all of these cases, you are asking, asking, asking, and then trying to fit the often fragmented pieces of the puzzle together. The culture of asking is the root of your information, and you need to have a lot of people asking as well as a system to get the information back to you promptly. History is full of examples of organizations that had critical information but didn't communicate it to the person who most needed it at the crucial moment. If you just gather information but don't communicate it, you aren't doing your organization any good.

I'm sure that you have noticed that I did not give you one source or even a set of sources that will necessarily meet all your information needs. Finding out about competitors is often a haphazard quest, with incremental progress in some cases and huge gains made in others. It will depend on the competitor, the situation, and your resources. But just because you don't think that you can get all the information you want immediately doesn't mean that what you *can* gather isn't important. It is. For your core competition, go after the information, keep it up-to-date, and use what you can to improve your own services and products.

C. FOCUSING ON YOUR CORE STRENGTHS

By using the techniques discussed in this chapter, you now know how to identify your competitors, how to find out information about them, and how to focus on the most important of your competitors. Now what do you do? Do you try to compete on all fronts, with all types of organizations, in all services, and for all groups of people?

Of course not. You don't have the resources, energy, or time to do that. What you need to do now is the third step in a three-part analysis. Let's review what you have done in the first two steps and then examine the third.

Step 1. Review the markets. You have done this (as described in Chapter 7) already. You should know who your markets are, how many there are, and which of them are your focus for the future and which aren't. You have applied the 80/20 Rule and know its implications.

Step 2. Evaluate the competition. You should have done this as well, as described earlier in this chapter. You know as much as you can gather about your competition, including an analysis of the competitor's strengths and weaknesses compared to yours.

Step 3. Look at your core competencies. It is time for this third, crucial step. Since you can't compete on all fronts, where do you focus your actions? One place to do that is where you are already strong. Remember the SWOT (Strengths, Weaknesses, Opportunities, Threats) analysis that you used to run when doing a plan? Do it again now with your board and staff, but stop after the Strengths and Weaknesses parts. Identify the things you do well and the things you should work on. (*Note:* If you have never done a SWOT analysis, it is a wonderful and worthwhile exercise. I have included much more information on SWOT analyses in Appendix A.)

Now, compare your strengths and weaknesses to the things your markets want. Are the things they want the things that you do well? If so, fine. If not, do you need to invest in improvements? Or, should you focus on a market segment that wants the things that you do well?

● **FOR EXAMPLE:** A sheltered workshop in western New York State recently told me of their decision to get out of the business of packaging as a way of employing people with disabilities. The packaging industry had become too price-competitive and too oriented to Just-In-Time, both areas where this organization did not feel it could compete well. Instead, it looked at what it *did* do well, and found that service — high quality service — was its strength. Over a three-year period it changed its focus to work with customers who valued high levels of service, rather than price or speed.

Now, look at the list of strengths and weaknesses again, in light of your competition's strengths and weaknesses. Do you compete strength to strength or weakness to strength? Do you need to bolster some areas to meet a competitor's strength, or should you compete in an area where they are weaker?

When you are done with this analysis, you should have defined a list of the things you, your staff, and board feel that you do well — your core competencies. Focus on those. Invest in keeping them state of the art. Buy the training, equipment, and staff that you need to keep these areas at high levels of excellence for years to come.

Remember, you are not your competition and you don't want to be. Your organization is unique in its own right. Certainly, study and learn from your competition. But don't try to copy them in every thing. Be yourself, focus on the markets you want using your own core strengths.

RECAP

In this chapter, we have covered the important points that will help you identify and learn more about your competition. We looked at how to analyze your competitors through the lens of your services, the people you serve, your referrers, and your funders. I then showed you how to use staff, board, volunteers, friends, and even vendors to continually gather information on the four key questions you need to answer about your competition:

1. *What services do they provide?*
2. *What clientele are they seeking?*
3. *What value do they give to the customer?*
4. *What are their prices?*

We then turned to the issue of finding out about how the competition is approaching your board, staff, and volunteers, and what they are doing in direct bidding. Finally, I showed you how to analyze all of this information in light of your organization's core competencies. Focus on the things that you do well, and match those competencies with what your target markets want.

One last reminder about the competition. Respect them, but don't fear them. They are organizations made up of people just like you, trying their best to provide a product or service in a chaotic and often confusing world. Don't ever assume that they can automatically do things better than you. Find out where they are good, and find out where they are weak. All organizations have some of both. The biggest mistake I see, as not-for-profits realize that they are entering a competitive arena, is fear. Fear closes your ears and eyes to information about your competitors. Fear incapacitates you, making you incapable of innovation and flexibility. Fear makes it impossible for you to take a risk on behalf of the people you serve. It will eat you up.

Don't fear the competition. Respect them. Respect yourself, and be proud — and at the same time realistic — about your organization's capabilities. Compete head-to-head when you have to and when you can. Focus on your core strengths, build customer loyalty by giving them what they want, and you will be successful.

In order to give your customers what they want, I have told you that you need to ask, ask, and ask. And that is the subject of our next chapter.

☞☞ **HANDS-ON REVIEW:**
- **Some competition assessment sheets**
- **Asking about your competition**
- **Asking in groups**

DISCUSSION QUESTIONS FOR CHAPTER 8:

1. Do we really know who are competitors are? How can we keep better track of them? Should we focus on the top ten or on the competition that is after our 80/20 markets?

2. Who competes for our referrers now? Are we doing enough for our referral sources? Can we do more?

3. What are our core competencies? Are we excellent in these? How can we maintain that excellence (improve our status)?

4. How can we keep up-to-date on all the techniques and knowledge that we need to maintain excellence?

5. In our target markets, do we need to worry about competition, or is there enough market for all of us?

9. Asking Your Markets What They Want

OVERVIEW

Ask, ask, ask, and then listen! I hope you are beginning to repeat that as a marketing maxim, because it is the best one I know. Only by asking, asking regularly, and asking the correct people the correct questions can you find out that all-important information: what your markets want. Only by asking regularly can you keep track of how those wants change with time. Only by asking and listening can you overcome the *marketing disability* that I described to you earlier. You need to ask.

But how do you ask? Whom do you ask? How often? In what format? What kind of outside help do you need? How much will it cost? Where do you start? Does the 80/20 Rule apply to asking? All of those questions will be covered in this important chapter.

Chapter Thumbnail
- ➡ **Surveys**
- ➡ **Focus Groups**
- ➡ **Informal Asking**
- ➡ **Asking Mistakes to Avoid**
- ➡ **After Asking**

First, we'll look at the most common way of asking: *surveys*. We'll go over survey methods, how to develop a survey, where to get help, and how many people you need to survey to be sure that your answers have meaning. We'll look at sample formats, review how many identifiers you should use, and examine ways to make tabulation and analysis easier.

Then we'll turn to *focus groups*, a favorite method of many market analysts. We will cover how to plan and run a focus group, what to ask, what not to ask, who to invite, and where to get help. We'll look at how to analyze the data gathered and what to do after the focus group meets.

Next, we'll talk about *informal interaction* as an asking tool. We'll cover ways to ask, what to ask, training your staff to be constant askers, and some problems that other organizations have had with regular asking. Then, we'll look at some fatal mistakes people make with their asking, ones that you want to avoid.

Finally, we'll cover what you should do after you ask. This will include tabulating, analyzing, and sharing the information, getting back to the people you asked, and integrating the information into your marketing plans. By the end of the chapter you should have a number of hands-on tools and ideas on how to proceed with this crucial part of the marketing cycle.

A. SURVEYS

We all know about surveys: they are expensive and complex, and get very little response. Right? Wrong, at least as a rule. Surveys can be expensive and complex and have undependable results. They can also be inexpensive, simple, and can garner nearly 100 percent return. In this section we'll look at what surveys are and some rules for keeping them affordable, useful, and easy to add to your marketing efforts.

Surveys, when done properly, gather *objective* data, that is, data that can have statistical significance. You can analyze this data over time, looking at the same questions every six or twelve months. For example, if you survey your staff you can analyze the percentage who respond that they are "very satisfied" with their job, and see whether that number goes up or down each year. This is called *trend analysis*.

Alternately, you can look at the same data and analyze it between groups in the same survey. Going back to the staff survey, you could examine whether the job satisfaction was higher in administration or in direct service, in one of your locations or another. This is called *cohort analysis*.

Another benefit of surveys is that, if done correctly, you can survey a small group of people and accurately transfer the findings of the small group to a much larger one.

● **FOR EXAMPLE:** I am sure that you see the results of survey data on television, or in advertisements regularly.

"Our most recent poll shows that Candidate X is ahead of Candidate Y by a 53 percent to 41 percent margin with 6 percent of the population undecided." Then the announcer (or the graphic) adds, *"Survey of 2,045 American adults conducted June 15-16. Survey results accurate ± 3 percentage points."*

The surveyors looked at a tiny slice of all Americans and then made an extrapolation of those results to the population as a whole. This ability to survey a small group is very, very cost-effective if you need to know what a large group thinks of your organization, but it is only useful if the survey is done properly. You can't just ask 15 people on your block a question and have any confidence that the results represent your community as a whole (unless the block *is* the entire community!).

Surveys have benefits that can really help your marketing. You can see how you are doing now, as opposed to last month. You can see which market segment is most in want of your services. You can find out who is happy and who is not. You can survey the *who,* the *what,* the *where,* the *when,* and the *how much.* What most surveys are not particularly good at is finding out the *why* in any depth. For this you have focus groups, interviews, and informal asking. More on these later.

We will define a survey as a standardized sequence of prepared questions given to a group of people to elicit information on a particular subject. The most important adjective here is standardized. You want to ask everyone the same questions, with the same tone, in the same sequence. The standardization is a crucial part of getting statistically reliable information from the survey.

Who could you survey? In theory, any market that you want to serve and in which you want to become or remain competitive. In practice, you would probably survey only your largest, your target, or your most crucial markets. You could survey consumers, donors, funders, staff, referral sources, even (though I don't suggest it) the community as a whole. You could aim your questions at need, at your competition, at the satisfaction of the survey group with your organization.

So, there are a lot of people that you can survey and a lot of information that you can get out of them. But, you only have so much money and time, so let's look at some suggestions for getting more out of your surveying. I want to ensure that all of your surveying dollars are well spent.

1. Have Instructions.
At the beginning of the survey, have instructions for the reader. Keep

them *simple* and *short*. Include the reason for the survey, any special instructions for how to fill it out, where to send it when it is completed, and the deadline for submission to have input considered. Also have a name and phone number for any questions that may arise.

2. Be Brief.

You need to be as brief as you can be. When people fill in a survey, they are doing you a favor, giving you some of their time as well as their opinions. Help them by keeping the survey as short as possible. I see a lot of people who think that they are being smart by asking everything they possibly can on one survey to "save money on mailing." What happens is that the longer the survey, the less likely people are to fill it in. Thus, the "savings" get eliminated since the return diminishes.

3. Be Focused.

This is one way to accomplish point 2. Focus each survey on a particular issue: customer satisfaction, needs analysis, product testing, etc. Don't mix the questions; you will mix up the survey and its resulting data. Be focused, be brief.

4. Don't Ask Too Often.

If you send a board member, staff member, or donor a questionnaire weekly, how many do you think they will fill out? I have already told you that you need to ask and ask regularly to track trends and keep up on new customer wants, but regularly does not mean daily. Again, value the time of the people you are surveying. Ask them, but only as often as you absolutely need to.

5. Ask the Questions in the Correct Sequence and Wording.

You can really mess up the data you get by asking questions in the wrong fashion, the wrong way, or even in the wrong order.

● **FOR EXAMPLE:** There is a wonderful story that I have heard repeated for years (and that I suspect is apocryphal) of graduate students in marketing who each year go down a busy street at noon, holding up an 8 x 10 inch glossy photograph of the current president of the United States. They ask the first 100 people they see the following question, "You know who this is don't you?" and get a 95 percent correct response rate. Then they ask the next 100 persons, "Who is this person?" and only get a 79 percent correct response. According to the story, this experiment is repeated annually by each class to make the point: be careful how you ask — it skews the answers.

You can really get valueless information by asking the wrong question the wrong way. Make a list of the information you want and then follow the suggestion in point 10 below.

6. Limit Your Identifiers.

Identifiers are the things you usually fill out at the beginning of a survey. Are you male or female? What age group are you in? Married, single, divorced, widowed? Income bracket? These are all identifiers. You will almost certainly want to have these in your surveys as well, since it is the one way you can analyze the data by groups of people (called cohorts). For example, if you do a consumer satisfaction survey, you probably would like to identify people with the different programs you provide, or the different demographic categories you serve, or even the county (city, zip code) where they live. This lets you look at your data in more depth.

Identifiers are terrific, but they have a big drawback. The more you put in your survey, the less people will fill it in, for two reasons. First, it makes the survey longer, cutting down on the response level simply because the form looks too long to some people. Second, the more identifiers you have, the more people feel that they will be identified as an individual. Thus, they will either not fill in the survey, or worse, they will fill it in but pull their punches, not being as frank as you would like. Then you have bad data, which is worse than no data. This second caution is, of course, moot in cases where you have people fill in their name. I suggest that for any survey where you ask for "satisfaction" levels, keep the survey anonymous. My experience is that you will get much more useful information.

☞ **HANDS-ON:** When making a list of what you need to know on a survey, particularly in the area of identifiers, make a list of the breakouts you would like to see. This might be by gender, age group, ethnicity, location of service, or countless other "slices" of information. Then look at the list and for each item on it ask the question, "What am I going to do with this information? Am I collecting it from curiosity or need? Will I be able to use the information I collect?" Be brutal on yourself in this area. The strong tendency is to ask for too much information. I have read countless survey reports that are demographically loaded but light on real information. The reports nearly go into the shoe size of the respondents, but don't have much hard information that is of use. Make a list and ask Why? Why? Why? before including the identifier in the final survey.

This is not to say that identifiers are not important. Some are crucial analytical items for statistical significance, others speak to important program and service needs or concerns. For example, if 90 percent of your program recipients are women, but 55 percent of your consumer survey recipients are men, extrapolating the survey data for all consumers may have problems. Thus having a gender identifier on that particular survey form would be valuable. Similarly, for surveys that have questions that seek concerns with program hours, services, and other indicators of satisfaction, knowing which services the survey respondent uses most, or their location of service, may be very important. But their zip code may not be.

So be selective. Ask for some identifiers, but only as many as you *absolutely* need. Your outside help (see point 10) can give you some assistance in this area.

7. For Trend Data, Be Consistent.

Trend data looks at information over time: For example, how many of your staff are "very satisfied" with their job this year as opposed to last year and the year before? That is trend data, and watching the trends is a crucial part of good management, good marketing, and being competitive. While data in isolation is *interesting,* data in context (compared to something) is *valuable*. The context here is the context of time. Are the trends positive or negative? Are you gaining ground or losing ground?

● **FOR EXAMPLE:** Let's look at a list of information gathered from surveys that you might be interested in tracking over time. Note that this is a generic list for not-for-profits and that you should add to (or delete from) this list to make it fit your unique circumstances.

- *Customer/Client Satisfaction (may be more than one survey depending on the breadth of customers you serve)*
- *Staff Job Satisfaction*
- *Staff Benefits Preferences*
- *Community Needs Assessment*
- *Funder Satisfaction*
- *Referrer Awareness and Satisfaction*

Each item on the list could involve a repeated survey (usually every 12 to 18 months) whose data could be compared with previous surveys. The trick in collecting trend data is avoiding the common pitfall of constantly amending (offenders in this area call it "fine tuning") the questions so that the data is skewed, making it, at best, less accurate and, at worst, worthless. You need to ask exactly the same questions over and over.

Having said that, if you have a question that is not giving you valuable information, definitely drop it. You save yourself and the survey respondents time. And, as circumstances change, you will need to add questions to accommodate those changes. But such amendments should be few and far between, and the wording of the questions that are repeated from survey to survey should hardly ever change at all.

☞ **HANDS-ON:** When you do change parts of your surveys, make sure that you note it in the report. For example, let's assume that your previous consumer surveys only had four choices in a question that asked, "Which of our programs do you use the most?" and your current survey gives six choices, as you have added two new services since your last survey. This change, while valid and worthwhile, will skew the comparative data, and thus the change deserves a notation in the report. Always make such notations to be fair to the reader. And, if the only reader is going to be you, *still* make the notations, so that in future years you can remember what changed!

Work for consistency in your data gathering. It allows greater utilization of the information that you have spent so much time and money gathering.

NOTE: There are many, many other trends that you should be tracking within your management team, including financial ratios, donated dollars, days payable, staff turnover, customer complaints, salary comparisons, administrative percentages, etc. The list could take three pages and, like any other, would need to be customized for your organization. Don't look only at survey trend data. There is a lot of information already inside your organization that you should be monitoring.

8. Include Closing Instructions.

At the end of the survey, tell people what to do with the survey once it is completed. Even if you included instructions about where to send the survey, and by when, in the introductory page, do it again here in large, bold typeface. If you are asking people to mail the survey to you, include a stamped, preaddressed envelope. Always include a fax number for their convenience.

9. Say Thank You.

At the end of your survey, thank people for their time and effort in giving you information. It seems like a small thing. It's not. Let them know you appreciate their time and also tell them what will happen to their survey, when they might expect to see results, and how the information will be used, by whom, and by when.

10. Get Help.

As you have probably gathered, surveying is not just something you wake up one day and start doing. It takes time, financial commitment, and a fair amount of expertise. It is easy to do poorly, a challenge to do well. Doing it poorly results in that most dangerous of products: poor, inaccurate, and therefore misleading information. Doing it well can give your organization a true competitive advantage: good, accurate information on which you can base policy, develop programs, improve services, and do more effective mission.

All of which is to say you probably need help, at least to develop your initial surveys and learn the ropes. There is lots of help out there. There are professional marketing and surveying organizations, including a growing number that work solely in the not-for-profit sector. There are instructors and professors at your local colleges and universities who teach marketing, surveying, and similar courses. There are professionals who work for large corporations whose job it is to develop their internal and external surveying. There are staff at regional planning commissions, agricultural extension offices, economic development agencies, and in your local mayor's or county/parish commissioner's office who develop surveys. All of these are resources you can tap.

What can this professional help do? A number of things. You should make sure that you get assistance in at least the following areas:

• *Selection of survey sample:* What is the best set of people to survey to get the information you want — that is accurate while being affordable? This is a technical and statistically challenging area.

• *To pilot-test or not to pilot-test?* If you are surveying a huge group, or making a multiyear commitment to a survey instrument, it may be smart to pilot-test the survey with a small group to make sure that it is working the way you want it to.

• *Question development:* While you should absolutely be in charge of what information is sought, the way that it is asked is crucial. Should particular questions be open-ended or "forced choice"? If forced choice, how many options should there be and what wording should be used? In what sequence should the questions be placed? Should there be confirming questions included?

• *Survey administration:* Your survey consultant can help you with administering the survey. Should you mail it or hand out the survey? Should it be anonymous? Should it be done in person?

The consultant may even mail out, collect, and analyze the data for you.

Don't scrimp here. If you try to be cheap, you may have correspondingly valuable data. Remember the old adage: you get what you pay for.

Sample Survey

In Appendix B, you will find a sample survey that I helped design for a West Coast organization that serves people with disabilities. As you review it, note that it is long and deals with a variety of issues related to the satisfaction of the people that the organization serves. Since the survey was administered by trained surveyors in the home, the response rate was very high and the group could afford to have as many identifiers as it did. Also note the format, with numbers associated with each response. This design was to speed data entry for the survey so it could be analyzed in a database.

If you plan to do surveying, I would strongly urge you to order a copy of an excellent basic surveying text. One I really like is titled: *How to Conduct Surveys, A Step-by-Step Guide,* by Arlene Fink and Jaqueline Kosecoff (1985, Sage Publications, ISBN 0-8039-2456-9). It is excellent and will arm you with the basic information you need to work with your outside expert.

B. FOCUS GROUPS

Focus groups are great. They allow you to easily do what surveys cannot do: to follow up on initial responses, accessing feelings, reactions, emotions at a much deeper and more personal level. Focus groups at their core are facilitated sessions of 8 to 15 people that focus on a particular issue. They are often used to test the reactions of people to a new product, a potential commercial, or to compare reactions to two or three different potential advertising slogans or campaigns. Politicians use focus groups regularly to test their messages prior to general distribution.

As a not-for-profit administrator, you have a number of potential uses for focus groups. These could include:

- Testing a potential new service with consumers, referrers, and funders.
- Following up on survey results that showed a problem (or an opportunity).
- Testing various themes and slogans for a capital campaign.

There are, of course dozens of other uses for focus groups.

From focus groups comes *subjective* information. They elicit immediate reactions, in-depth commentary, and emotive responses in ways that surveys cannot.

● **FOR EXAMPLE:** Let's say that you are surveying a core constituency and on one question you ask, "Overall, how would you rate your satisfaction with the services you receive from our organization?" You give the respondent a scale of 1to 7 with a 7 being equivalent to "Terrific!"" and a 1 being equal to "Awful." The responses are consistently 4s and 5s, where in previous years they have been mostly 6s and 7s. What's going on? Surveys are not the best way to find the answer. By the time you receive the data and analyze it, the respondents are on to other things. But you can ask the question in a focus group. "How do you like our services? Why? Is your level of satisfaction lower, higher, or about the same as last year? Why?" And, when someone in the group says something like, "Well, I'm not as happy because the staff just aren't as friendly," follow-up questions can be asked right on the spot by the facilitator, honing in on what the problem may be. None of that can be done efficiently by survey.

As in surveying, there are some suggestions to make your focus groups more valuable, less expensive, and more productive.

1. Get a Facilitator.

This is absolutely crucial. You need to have a person *from outside your organization* who can plan and run your focus group. Focus group facilitation is a real skill, and it is much more important that your facilitator be strong in facilitation than an expert in your area of service. You can teach them about what you do.

Why have an outsider? Because the people in the focus group will be more frank with an outsider, and an outsider will be more objective about what she or he hears than you or anyone in your organization can be. Thus you get better, and more objective, information.

Facilitators are available in a number of places. Ask your Chamber. Call a marketing organization. Talk to the marketing department of a large company or bank in your community. Get references, and check them. You want someone skilled in facilitation, who is willing to work with you, eliciting the information you need.

2. Focus Your Questions.

After all, it is called a **focus** group. You need to focus your questions on a few key subjects. Your facilitator should help you with this by turning your information needs into open-ended questions that lead people to open up and share their opinions, reactions, and emotions. You only have a limited amount of time (see point 4) and so you want to have your issues focused and in a priority order. Don't ask a group that is supposed to focus on a new service how they like your existing ones. It will get them off track and use up valuable time.

3. Have a Homogeneous Group.

Here's another key ingredient to a focus group that succeeds: put like people around the table. For example, if your organization is a science museum, and you want to study the reactions of all your consumers to a potential new exhibit, don't have a group that includes high school students, graduate scientists, and senior citizens. Inevitably, one portion of that group will dominate the discussion and the others will feel disenfranchised and not participate. Again, focus your efforts on one type of person, and you will have more responses, better information, and an increased value from your investment.

4. Don't Wear the Group Out.

You have between 90 minutes and two hours. Then people's creative brains turn to mush. A good facilitator will keep track of the time, ask your questions in priority order, but will also tell you that after one and one-half to two hours you should let the group go. No sense in keeping people when they are not going to be productive.

5. Compensate the Group.

In the commercial world, people are often offered between $100 and $250 to participate in a two-hour focus group. You probably can't afford that and, in fact, may insult people who are associated with your organization by offering them money. But do offer them something: coffee and doughnuts, lunch, transportation, a parking voucher. Hold the session in a safe, comfortable space. After the session, thank each participant by letter, perhaps accompanied by a "token" of appreciation like a coffee mug, attractive paperweight, or other premium. Talk to your facilitator about what the community standard is for compensation, and don't be stingy. These people are providing you with literally invaluable information.

6. Analyze the Results Between Groups.

After each session (which should be audiotaped), analyze the results. Are you hearing similar issues? Are there enough issues left incomplete that more sessions are merited? Do you want to add another group made up of the same type of people, or an additional one made up of a different category of people? Have your facilitator tell you about body language, inflections, and other things that he or she may have picked up. Have the facilitator give you his or her overall impressions of the group, and list where he or she thinks you have opportunities to improve.

Sample Focus Group Questions

In Appendix C, you will find the actual questions I asked at a focus group for a product to be developed by a sheltered workshop in the midwest. Note how the questions are open-ended and in the priority order that the organization wanted answered.

How many groups should you run? Like any other question of this sort, the answer is: it depends. Focus groups are expensive to administer, but many experts suggest that you run enough so that you begin to hear the same information repeated. Thus, if you are a school, you may run groups of parents, students, faculty, and alumni. You might run only two of each type at first, and hear the same thing in each group except the parents, who might have so many different issues that you would want to run three or four sessions. Again, you don't want to mix groups, and you don't want to work them to death, so plan your strategy carefully.

If you want to pursue focus groups, I again have a resource for you to read before you hire your facilitator. It is a good, basic guide to the subject. It is entitled: *Focus Groups, A Practical Guide for Applied Research*, by Richard A. Krueger (1988, Sage Publications, ISBN 0-8039-3186-5).

C. INFORMAL ASKING

Here we confront a major cultural change for many organizations. Developing that regular "culture of asking" that I have referred to over and over takes time and the belief of everyone in the organization that they are on the marketing team. Only a total team effort will gather all the information, elicit all the wants, pick up on all the problems and opportunities that are out there. Your staff and volunteers need to be urged, cajoled, and led to ask, and ask regularly. They also need to be trained to ask, because there is a lot of "bad asking" going on out there.

● **FOR EXAMPLE:** Here is an experience that most readers have shared. You go to a restaurant, eat, then get your check. You approach the cash register to pay, and you are asked by the person behind the register about your meal. This can happen in two ways:

OPTION ONE: The person looks down at the register, and, while keying in your bill, asks, "Was everything okay?" To which most of

142

us answer, "Yes." This person was told to ask every customer how things were, and they are complying with the letter of the training, but not the spirit. The question suggests that everything was okay. They are on what I call *asking autopilot.* I even had someone recently ask me whether "everything was okay" and I said "No." They finished up printing out the receipt, gave me my change, and said, "Well that's great. Have a nice day and come back soon!" Asking on autopilot.

OPTION TWO: The person behind the register stops, looks you in the eye, and says, "How was everything tonight?" Then he or she waits for your answer and responds appropriately. This person was trained to ask the open-ended question that forces customers to come up with their own answers. Even if most of us respond with the stock, "Just fine," we still are more likely to let the clerk or the manager know about problems with this question than in the question posed in Option One.

Train your people that asking is important and then give them the tools to ask correctly, without skewing the answers.

1. How to Get Started.
Informal asking comes in many shapes and sizes. Different staff will be affected differently. Here are some ideas of where to start in developing some informal asking:

a. Have your staff trained to ask new customers where they heard about your organization. This might mean a receptionist, intake worker, someone sitting at an information booth, or any other person who would be the first point of entry.

b. When you interact in the community try to ask people regularly, "What do you hear about our organization? Do you know anyone who uses us? If you do, how have your experiences been?" If it's a friend or family member, ask how have their experiences been.

c. When you see your key vendors — your banker, insurance agent, auditor, office supply company, printer, and the like — ask them: "What do you hear about us on the street? Do you have ideas about things that are not being done now that we could do?"

d. Most importantly, whenever anyone in your organization interacts with anyone who you serve, who donates or contracts for services, who is a member, or who in any way can be considered a market, the final interaction should be this question: *"Is there anything else we can do for you today?"* This question, consistently and politely asked, will generate a constant stream of opportunities for service and improvement.

2. Following Up on the Answers.

One danger in informal asking is that, since it is just that, informal, you don't have a formal path for the information gathered to flow to the correct place. For example, if a caseworker asks someone how their visit was, and the client answers: "Great. Oh, but the toilets really smell. That's a real turnoff to me," the information has *got* to get to the maintenance or janitorial staff. Otherwise, even though your people asked, the information was not put to good use. Make sure you train staff in *what to do with what they learn*. You must be sure that there is a clearly spelled-out path for information to flow. If this is not put in place, much of your asking will be wasted.

More than any other kind of asking, consistent informal asking shows that you and your staff and volunteers care about the kind, quality, and level of service that your organization provides. It forces you to interact one-on-one, taking the chance of getting criticism or complaints face-to-face. People take note of that kind of risk-taking and appreciate it—unless you don't follow up the asking and make one or more of the mistakes listed in the next section.

D. ASKING MISTAKES TO AVOID

Of course, things can go wrong. You can ask and ask and ask, and have problems. Let's take a minute and review the common mistakes that other organizations have made in the hopes that you can avoid them.

1. Not Expecting Criticism.

If you ask, people will tell you. And, it is naive to think that no one will ever have any problems with the way that you do business. They will. But I regularly see staff people wailing and gnashing their teeth about the criticism that their organization has received. I have literally seen organizations who send staff members to counseling to get over the shock of reading the survey responses that they have gathered.

Come *on*. No organization is perfect. People like to gripe. And, you asked. What did you really expect?

The key here is to expect and even welcome criticism. I tell my clients all the time: *criticism is an opportunity to improve*. If your organization is dedicated to continuous improvement, you have to ask and have problems pointed out to be able to make those improvements.

Just don't get gun-shy. If people take a shot at you, analyze what they said. Was it fair? Was it accurate? What want of theirs did it show you? Can you accommodate them? If the complaint is regularly repeated (in other words, not an aberration), then fix the problem!

2. Not Listening.

This mistake is the logical end point of the marketing disability that I discussed earlier. You know all the answers, so why listen to what people want? You are the expert, so let's just appease people's sense of involvement by asking them, and then go on about our business. Chrysler did that in the early 1970s. They ignored what people were telling them about wanting small, fuel-efficient cars, and almost lost the company. Then they started to ask, and listen, and respond. In their responding they innovated. Not only did they save the company, but they invented new products including a whole new (and highly successful) category of vehicle: the minivan.

You have to listen to what people tell you. That is not to say that you need to knee-jerk your responses and change your entire organization because two out of every 1,000 people are unhappy. But you do need to give each comment, each criticism, each idea a fair hearing. Otherwise you are wasting your asking dollars and missing significant competitive opportunities.

3. Not Responding.

So you asked, you listened, but it's too much trouble to change, to respond. You don't have the time, or the money, and, anyway, you can't make all the people happy all the time. True, but you better work to make your target markets happy nearly all the time. And you'll do that by being responsive to their wants.

● **FOR EXAMPLE:** Imagine that I come out to your organization to do a speech for your board and staff. I start off and am really moving along. At the intermission I ask you how you think that things are going. You tell me, "You are going too fast for some of our board members. Can you slow down and take some more time for questions? What you are saying is really good, and I want everyone to get a good grasp of it. We're in no hurry. Take your time."

What is my response? Do I tell you that I need to get through because your staff and board showed up a half an hour late and I have a plane to catch? (The customer is not always right, but the customer is always the customer!) No, I tell you: "Thanks for the input, I'll pay more attention and take some time for questions. Let's get the people back in their seats and try to get back on schedule." When we reconvene, I ask for questions on the previous material and then proceed at a more leisurely pace, still paying attention to the clock.

Here, I made a reasonable response to a reasonable request. I asked, I got an answer that I really didn't want to hear, but if I had just gone on, my customer would have been justifiably upset.

You need to respond as well as you can, as promptly as you can, as reasonably as you can. And you need to empower your staff to do the same.

E. AFTER ASKING

Now you have asked, what next? Asking again? Well, of course, but there are some things you should do after you have gathered the data. These include the following:

1. Analyze the Data.

Look at your information critically and soon. Make sure that an interdisciplinary group of staff and board give the data close scrutiny. Was the survey sample significant? Are the results valid? If so, what did we learn? What can we apply? What trends pop out? What follow-up inquiries should we do?

You have taken time and paid good money to gather the information. Now, examine it carefully. I see too many groups that do a survey and either ignore what they learned or don't examine it until the information is so out-of-date that it no longer is relevant.

2. Respond to the People You Asked.

You have just imposed on the people who gave you valuable information. Do the right thing. Tell them what you learned. Send a memo, put a report in your newsletter, or make an announcement at a staff meeting, but let people know that you asked and you appreciated their input. Be sure to list the key things that the most people said.

☞ **HANDS-ON:** Make a list of what you learned and then tell people what you are doing about it. It may look something like this:

WE LEARNED THE FOLLOWING THINGS AND HAVE TAKEN THE FOLLOWING ACTIONS:	
ITEMS A, B, C, D	We have already implemented changes to respond to these excellent ideas.
ITEMS E, F, H, J	We are budgeting these for the next fiscal year.
ITEMS G, I, L	We cannot accommodate these suggestions because of regulatory restraints.
ITEMS K, M	The board will discuss these policy change ideas at their next meeting.

By doing this, you not only allow people to learn from each other, you acknowledge their input and take credit for taking action — something that most people are pretty cynical about. They often assume that their ideas go into a large trash barrel. So don't do that. Instead, tell them what you heard and, equally importantly, what you have done about it. Show them that you are responsive.

3. Accommodate to the Wants of Your Markets.

If you ask, people will tell you what they want. Now that you know, make the changes that you can to accommodate the wants. This, of course, is the other side of two of the errors people make that we just reviewed above: not listening and not responding. While you should never make promises you cannot keep, you should always try to accommodate your markets as best you can. This means that you should review your survey or focus group information with the people that provide your services, and try to come up with ways to accommodate what your customers have told you. Don't just tell staff what to do. Have them become part of the marketing team by learning how to use the information that you are gathering to do a better job.

4. Incorporating Your Information into Your Marketing Plans.

Later, in Chapter 12, I will show you how to put all of your marketing information into a cohesive plan. Suffice it to say here, don't ignore the data that you gather as you go about putting together your initial plan and adapting your marketing methods to changing circumstances. It is very easy to say: "Well, we've decided our goals for this year, and we'll review this new information that we've just gathered next year during our annual review." Next year? That may be too late. If you are confident of your data, use it. Good planning takes into account changes in the situation. If you have new information, even if it conflicts with the course you are on, use it! Imagine a ship captain whose vessel is set on a particular compass heading. He gets information from a satellite that there is a huge ice pack ahead. Does he stay on course (going with the plan), or does he use the new information, go around the danger, and eventually achieve his goal — reaching his destination safely?

RECAP

In this chapter, we have covered the crucial function of asking your markets what they want. You need to develop a culture as well as a system of asking to maintain your competitive edge. If you don't ask, how are you ever going to keep pace with the constantly changing wants of your target markets? Answer: you aren't.

First, we looked at surveys and discussed the ways to and ways *not* to survey. I suggested ten rules for surveying which, to review quickly, were:

1. **Have Instructions.**
2. **Be Brief.**
3. **Be Focused.**
4. **Don't Ask Too Often.**
5. **Ask the Questions in the Correct Sequence and Wording.**
6. **Limit Your Identifiers.**
7. **For Trend Data, Be Consistent.**
8. **Include Closing Instructions.**
9. **Say Thank You.**
10. **Get Help.**

We then moved on to focus groups, noting how they obtain qualitative data rather than the quantitative data that surveys can gather. Again, we went over some rules, this time the following six:

1. **Get a Facilitator.**
2. **Focus Your Questions.**
3. **Have a Homogeneous Group.**
4. **Don't Wear the Group Out.**
5. **Compensate the Group.**
6. **Analyze the Results Between Groups.**

We then turned to how to get the most out of informal asking, noting that this kind of constant attention to customers really pays off in a variety of ways, but that it takes training and motivation, and the involvement of everyone in the organization to do it well.

We next reviewed what *not* to do by looking at some common mistakes people make in their asking. These included not anticipating criticism, not listening, and not responding to what you have learned.

Finally, you were shown what to do after you ask, including analyzing your data, responding to the people you asked, and making sure that you take appropriate actions to respond to your new knowledge base.

Asking, listening, and responding are parts of a constant cycle, a vital part of the marketing process. Now that you know how to ask, we can turn our attention to the next issue: letting people know what you do —making better marketing materials.

☞☞ HANDS-ON REVIEW:
- **Limiting the number of survey identifiers**
- **A hint for modifying your surveys**
- **A follow-up listing for a survey or focus group**

DISCUSSION QUESTIONS FOR CHAPTER 9:

1. How often do we formally survey our target markets? Is this often enough? How recently have we updated the surveys that we do? Do we look at trend analysis now?

2. What about focus groups? Are they a good tool for us? For what kind of customer?

3. Can we get survey data from our competition? Is any of it public information?

4. Do we respond to customers after we survey now? Should we? How?

5. How can we get better at both asking and listening? What about making sure that ideas from the line staff get to us?

10. Better Marketing Materials

OVERVIEW

You now know who you are trying to serve (your markets) and what their wants and needs are. You know about your competition and what they are offering to your markets. Now comes a critical part of *both* your marketing and competitive cycle: letting your markets know about you — who you are and what you can do for them. In the marketing cycle this step was called "Promote the Product or Service." In this chapter, I'll show you how.

Marketing "materials" covers a lot of ground. It can be the traditional three-fold brochure, or stacked handouts that come in a larger folder. It can be advertising in a local newspaper or magazine, or a flyer placed under a windshield wiper. It can be your business card or your homepage on the World Wide Web. It can be your promotional spot on local television or radio, the notices you send out in direct mail, or the educational materials you give free of charge to the people you serve. It can be information on memberships, donations, or even a promotional trinket such as a key chain, calendar, or coffee mug. For most readers, their organization will be promoted through a mix of these vehicles in addition to word of mouth, referrals, and face-to-face sales.

But whatever it is, the mix has to address some similar issues. Many not-for-profits, like their for-profit peers, do a great job at developing and appropriately using their marketing materials. Many, however, do not. And, many not-for-profits are still doing that job as if they are living in the old, less competitive economy. They focus on *public relations* and *promotion* rather than *marketing*. There is a *huge* difference.

There is an overarching rule for marketing material: it must connect with the targeted market *from the customer's point of view*. This means that good marketing material grabs the customer and shows that person that you understand their wants, who they are and can solve their problems. By reading your brochure, listening to your radio spot, or looking at your television ad, can the customer quickly understand the benefit of using your organization's services? If not, you have not made the connection.

Chapter Thumbnail
➡ **The Problems with Most Not-For-Profits' Marketing Material**
➡ **Solving Customer Problems**
➡ **Things to Include in Your Marketing Material**
➡ **Things to Avoid in Your Marketing Material**
➡ **Developing Different Materials for Different Markets**

In this chapter, we'll talk about *marketing* materials as opposed to *promotional* tools. First, we'll cover this difference in emphasis as well as a number of other problems that I regularly see in not-for-profit marketing materials. Then, we'll focus on the issue in sales: solving customers' problems. I'll show you how to tell if your current marketing material does this and, if not, how to improve it so that it does. Then we'll turn to the seven things that you should *include* in your materials, and then a list of seven things to *avoid*. Finally, I'll give you some ideas on developing different materials for different markets, which sounds like a very straightforward and no-brainer idea, but apparently isn't, because a lot of organizations ignore it.

By the end of the chapter you should be much better able to analyze your existing marketing materials and to create new ones that really speak to and excite your many markets. Remember, your marketing material is out there speaking for you every day. If it is speaking in some unknown tongue, you are losing opportunities to connect with people who you could serve.

A. THE PROBLEMS WITH MOST NOT-FOR-PROFIT MARKETING MATERIAL

You have already read that the critical sequence in marketing is identifying your markets, asking those markets what they want, and then developing or amending services to meet those wants. This is called being *market-oriented,* and it is much preferable to being *service-oriented* where an organization just pushes its available services with little regard for what the market actually wants.

And here is the problem. Most of the marketing material that I see is *service-oriented,* pushing the existing service array, usually in jargon, and hardly ever in a way that really appeals to the wants of the markets. It is dull, dense, and not of interest to most people other than the individual who wrote it. It is also often poorly written, unprofessional looking, and out-of-date. It doesn't spell out the benefits of using the organization and makes no attempt to connect with the customer.

Why? Why, in an era of dirt-cheap, easy-to-use software and excellent low-cost color printers, do not-for-profits scrimp on marketing material? Why shoot yourself in the foot every time a potential customer, donor, referral source, banker, or board member sees an advertisement or promotional piece? The answer is multifaceted and it has to do with the marketing disability, tradition, being penny-wise, and a misunderstanding of the true nature of marketing. Let me expound on each of these.

1. The Marketing Disability.

Remember that the marketing disability springs from most not-for-profit staffs' professional training in diagnostics. This results in an attitude of "We know what you need" and the corollary (but unspoken) attitude of "We don't care what you want." This shows up in marketing material that contains:

- A history of the organization (a self-congratulatory one at that)
- A list of services (usually in jargon)
- A description of hours and locations available
- A phone number

What have we here? Otherwise useful space taken up with old news (the history that no one outside the organization really cares about), a cold list of jargon-filled services that anyone without a master's degree *in your discipline* has trouble understanding, a "come and get it" listing of times and locations, and an impersonal phone number.

Great first impression. Push your services, make no personal connection, confuse the reader with jargon. Often the marketing piece will add insult to injury by including a request for money!

● **FOR EXAMPLE:** I see marketing material like the one described above in all parts of the not-for-profit sector. In my work with organizations who provide vocational services to persons with disabilities, I often see brochures or pamphlets that list the services that the organization can provide to such persons and their families. Here is a sample list, taken from a real (unfortunately, typical) brochure that came across my desk recently.

- Employment Assessment
- Job Placement
- Family Respite
- Vocational Transportation
- Work Supports
- Work Hardening
- Supported Employment
- Employee Enclaves
- Occupational Therapy

All of these terms are legitimate technical descriptions of services in the field. But to anyone outside (like parents, funders, donors, and anyone else not intimately involved in the field), most of these terms are Greek. I once asked a group of management staff from an organization that provides services such as these what the term "work hardening" really meant, and whether they really expected people outside their organization to grasp its meaning. "Heck," said one, "90 percent *of our staff* don't know what it means, and I'm not sure that I could give you an accurate definition." I then asked why they included it in their marketing material. "Sounds impressive," was the answer. The marketing disability — in full swing.

☞ **HANDS-ON:** Try this jargon test. Hand your marketing material to a neighbor or friend who knows *nothing* about your services. Ask them to read it carefully, circling every word that they do not *fully* understand. Make sure that they know that this is not a test of their knowledge, but a way of helping you make your materials more understandable. Try this with two or three friends, and include your newsletters, if you print those. Don't overload individuals, just give them one or two things each to review. You will learn a lot about what is jargon and what isn't.

2. Tradition.

"We have a grand tradition here at our organization. We have a great reputation. We want to build on that." I hear this regularly but, interestingly enough, most often from organizations that have really poor marketing materials. They are so focused on their past that they can't even see their present, to say nothing of their future. Good marketing, competitive marketing, is interested in what the markets want today and in predicting what they will want tomorrow. If your marketing materials are focused on the past and look like they were designed in 1965 (perhaps because they were?), you are not going to appeal to today's markets.

Let's look at the quote above: first, the term *tradition*. As I said in the last chapter, traditions are great, as long as you build on them. When traditions appeal to a market, they really help an organization. An induction ceremony for a club, fraternity, or sorority, a dress code at a restaurant, a particular emphasis on customer service at a hotel — these are all traditions that *could* really appeal to customers. My family and I go to a family camp in New Hampshire every summer, and at that camp July 4th is celebrated with a "tradition" of a parade, picnic, and games. We return, in part, every summer because we enjoy this tradition.

But traditions can also be customer-aversive. Let's look at the same set I listed above: an induction ceremony ("demeaning"), a dress code ("stuffy"), or customer service ("they weren't *that* nice"). So you need to build on your positive traditions and get over your negative ones, remembering that it is not your opinion that counts, it is that of your markets. If your marketing materials are lost in the past, you will look like you are out-of-date, which is right up there with out-of-touch.

3. Penny-Wise and Pound-Foolish.

This is a problem that is a holdover from ten years ago and can be summed up in the statement, "We can't afford nice-looking materials. They are too expensive, and they are unseemly for a charity." Wrong on two counts.

Count One: With inexpensive software and color printers, anyone with a mouse can develop very high-quality marketing materials that can be updated easily, quickly, and inexpensively. Ten years ago, you might have spent $1,500 to $3,000 to design a brochure, letterhead, and business cards and get them printed. Today, less than that amount will buy you the computer, software, printer, and the predesigned stationery to do all of that yourself. And, of course, the computer and printer can be used for other things as well.

Count Two: Your material, if it looks good, doesn't look *unseemly*. It looks *professional*. Tacky material — outdated, cheaply produced — speaks of a cheap organization. That you cannot afford to be. At any price.

Spend a little money for a lot of return. This does not mean that you need to go out and put all your money in a 40-page, four-color glossy catalog when a three-fold brochure will do, but it does mean that you shouldn't be sending your information out on a hand-typed and then photocopied piece of paper. Raise your sights and your standards here. Look at what your competition is doing. Look at what your markets want. Show that you know their wants in the quality of the marketing materials.

> ☞ **HANDS-ON:** When was your marketing material last revised? Your logo, slogan, letterhead, and other items? If you can't remember, or can't find the documents, it is too long ago. Refresh your materials now!

4. Public Relations or Marketing?

I've lost track of the not-for-profit marketing material I have seen that tries to cover all the bases on one or two sides of an 8½ x 11 sheet of paper. It includes the things I listed above (history, jargon, money requests, etc.) but never focuses on a core marketing sequence of targeting a market, asking that market what they want, and then providing it. Instead, the organization has hired a public relations staff person whose training is really in dealing with the media and giving your organization a good image in the community, but not in marketing.

I don't intend to denigrate public relations. A lot of organizations that I know could use some talented PR help. But PR alone is *not* marketing. Good public relations can supplement a marketing effort, raise positive image, let large numbers of people know that your organization is there, and give a positive opinion about you. But that still does not necessarily mean much to the marketing effort.

> ● **FOR EXAMPLE:** A few years ago, I was assisting an organization that provides rehabilitation to people with spinal cord injuries in the Northwest with the development of their marketing plan. During my first visit, the planning committee told me that they were going to spend $15,000 on a public relations firm to raise the image of the organization in the community. *"Why?"* I asked. "We did a survey, and only two percent of the community knows what we do. So we need to raise our visibility," they replied. *"Why?"* I repeated. "Because people need to know about us." *"Do you get a substantial amount in small donations, or are you planning on expanding your grass-roots development efforts?"* "No." *"Do you get referrals from the general public?"* "No, from physicians, insurers, and hospital patient advocates." *"How many of them know about you?"* "We don't know." *"That is the group where your visibility needs to be highest."*
>
> The group had fallen prey to the PR ego bug. *"Everyone* needs to know about us!" But *everyone* wasn't their market, and the best way to focus your limited marketing resources is on the target markets that you have chosen.

Make sure that your board and staff understand the differences between marketing and public relations.

These four all-too-common problems lead to unfocused, service-based, poor-quality materials. Now that you know the reasons for poor material, let's look at what your marketing material *should* be doing and then at two checklists of things to include and things to avoid.

B. SOLVING CUSTOMER PROBLEMS

All successful salespeople know that you develop a long-term relationship with a customer by repeatedly being there to connect with the customer and then to solve his or her problems. As you watch television the next few weeks, notice how many advertisements talk about (or demonstrate) a problem first, and then state that their product has the solutions. Backed-up toilet? Hemorrhoids? Expensive long-distance? Flabby stomach? Have to get a package absolutely, positively, there overnight? All of these are the problems shown in one five-minute stretch of commercials on the evening news recently.

Note that they are focused first on the problems, *not* the solutions. That is because selling solutions without a problem is being service-based. Selling a solution to a market problem (want) is being market-based. Thus, your marketing material should demonstrate that you understand what your market wants, what their problems are, and that you can solve them.

● **FOR EXAMPLE:** I recently saw a brochure for an art museum that gave a great deal of information, but never really connected with me (or apparently, many other people, as attendance was down). On the cover was the name of the museum, a picture of the building, and a lost-in-the-past slogan ("Providing Access to the Arts for Adams County since 1910"). Inside was a description of the museum in very dry terms ("250,000 square feet of exhibit space, a permanent and rotating collection, lecture hall that is also used for small music performances and poetry readings," etc.). Then there was a listing of some of the artists whose work was displayed and a list of the collections on display. The back cover was a map, hours, and a place to call for more information.

All of this information (with the exception of the slogan) was factual and, to some people, important. But was it to a potential visitor? What about statements such as "Art comes alive at the Adams County Museum! If you are an art enthusiast, come see a local collection of the masters close to your own home. If you are an art teacher in need of exhibits to view and discuss, the Adams County Museum is a great field trip. If you are a parent who wants to expose your child to art, bring your child for a visit and then return for one of our art classes."

Each of these statements connects with a target market that the museum had identified but not addressed in the marketing information. They had assumed that parents, patrons, and teachers could glean what they needed from a generic brochure. In fact, what they needed was four brochures: one general one, one for art patrons, one for art teachers, and one for parents. Each of these carefully aimed brochures could be headlined in a focused manner such as "RESOURCES FOR ART TEACHERS FROM THE ADAMS COUNTY MUSEUM." (Teachers are attracted to the word "resources" like bees are to honey. Their problem: never enough resources to meet the needs of their students.) "ART ACTIVITIES FOR KIDS AT THE ADAMS COUNTY MUSEUM." (Parents have a problem: bored children. The word "activities" addresses that issue). I'm sure you get the idea now. Figure out who your target markets are and write your material to speak to them.

☞ **HANDS-ON:** Never, ever assume that a market will make the connection between your resources and their problem. They won't. And, in fairness, it's not their job. It's yours. In asking the market about what their wants are, you should be asking about their problems. This information comes best through the focus groups and informal asking that we discussed in Chapter 9, but it also comes through reading the general and business press. You will read, for example, about the problem of Americans feeling their days are too short. Lesson? If you can save them time, you can attract them. You will read about their concerns about education, the breakup of the family. Can your organization make a connection here? Do you provide some kind of educational experience? Do you focus on the family unit in a definable way? If you do, these "buzzwords" should show up in your marketing material.

Solving people's problems puts the focus on *them,* not on *you.* It develops empathy for them, not emphasis on your services. It makes a connection, and avoids the hard sell. And it works. I should also point out that solving people's problems should be the process by which your staff connect with individuals in person or by phone. Your staff and board, in their informal asking, should be willing to listen to problems, and then be thinking of how your organization can solve those problems.

C. THINGS TO INCLUDE IN YOUR MARKETING MATERIAL

Now let's turn to a list of things that you should make sure are included in your marketing material. Review all of your materials, commercials, handouts, and presentations for the following seven components. And, remember, you have to *connect with your customer,* showing him or her the benefits of using your services.

1. Your Mission. If your mission statement (or charitable purpose) is succinct and not full of jargon, it is an excellent thing to include in most of your marketing material. If it is so long that it will take up 90 percent of your space, forget it. But your mission is the defining statement of what and who your organization is, and you should be able to lead with it.

2. Focus. Each piece of marketing material should focus on a target market or a service component. The art museum in the example above could develop a piece for art lovers, parents, and art teachers. That would be an example of focus on target markets. A YMCA might have a piece on summer camp, one on its aerobics classes, and one on its basketball and soccer leagues. That would be an example of focus on a service. But, and this is very important, even within the "service pieces," it is critical that you use terms that connect to the market wants. If you just focus on the service you are back to that service-oriented rather than market-oriented mentality.

3. Brevity. Blessed is the person who can say it in the fewest, clearest words. Remember that no one is forcing the reader to spend time reading your material. It needs to be *brief,* or they will get bored and stop reading. No run-on sentences or minute detail. Give essential information only.

4. Connect Problems and Solutions. Does the material clearly show that your organization understands the problems of the target market(s)? And, does it clearly state that you can help solve those problems? If not, you are trusting the reader to make those connections and that is a mistake.

5. Appearance. As I mentioned earlier, there is no excuse for sloppy material, poor writing, and cheap-looking paper or graphics. They speak volumes about your organization. Word processing and printing are so inexpensive now that there is little impediment to developing professional-looking materials at a very reasonable cost.

6. References. In certain materials, it will be important to list well-known customers. For example, if you are a health care organization, it may be important to list the large employers with whose employee health plans you qualify. Other organizations need to make connections to state and national associations to show a level of quality ("Certified by the National Association of XYZ") or to a community standard ("A United Way Agency"). As with your other text, be brief and put only those references that mean something to the target market for that particular marketing piece. For example, being accredited by the Joint Commission on the Accreditation of Hospitals may be important to a referring physician but meaningless to a patient. Be selective and focused.

7. A Source for More Information. Always include a phone number where people can call for more information. Include the number, hours of availability, *and the name* (not the title) of the person to contact. I realize that this means that you will have to update the materials when that person changes jobs, but the personal listing is valuable in two ways. First, it is just that — personal — and gives a name to an otherwise impersonal organization. Second, it routes the questions to the right person immediately. One thing that nearly all of us despise is being put on hold or handed off endlessly from person to person trying to find out some simple fact, figure, time, or other answer to our question. By putting the name of the correct person on the brochure, you simplify the process and usually avoid the problem.

All of these things should show up in some fashion in your material. Now, let's look at the other side of the coin.

D. THINGS TO AVOID IN YOUR MARKETING MATERIAL

I assume that you have now gone through your material to make sure that the items above are included. But there may well be things that are in your material that you should pull out. There are certainly things to avoid. I've provided you with a list of seven common items you need to make sure you keep out of your material.

1. Jargon. The worst offense in marketing material is to speak in a language people don't understand. You don't impress people by confusing them. Using jargon puts a big barrier between you and most audiences. I have long contended that if you can't explain or describe what you do in words that a fourth-grader can understand, you don't really understand what you do. Simplify. Clarify. And remember that the average American reads on a mid-high-school level.

Having said that, there is a time for jargon. If your marketing material is to professionals in the field, jargon is the language of the profession and thus appropriate. If, for example, you were developing a brochure to advertise a continuing education program in computers the terms DOS, ASCII, PC, icons, Internet and modem would probably be appropriate. If you were training on labor law, citing of the laws, and using common labor law terms would be important. Write for your audience.

2. Inappropriate Photos. Here is the sad truth. Most people don't care about how your building looks. You do, because you probably put a great deal of blood, sweat, tears, energy, and money into the property. But most pictures of buildings are a waste of precious space in a marketing brochure. Pictures of people are usually much more effective, but even those can be counterproductive if they are grainy, blurred, or so small as to be unrecognizable. Make sure each and every photo (or graphic) that you include is valuable and, like the text, simple, well-aimed, and understandable.

3. Lack of Focus. There is nothing wrong with a general purpose brochure, but there is something definitely wrong with having *just* a general purpose brochure, or with having a general purpose brochure that tries to do everything for everyone. Focus is the heart of good marketing material. Ask yourself, "What is the purpose of this piece of paper?" If the piece goes much beyond that central purpose, it is almost certainly unfocused and too long.

4. Asking for Money. With the exception of fund-raising letters and brochures whose purpose is explaining the various ways to give to your organization, asking for money is outside of the core purpose of the marketing material and thus inappropriate. I know that it is tempting to just throw in a sentence or two about donations, particularly if you are desperate for money, but that desperation will come through, and some markets may well be turned off. Stick with your primary aim.

5. A History Lesson. Very few people care about your organization's history, or even how long you have been in existence. Having said that, some organizations need to validate their experience and stability by saying things like "Serving the Finger Lakes Region since 1965." But more often I see people who use 400 words to explain the origins of their organization in great (and agonizing) detail. They list the initial incorporators, the first few office addresses, and even give pictures of some of the sites that they have occupied, noting additional important dates in history.

There is nothing wrong with history, and we certainly can learn from it. But is a recitation of your organization's past (however laudable) "on-message" for the marketing piece you are developing? Probably not. But if it is, is your recounting of the development of your organization brief and readable?

160

6. Out-of-Date. I really love pictures of staff, board, and service recipients in bell-bottoms, with shag haircuts, or in leisure suits. They make me want to run right down to the disco. The problem is the disco is closed, a part of the past. Pictures that are from a bygone era will set you up for ridicule, not respect. They will disenchant people, who will wonder whether it is your programs or just your photos that are outdated. Again, in this era of quick and easy software that includes photos at the click of a mouse, there is no excuse for having your brochure look like a retrospective.

7. Boring. If you wrote the text for a particular piece, you probably won't be a good judge of this. Get it read by people inside and outside the organization. Ask hard questions: Is this boring? Does it run on? Can we say more in less words? Are we "on-message," focused, and connecting with the intended audience? Don't trust your own instincts here. Get outside opinions. I usually am pretty happy with my own writing, but it is *always* improved by the friends, coworkers, and (in the case of my books) the editors who read it. Don't be boring to your target audience.

E. DEVELOPING DIFFERENT MATERIALS FOR DIFFERENT MARKETS

I noted above the need to focus on different markets. Look now at the different markets that we discussed in Chapter 7. You may have donors, staff, volunteers, board members, United Way, government, users, insurers, members, or other markets and you can't adequately address all these markets and their wants with one three-fold brochure. You need different materials for different markets. But you probably don't need a great many different pieces. Nor do you have unlimited resources or time to develop lots of materials.

You want to have a set of materials focused on your key markets, and you probably will have to develop them over time. Here are some tips for developing the best materials for the least money.

1. Use a committee to plan. Don't try to do this alone. Get a group together and then plan your materials. Which markets are big enough and important enough to merit an individual piece or pieces? What are their wants? What should each piece address? What kind of look should it have? Brochure, 8½ x 11 sheet, booklet? How much money do you want to spend and when?

2. Get a common "look." You probably have a logo of some kind. If you haven't updated it for 20 years, now might be a good time to think about it. Whether you develop a new logo or keep your existing one, get a scanned, digitized version of it. You'll need that for your remaining work. Have a common paper color, typeface (font), and setup to your materials. One excellent way to "jump start" this is to look through catalogs that sell paper in "look" sets. You can get 8½ x 11 sheets, brochures, cards, even announcements all in the same look, and just add your text and graphics to them. But, however you approach this, you want to have an identifiable and consistent set of colors, text, and graphics in your material.

MARKET	Want	Possible Marketing Material
Board	Initial information, ongoing information	Board orientation manual, newsletter
Staff	Initial information, ongoing information about the organization	Staff orientation materials, regular newsletter, or management updates
Donors	Information on ways to give and what happens to the donation, a number to call (with a name)	Specific piece designed for donors
Government	Information on program quality, program availability, meeting of regulations	Specific piece designed with needs and keywords of government — emphasizing outcomes, quality, and certification levels
Foundations	Demonstration of expertise and experience in the field of the foundation's interest	Probably a general informational piece, with a specific application for funds, perhaps a piece on the mission statement, endorsements
Membership	Information on the benefits and costs of membership, a number to call (with a name)	Specific piece on the value of becoming a member —from the member's perspective
Service Recipients	Information on services and outcomes, a number to call (with a name)	Pieces designed with target groups in mind (parents, teens, seniors) or regarding specific services for larger groups (camps, congregations, tours)
Referral Sources	Information about the quality of the program, and its array of services	A piece that might use professional jargon if designed for a professional referrer

3. Meet the wants of the different target markets. "Well," you say. "I have identified 100 different markets. Do I need 100 different brochures?" Probably not. But you do you need to focus your marketing material on your primary target markets. Look at the types of materials that you might develop, and the target markets that they might address. Always focus on your target markets.

These are just a quick set of ideas. You will undoubtedly have many more. The bottom line in this area is to remember to meet the wants of the markets and to recognize the virtually impossible task of doing that in a single, general brochure.

RECAP

Now you know how to improve your current marketing materials, and how to develop new or modified material as you enter new markets. You should realize that marketing material needs to solve problems and identify with its target audience, and not just sell products and services. You should be able to recite the seven things to include in your marketing material:

1. **Your Mission**
2. **Focus**
3. **Brevity**
4. **Connect Problems and Solutions**
5. **Appearance**
6. **References**
7. **A Source for More Information**

And, you should know the list of things to avoid, including *jargon, inappropriate or unnecessary photos, a lack of focus, asking for money, including a history lesson, being out-of-date, and being boring.*

Finally, you learned about making different materials for your different markets, and how to remained focused within that material on the markets problems (their wants) rather than on your services, no matter how wonderful these services are.

Remember, your marketing material speaks for you when you are not there. It has, in a very real sense, been delegated the responsibility to be your salesperson, to answer questions, promote your services, and establish a rapport with a potential customer. All without any supervision, and often without the opportunity for follow-up or evaluation.

If your marketing material is good, then you have hundreds or even thousands of "spokespersons" out in the community that are helping interest people in your organization. If your material is not good, the best you have done is simply wasted time, money, and paper. At worst, you are hurting your organization every time someone looks at your brochure, sees your ad, or hears your piece on the radio.

Spend the time and the money to get it right. Follow the list of things to include and, remember, you aren't just in the promotional business any more. If you build it, not only will they *not* automatically come, but they won't even care. But if you build what the market wants, and then show them how it solves their problems, they will come in droves.

☞☞ **HANDS-ON REVIEW:**
- **A jargon test**
- **How old is your material**
- **Connecting the service to the customer**

DISCUSSION QUESTIONS FOR CHAPTER 10:

1. Does our material include jargon? How do we know?

2. Does our marketing material sell services or solve problems?

3. How do we measure up to the list of things to include?

4. How do we do on the list of things to avoid?

5. Let's look at our target markets. Do we have marketing pieces that are developed specifically for them? How can we improve in this area?

11. Incredible Customer Service

OVERVIEW

In a monopoly, you can treat your customers in whatever way you want, and they will still stay as customers. Why? Because they don't have any choice. But in the competitive economy, you need to appeal to customer wants and give exceptional, even incredible, service to stand out from your competition.

We can all name organizations that do this. Why? Because these organizations give us a positive experience that we don't soon forget. Nordstroms, Disney, Lands' End, Marriott, Federal Express are all examples of organizations where exceptional customer service is the *minimal* standard from day to day and from employee to employee.

Chapter Thumbnail
- ➡ **Three Core Customer Service Rules**
- ➡ **The Customer Is Not Always Right**
- ➡ **Don't Sell Services, Solve Problems**
- ➡ **Customers Have Crises, Not Problems**
- ➡ **Regular Customer Contact**
- ➡ **Turning Customers into Referral Sources**

In this chapter I will show you many examples of incredible service and some tangible ways to make your organization a place where customers are more than just pleased with you. First, we'll look at the issue we touched on in Chapter 7—how to treat everyone, even your funders, like valued customers. The attitude in your organization from top to bottom, from staff to volunteer, has to be that the people outside the organization are always customers. I'll show you how to instill that philosophy and what results when you do.

Then we'll turn to the application in customer service of the marketing technique we discussed in the previous chapter: solving customer problems. I'll show you how to implement this technique with customers and also six rules for how to deal with unhappy customers.

To treat people well and to solve their problems, you need to solve them *quickly*. Since you cannot be everywhere at once, and since problems can and do occur at any time, you need to empower your staff to correct the problem promptly. For some readers this is a really scary idea, and I'll show you how to implement it with the least pain and risk.

Next I'll show you how to make and maintain regular contact with your key markets and customers. These regular interactions are the foundation of the communications flow that you want to establish with your customers so that they will tell you their wants and problems.

Finally, I'll take you to the next level. Not only do I want you to have incredible service, not only do I want you to solve customers' problems with an empowered staff, I also want you to take your good customers and turn them into a referral sources-ones that continually send you new customers.

By the end of this chapter you should have a very good idea of how to improve the standards of customer service in your organization, the reasons why it is so important, and some techniques to apply right away to empower your staff, and work toward a new level of incredible results for your markets.

A. THREE CORE CUSTOMER SERVICE RULES

In a protected economy, it really doesn't matter if you don't treat your customers well. If you are the only game in town, they must patronize you anyway. Choice, or in other words, competition brings about a need to treat everyone well, to treat everyone like a customer, even though you may never have thought of them as anything but the enemy. You simply have to treat everyone — staff, board, volunteers, service recipients, and funders — like a customer if you are going to succeed as an organization in today's economic and political reality.

We discussed everyone as a customer in Chapter 2 and at more length in Chapter 7, but it is so important (and so often ignored by not-for-profits) that I want to go through it again, this time with some ideas for how to bring your staff and board along. Let's review the three core rules of excellent services to all of your customers:

1. **The customer is not always right, but the customer is always the customer.**

2. Don't sell services, solve problems — from the customer's perspective.

3. Customers don't have problems, they always have crises.

Incredible customer service starts with those three statements. Not, of course, with just making the statements, but with believing them, and with structuring your organization to accommodate them.

First, of course, you need to look at everyone as a customer. I know that this is a real stretch for many readers, and a nearly insurmountable one for certain staff and board. For you, it may be difficult to think of your board as customers, when they have always seemed like a group of nice, but sometime meddlesome, burdens. It may be tough to equate staff, who you are supposed to monitor, supervise, and (sometimes) discipline, as customers. It may be a challenge to think of a funder as a customer at all, particularly if you have spent the past 15 years fighting with them over regulations, funding criteria, and oversight.

But they all *are* customers. That is why they made the list of key markets in Chapter 7. You can choose to treat them as such and have a much higher likelihood of success. I will assume for the rest of the chapter, in fact for the rest of the book, that you will make the effort for the benefit of your organization and of the people you serve.

So, everyone is the customer, the customer can make mistakes, but the customer is still and always the customer. Sometimes they are happy, sometimes not.

Let's look at each of the rules in much more detail:

B. "The customer is not always right, but the customer is always the customer"

All of us know that we are not perfect. We all make mistakes. We also know that we are customers for many organizations and businesses. Thus, as customers, we are fallible. Your customers are the same: imperfect. In organizations that continue to tell their staff the old fable that the customer is always right, I have seen tremendous resentment against both management *and customers* develop in employees. To say the least, this is counterproductive. A much more sensible way to look at it is that even though they may be wrong at times, their perspective is what counts, they *are* the customer.

For many of your customers, simply asking regularly will suffice. If you are in regular contact with them, they will tell you about their problems while they are still small, and not have major issues with you. But about ten percent of your customers will have a more serious problem. And dealing with them, in a courteous, helpful, and ultimately successful manner, is a skill that everyone on your staff needs to develop and to practice. Let's look at how to deal with this unhappy, often angry customer. Sometimes they are unhappy for a valid reason (from our perspective), sometimes not. Remember, the customer is not *always* right. But they are *always* the customer. Thus, you and your staff need some guidance in how to deal with the customer who calls or comes to your office door with a head of steam up. As you read these ideas, think about the last time such a customer vented their wrath on you. How many of these techniques did you use? What happened?

☞ **HANDS-ON:** When dealing with an unhappy customer, follow this checklist:

1. Listen to their whole complaint. Do not interrupt, cut them off, or in any way impede them from venting. If they are mad enough to complain, they want their whole say. Don't make them madder by correcting, interrupting, or explaining, at least not until they are through. Let them finish.

2. Acknowledge and apologize. Say, "Mr. Jones, I understand your frustration and I'm sorry you feel that way." Acknowledge that you heard their problem and sympathize with their feelings. Make sure they know you heard them.

3. Ask them what they want. Here is the place most of us mess up. We offer a solution to an unhappy person without asking what they want. Don't. Ask first, and if they don't know what they want, then offer some suggestions. More often that not, they really don't want anything other than to feel better and for the problem not to reoccur. Ask first. Let them choose.

4. Never make promises you cannot keep. As helping people, we want to make our customers happy. One way we think we can do that is by giving them *anything* that they want. It makes them happy now, but really unhappy later when we can't deliver. When you say, "We'll have the material mailed to you today," or "We'll be able to make your first appointment in a week" or "Check in for a first-time client only takes 30 minutes" are all of these absolutely true? Can you do what you say, and to the letter? If not, don't say it, and make sure that all of your staff understand this. Here is an area where the person on the line of service can really make headaches for you. Tell your staff: *make only promises we can keep.*

5. Keep excellent notes. Particularly if you have a problem customer, keep excellent notes about what was said, who promised whom, what, and by when, etc. Documentation like this not only protects you, it also *reminds* you of what your obligations are, making it more likely that you will keep your promises.

6. Never assume a customer is happy. Ask. Measure. Interview. If you do receive a complaint, call those who complain yourself. This action alone will diffuse 90 percent of complaints. But don't wait for them to complain — only 10 percent of people do and the other 90 percent (that don't) tell many other people, and *exaggerate their problem.* So get out ahead of the customer problem. Ask, ask, ask.

Now, when things do go wrong, what do you do? Do you fix the problem? Of course, if you can. Unfortunately, you only have 24 hours in your day. So others also need to have the authority to fix problems, and that is what we will turn to in a later section on empowering staff. But first, let's look at aggressively solving problems that are not your fault.

C. "Don't sell services, solve problems — from the customer's perspective"

If I try to sell you my kitchen widget, and I just say, "Look at how great this widget is! It can do anything you need done in the kitchen!", you may buy it, you may not. But if I ask you how you are doing, and you tell me you spend too much time in the kitchen, then I can whip out my kitchen widget and show you how it saves you time. If you believe my demonstration, you will buy it. Because it solves a problem you have.

In the previous section, I told you how to deal with customers who are unhappy with you or with your organization. Here we will discuss how to make people happy with you because you solve a problem for them. This is great marketing. If you ask a lot, ask regularly, and *listen*, people will tell you their problems. And if you *understand* their problems, then you will be able to make the connection between your organization's services and those problems. You can solve those problems, or at least give it a good shot.

This type of asking is best done informally or in focus groups, as we discussed in Chapter 9, and all of your staff need to be part of the culture of asking. Also, don't depend on customers to automatically make the connection between the services you provide and their needs and wants. They won't and it's not their job. It's yours. I see too many organizations that are stunned when people go elsewhere for services. The organization says "but didn't they know about us?" Well, perhaps they did, but did they know what you could do for them or how you could solve their problems better than the competition? Obviously not.

Solving customer problems also means that you need to learn to look at things from the customer's perspective. How do they view you? How do they see your staff, your board, your buildings? If you only assume what they are thinking, if you say "I know what they need, because I've been here 25 years," you are not going to be getting to the issue: what is the customers' perspective on this?

Paying attention to the perspective of the customer is the corollary to listening to their wants. Incredible customer service starts with trying to be in the customer's shoes, showing that you pay attention to their wants, their issues, their problems. Not paying attention to their perspective is an outgrowth of the not-for-profit marketing disability. Recognizing that the problem is *always* a crisis and attending to it accordingly is essential.

Do you pay attention? I hope so. Do you think through the way you provide services from the customer's point of view? I hope so. Let's look at just a few of those perspectives:

1. Safety. Is the location that you ask a customer to come to safe? Can you make it more so? Do you provide adequate lighting, locks, security, escorts, supervision, or whatever else it takes to make your customers feel secure?

> ● **FOR EXAMPLE:** A number of years ago (under a previous director) my wife and I both had our lockers broken into and items stolen at our local YMCA. After these robberies, I discussed them with other members and found a widespread concern with security, at least in the people with whom I spoke. I took these concerns to the executive director, and offered to volunteer for any committee that might be reviewing security and suggesting improvements to the board of directors. I told him that other people were concerned, and that if unresolved, the concerns might well affect his membership numbers. His response was, "We dealt with this issue two years ago. There are thieves everywhere. Whoever wants to leave can leave. They'll be back." Not exactly a customer-based perspective.

2. Parking. Is there low-cost (or, better yet, no-cost) easily accessible parking for patrons of your services? Ease of access is very important.

3. Cleanliness. Are your facility and grounds cleaned regularly? (And I don't mean annually!) Do they pass the white glove test? Do the lights/HVAC/toilets/phones/vending machines all work? All of this weighs heavily on how people think of you and your organization. This is an investment and an obligation, but all it takes is one cockroach, one backed-up toilet to send some customers elsewhere.

4. Ease of finding where to go. Is your facility easy to find? Is it easy to navigate from one area to another? Are there clear signs or helpful people nearby, or is a visit to your facility like a trek in the wilderness without a compass?

5. Greetings. Do all of your staff greet all of your customers in a friendly, helpful manner every time they meet them? Are friendly greetings exchanged in the halls, lobby, galleries, or wherever and whenever they interact?

6. Bathrooms. Are they easy to find and easily accessible? Are they CLEAN? Are they safe?

There are many other ways that customers look at your organization, but if they are unhappy with these (or other issues), they will not want to return, or they will tell others about their bad experience.

It is very, very important to look at your organization through the eyes of your markets, your customers. That is why you ask and ask and ask. But you also need to make sure here, as in other parts of your asking, that you are truly listening and not merely waiting your turn to talk. Listen and give them what they *want!*

> ☞ **HANDS-ON:** Find a friend who is willing to come in to your organization as a potential customer. Ask them to come in at their convenience and to take notes of everything that they see that they like, and everything that they see that they dislike — even in the slightest way. Pick a friend you feel will be tough on your organization, and emphasize to them that you want to improve things. After the visit, have your friend list the good and bad parts of the visit and, if he or she is willing, have them do a "debriefing" with your marketing team or management team. It will be an eye-opener, I assure you.

D. "Customers have crises, not problems"

Now we turn to the third part of the customer service maxim. From the customer's perspective, if they have a problem, it is not mundane, it is not run-of-the-mill, it is one-of-a-kind, and it is critical to them. If you or your staff treat it as no big deal, simply because you see this certain kind of problem all the time, you will not address it quickly or with the empathy it deserves. We have all experienced this personally from the point of view of the customer.

● **FOR EXAMPLE:** You wake up feeling awful. You have a headache, fever, chills, achy joints, runny nose, and a cough. You make the decision to stay home, and then wait for 9:00 AM when your doctor's office staff get in to call a nurse. At 9:02 you talk to the receptionist, give her your symptoms, and say that you want to talk to a nurse. The receptionist assures you that one will call you as soon as possible. You hang up. And wait. And wait. And WAIT.

The receptionist and the nurse have had 300 calls for this kind of ailment in the past two days, and yours is just number 301. Your illness is not life-threatening, the treatment is what you are already doing (rest, fluids, pain reliever), so, from their perspective, it is not critical to call back immediately. They have bigger problems, such as the ten people who just showed up unannounced asking to be seen as soon as possible (probably suffering from the same bug as you). Your call can wait.

Back at home, you are still feeling awful. You look at the clock every five minutes wondering: "Where the heck is that nurse?" By noon you are really angry, and by 1:00 PM you call back to find that the nurse is on her lunch break. Now you are both sick *and* really mad. It doesn't matter that the nurse is pleasant, sympathetic, and helpful when she does call at 4:30. You are too angry to appreciate it.

● **FOR EXAMPLE:** Once you get well, you decide it is time to get a new clock. You go to a local department store, find one that will look perfect in your home, and take it home. When you put the batteries in and put it on the wall, you find that it keeps double time, moving two hours for every 60 minutes. You take it down, get the receipt, box, and bag and return to the store, going up to the RE-TURN/CUSTOMER SERVICE counter. There is one person behind the counter and two people ahead of you. You wait. The counter staff person is friendly and helpful, but the first person is simply angry and wants to spout off for ten minutes or so. You wait. You see another staff person on break in back of the counter and wonder why they can't help you. You wait. You finally are next in line, and the person waiting on you pushes a form in front of you to fill out that takes ten full minutes to complete and seems more like an inquisition than simple information. You leave very frustrated at the long exchange. All you wanted was a working clock.

172

● **FOR EXAMPLE:** You pull into a gas station with a car that is running rough. The service manager listens to the engine and says, "Yeah, you need a tune-up. Take about 45 minutes." Of course, it takes two hours, since they need a coffee break, there are customers for gas, etc.

In all of these examples the problem (illness, a return, a broken car) were made worse by the attitude of the employee. In every case, their attitude was natural and understandable. And wrong. The nurse heard dozens of such calls every day, knew that there was no life-threatening issue, and made a professional judgment. She ignored (or had never been trained about) the fact that you, from your perspective, were SICK. You didn't do this dozens of times every day, and you wanted a little assurance that you weren't going to die.

The entire methodology of returns when the clock was brought back was a mess. Many customer service counters in "customer-friendly" stores are now overstaffed, just so people won't have to wait to get their refund or exchange. Why? Because someone finally figured out that the customer is already put out, so why make them more angry by putting them through the third degree? I regularly go to customer service counters now to exchange something, and the service staff person will say, "Do you want another item like this? Do you want one of our people to get it, or do you want to select it yourself? Just bring it back up here, I'll stamp it and you will be on your way!" Or, if it is a return for cash, it takes 45 seconds. They recognize that I want to be on my way *now!*

The service station sees poorly tuned cars all the time. What the manager forgot was that not only is the customer's time important, so are promises. She promised 45 minutes and that became the "contract." This commitment was not met. Additionally, when your car is broken, or at least up on a lift, many of us feel truly stranded, thus aggravating the frustration and impotence that we have in the situation.

In all of these cases, viewing the situation from the *perspective of the customer* had not been trained and regularly reinforced. You may see 50 sick people today, but their illness is their only one. You may have 150 irrational customers returning things, but what they want is to (a) gripe, and (b) get their money or a working product. And soon. You may see cars like this all the time, but the customer needs to get on her way as soon as possible.

Now you know that every customer problem is a crisis, not just a problem. You may feel that you solve customer concerns quickly and efficiently, but does everyone else in your organization do the same? You may believe that they do, but here is the test. Ask yourself this: when I am out of town for two or three days, or on vacation for a week, things break, stuff goes wrong, customers have problems. What happens then? Do my staff fix the problems, or do they wait for me to come back?

If you have told staff to fix customers' problems, do you then upbraid them about their solution? If so, they won't take such a risk again, and your customer will be poorly served. Staff must be empowered to fix customers' problems. They must be coached, encouraged, shown how, and then entrusted to fix things when Mr. Murphy arrives, because he will.

● **FOR EXAMPLE:** All staff of Ritz-Carlton Hotels have the authority to spend up to $2,000 (as of this writing) on the spot to fix any problem that a guest brings to their attention. All staff: housekeeping, maintenance, front office, and security.

● **FOR EXAMPLE:** Lands' End Catalog is a business where 95 percent of the customers are never met in person by the staff. No chance to smile, to shake a hand, to look concerned. Yet whenever I call, I am always made to feel welcome, like an honored guest or even an old friend. And the staff will fix *any* problem I have with clothing, even after I have worn it and washed it a few times. "Send it back, Mr. Brinckerhoff, and we'll send you a replacement, credit your account, and we'll also pay for the shipping."

● **FOR EXAMPLE:** I once arrived at a Marriott Hotel at 2:00 AM with the mistaken idea that I had a reservation. The hotel was sold out, and it turned out that my reservation was at a Marriott on the other side of the same city. What did the clerk do? Did he say to himself, "This guy is an idiot. We're full. Let him take a cab to the other hotel"? He could have. But no. He saw a customer with a problem/crisis. It was 2:00 AM. His hotel was full, but he did have the Presidential Suite available. The president hadn't shown up yet, so he let me use an exorbitantly expensive room for $139. He solved my problem. At other hotel chains, he might have been reprimanded, if not fired. At Marriott he got commended for helping a customer. Marriott empowers its people. Since then this customer has told the story to literally tens of thousands of people.

The bottom-line question here is: do you really *empower* your staff to fix problems or just tell them to and then not support them? Empowerment means to delegate *and* support staff in their customer relations. It means that customer satisfaction is an organizational priority for everyone, and that you, as a supervisor, will go just as far to support a staff person in their customer relations as you will to actually satisfy the customer.

And let's face it. This is risky. All delegation is. But you need to have the attitude that you, as well as everyone else, learn from trying, and often learn best by making mistakes. Just the way competition is risky, so is letting staff fix problems in your absence. But if you encourage innovation, encourage initiative, coach and support your staff, and train them in the outcomes you want, then most people will rise to the occasion. You will find that some, perhaps many, of your staff have different ways of solving a problem, of meeting a want than you do. And often you will find that those solutions are *better* than yours.

Is this risky? Sure. But go into it with the understanding that the alternative is much, much more dangerous. If you don't delegate customer service, if you don't make sure that everyone is empowered to fix customer problems, if you make every issue wait for you to intervene personally, you will absolutely be losing customers. A competitive environment doesn't wait for you to personally get involved in every decision. It moves too quickly. Empower your people to fix problems (oops, crises!) and fix them *now*.

I've spent a lot of time talking about fixing problems. But what about preventing problems before they occur, or catching problems when they are minor? And, what about that constant asking I have been talking about throughout this book? All of those things happen better with regular customer contact, which is the subject of our next section.

E. REGULAR CUSTOMER CONTACT

Another crucial part of customer service is to regularly check in with them. Through regular contact, particularly for the target group of customers, you will not only learn more about them but will have the opportunity to see their problems, sometimes as they occur, allowing you to offer a solution, sometimes with just your presence.

● **FOR EXAMPLE:** I regularly contact my key customers, just to chat. I don't try to sell, I don't try to tell them about new training sessions I may have developed, or new publications that we may offer. I just call up, or drop in and chat for five minutes. I ask them what is going on in their lives, in their industry, at their workplace. If they bring up a problem in an area where I have expertise, I will offer some ideas and suggestions on potential solutions.

I *never* sell on these calls. But I get lots of work from them, often on the spot. The reason? Because I am visible and available, and show that I care about them. Highly successful sales people that I talk to all say the same thing: you have to stay in touch, you have to be visible, you have to be available, and that means personal interaction.

● **FOR EXAMPLE:** Why do you think your insurance agent calls you on or around your birthday each year? To wish you a happy day? To remind you that you are getting older? No, it's to maintain contact and to ask if there are any insurance needs that you might want to discuss.

● **FOR EXAMPLE:** Why do ministers greet their parishioners after services? Why do many make house calls, sometimes unannounced? To catch you being bad? No, to get to know you better and to be available to help you if they can.

There are a number of elements to keeping in touch with your key customers that I would like you to consider. These are listed below. I do want to point out that I recognize that you don't have time to do all of these for every market, but you should focus on your most important markets, using the 80/20 Rule. Also, remember that a key customer group is your funders. Don't leave them out of your regular contact planning.

1. **All key markets (payers, board, staff, volunteers, clients, contractors) should be offered the opportunity to have input into the organization.**

   For example, you can include customers in strategic planning by letting them review a draft of the plan. When you drop by to talk, ask them for ideas on how to solve one of your problems. Increase their ownership in your organization.

2. **Keep up on customers' important issues.**

   Read widely, and make notes of things that may affect your customers, whether an industry or a family issue. Ask them about it the next time you see them and let them know you understand their issues, their experiences.

3. **Tell them if things aren't fixed immediately to call YOU.**

   When there is a problem, let them know that if the normal solutions are not satisfactory, they can come back to you personally. Then, take the initiative and call them yourself to make sure that they are happy.

4. Send a note thanking them for each payment, gift, or effort.

This is a small thing but easily done. A small postcard can be pre-printed to accomplish this.

5. If you make guarantees, make *sure* you can live with them.

Don't promise what you cannot deliver!

6. Make intermittent "quality checks."

Show up or call up and just have one question: is everything okay? Make sure that your staff know that you are doing this, and you will get two benefits: fewer mistakes and a customer who knows you are committed to quality.

7. Always follow up with a new customer.

For new large markets, a personal greeting and quality check is mandatory, and this is a senior manager's job.

8. Be pleasant.

Even when you are down, tired, frustrated, or sick, work as hard as you can to be pleasant to others. Remember, you are always a member of the marketing team, and therefore always "on." Smiles, courtesy, and a pleasant attitude will buy you a lot of goodwill — goodwill that you may well need later.

Of course, all of this is a lot of work, but you want customers to be customers forever. Invest time and effort in them and they will repay you tenfold. One of the ways that they will do that is by sending new customers, new clients, new students your way. That is the subject of our next section.

F. TURNING CUSTOMERS INTO REFERRAL SOURCES

How would you like a "free" source of customers? A source where you don't have to sell, make cold calls, send written material, or make a personal visit? Sound good? Well, there is such a source: it is your current customer base.

In the previous sections I noted that unhappy customers go and tell people (a lot of people) how unhappy they are. The same is true for happy customers. And it is really true for customers who feel that you are giving them incredible customer service. Thus, if you implement the ideas in this chapter, you should wind up with customers who are happy enough to be willing to send you other customers. But do you just wait for it to happen, or are there some things you can and should do to move the process along? There are, and I have listed them below.

1. Referrals are not truly "free."

You need to work for them and work at them. But if you have done a good job at customer service, the happy customer is a resource that is available and that you should not waste.

2. Don't be too eager with new customers.

One of the most common mistakes I see is people who have a new customer, and then they immediately make him or her uncomfortable by asking for references or other referrals. Give a new customer time to experience your organization fully. Additionally, if I call a reference, I usually ask, "How long have you been a customer?" If the answer is "a week" I know that the referral, while perhaps sincere, is not based on enough experience to be meaningful. Be patient.

3. *Always* ask for permission to use a name as a reference.

Never, ever use someone's name or the name of their organization without permission. Most people will happily agree to be a reference, but there are many who will be really upset if they hear you are spreading their name around without their knowledge or approval. Do you really want to make customers mad? I don't think so.

You can ask for many things in this area:
- Other organizations who are potential customers.
- Permission to use their name as a referral/reference.
- Mentioning your organization to peers.
- Names of trade associations that they belong to.

All of these things have use to you as you expand your marketing effort.

4. Remember to meet referrers' wants.

Your customers are giving you help. Do they want anything in return? Find out. For most people it may just be thanks, but make sure. Some people want their *title* always put with their name, some don't. Ask.

5. *Always* call or write a note of thanks.

I assume that you are tracking where your customers come from. Whenever you find out that you received a referral, call or write a note of thanks. Every time.

Don't ignore the benefits of all the hard work you have put into improving your customer service. Ask for help from your customers in getting more work. Nearly all will be glad to help you. They want you to succeed so that you can be there to provide more services to them.

RECAP

Incredible customer service? There is nothing incredible about it. It is an attitude and it is hard work — the consistent application of a few basic rules, and a team effort. But incredible service is something that is achievable, and it is something that is very important to your marketing effort in a competitive economy.

In this chapter I showed you why incredible service is the *minimum* standard to apply in a competitive environment. We discussed incredible service and the issue of solving customer problems. We reviewed the falsehood that the "customer is always right," but also reviewed the fact that "the customer is *always* the customer." Thus, it is essential to fix the problem when it arises, but also to ascertain what the problems in a customer's life are and try to make a connection between the problems and your services.

I showed you why it is so essential to empower your staff and to have them able to fix what breaks immediately, not just when you are available to tell them what to do. Then, we looked at ways to make and then maintain regular customer contact as both a means of ferreting out small problems before they become big ones and, just as important, as a way of learning about customers' wants on a regular basis so that you can propose solutions that you or your organization can provide. I noted that this is especially important to do with funders and gave you eight ways to make your customer contact more fruitful.

Finally, we talked about how to reap the benefits of incredible customer service by turning your customers into referral sources. I walked you through six ideas on how to get more from your customers and have them have ownership in getting you additional work.

Incredible customer service is the way to keep your existing customer base in an ever-more competitive world. It is a standard that more and more not-for-profits are aspiring to, and one that you need to strive for. It is a lot of work, and an investment, but one that will pay off very, very well.

☞☞ **HANDS-ON REVIEW:**
- **A checklist for customer complaints**
- **An outsider check of customer service**

DISCUSSION QUESTIONS FOR CHAPTER 11:

1. Are our staff empowered to fix customer problems, or do they always rely on us? Do we encourage creativity and reward making customers happy, or do we punish our staff for not asking us?

2. Do we sell service or solve problems? Do we ask and then listen, or start with our hand out?

3. Do we regularly see all of our major and targeted customers? How can we do better in this area? Are the right people visiting these markets in the right way at the best intervals?

4. How much of our work is referral? Do we know who we are getting referrals from? Do we thank them every time? Who else can we encourage to refer to us?

5. Think about the most recent experience with a business (restaurant, service, product, store) you had that was exceptional. What was it? Why was it exceptional? Do you think people go away from our organization feeling that way? How often?

12. The Marketing Planning Process

OVERVIEW

Now we need to put it all together. You have all the philosophical and technical information you need to move your organization toward becoming market-driven and mission-based. But to get from where you are to where you want to go, you need a plan.

Remember earlier, I said that you needed to improve, to change incrementally, 1 percent at a time. I also noted that if those 1 percent changes weren't directed by a plan, that they could result in just going around in circles. It has been said that, without a plan, the only way you get where you are going is by accident. I agree, and you certainly don't want to have the results of all your marketing efforts be haphazard or accidental. You don't want to have one part of your organization target one group of people and ignore another, especially if that second group is the target market for a different part of your organization. You don't want to show multiple "identities" to the public, nor do you want to survey one part of your markets five times and another not at all. Good marketing planning will allow you to do all the things that you need to in a coordinated, efficient, and effective manner.

Chapter Thumbnail
➡ **Developing Your Marketing Team**
➡ **An Asking Schedule**
➡ **Targeting Your Marketing Effort**
➡ **A Marketing Plan Outline**

180

This chapter will show you how to begin the planning process. We will start at the beginning. That means putting together a winning marketing team. I'll make some suggestions on who to pick, how to put the group together, and what their job descriptions should be.

Next, we'll examine how to develop an asking schedule. You may remember that in Chapter 9 on asking, I noted that one of the mistakes people make is in asking too often — or too infrequently. This schedule will help avoid that. But how do you choose which market to ask and when? I'll show you. And, that will lead nicely into the third part of this chapter, which will have practical applications for targeting your marketing. You have already heard me say how you need to focus and target, focus and target. Here, I'll show you how.

Finally, I'll provide you with a fairly detailed outline for a marketing plan, showing you the content areas that I think are essential, as well as an example from a real marketing plan. We will also review how you can integrate your marketing planning into your organizational strategic plan. By the time you are finished with this chapter, you will have a good handle on how to get started with a coordinated, planned marketing effort.

A. DEVELOPING YOUR MARKETING TEAM

I said early in this book that marketing is everyone's job, not just the executive director's or the director of marketing's. Everyone is part of the marketing effort, but not everyone can sit on the committee, or team, that develops and implements your marketing plan.

You do need a team. You need it to be broad-based and with a variety of experience and perspective. You need the team to develop the marketing plans, develop your asking schedule, allocate the marketing portion of your budget, and do the lion's share of the regular customer contact. Let's look at the makeup of the marketing team, and then review its responsibilities. I think you will find that by developing such a team, you will greatly improve the results of your marketing efforts.

1. Who should be on the marketing team?

I always like teams or committees that are broadly based. Thus, I do not think that this group should be just board members, nor do I support teams that are only made up of senior management staff. I have found that the wider a representation you have from throughout the organization, the better the work product is. So who do I think needs to be involved? These people:

• *CEO.* The top staff person in the organization needs to be involved, at least in the selection of target markets, marketing planning, and other strategic issues. He or she probably shouldn't chair the committee, though.

• *Board Member.* You should ask one or two members of the board to be involved in this critical part of the organization, particularly if you have a board member who is involved in marketing in his or her regular job.

• *Marketing Director.* Whoever on your staff has the core responsibility for marketing should not only be on the committee, but he or she should most likely chair it.

• *Director(s) of Services.* Whether this is one or more staff, the people in charge of your core services need to be part of the asking and the listening!

• *Mid-Level and Line Staff.* You need people from throughout the organization. Many of these people have more direct contact with your customers than senior management, and thus their input is critical. It is also a great staff development experience for them.

• *Outside Expert.* Some organizations find it helpful to have one or two outsiders on the marketing team, almost always people who have specific expertise to offer.

The team should probably not be any larger than ten to twelve people, nor much smaller than five to six. That is the best size for a working group such as this.

2. What are the marketing team's responsibilities?

Once you gather your group, what do they have to do? The following is a list of outcomes that the Marketing Team should consider their responsibilities.

• Develop a marketing plan coordinated with the organization strategic plan. This plan should include strategic as well as one-year goals, objectives, and desired outcomes.

• Develop and administer a marketing budget.

• Develop a schedule of asking.

• Develop and keep up-to-date all marketing material

• Develop and keep up-to-date the organization "look" and logo.

• Monitor trends in the industry and advise the board and management team as appropriate.

• Implement adequate surveying, focus groups, and interviewing to stay in constant touch with the wants of the markets.

• Sponsor in-house training on customer service, marketing, asking, and other related subjects for all staff.

• Keep in regular personal contact with key market segments.

• Regularly train themselves to further their own marketing expertise. Get outside education for team members on surveying, interviewing, market analysis, and materials development. Develop internal expertise.

I know that this sounds like a lot to do, and it is. But if the group meets every two weeks (for two to three hours) for the first six months and then monthly on a permanent basis, there should be adequate time to get it all done. And, to get you started, I have broken out some crucial things you need to get accomplished in your first six months.

3. Outcomes for the first six months.
The following are some suggestions of things that your marketing team should aim to accomplish in the first six months.

• *Build Common Ground.* It is important that you come to common ground on definitions and on methods of achieving common goals. I would suggest that you have all team members read this book.

• *Identify Your Target Markets.* Go through the market identification process that you learned about in Chapter 7. Work toward a consensus on who your target markets are.

• *Identify a Contact for Each Target Market.* Identify an individual within each of your target markets with whom you will keep in regular contact. This is easier for a funder and more difficult for a target market such as "teenagers" or "nursing home residents," but even within those broad markets there will be representatives, advocates, family members, or others who can fill that role.

• *Assign a Team Member to Each Target Market Segment.* Each member of the team will have at least one (and probably more than one) market to focus on. They will develop expertise over time, something you will really want to have.

• *Develop Baseline Benchmarks.* Look at the status of your markets now. In many cases you will already have internal data you can look at. How large is the market? How many customers return? Where are our referrals from? How happy are the markets with us? How many complaints do we get? All of this information goes into your baseline benchmark setting. These will be your starting point for improvement, because if you don't set them up now, you won't be able to tell later how far you have come!

• *Develop an Asking Schedule.* See section B in this chapter for more on how and why to develop an asking schedule. You need to plan and coordinate your asking *now,* not later.

• *Develop a Rough Draft Marketing Plan.* See section D in this chapter for more on this.

Your marketing team is a crucial component of your overall marketing effort. Choose the people carefully, give them support and resources (including time away from their other duties), and make marketing a priority for them. Don't try to do this with one or two already overworked staff people. Get a group, motivate it, support it, and have high expectations of it.

B. AN ASKING SCHEDULE

In Chapter 9, I showed you the way to ask your markets regularly what they want. You will remember that there were surveys, focus groups, and, of course, informal and constant asking. So you know that asking is important, and you know how to do it. But asking, especially with focus groups (and to some extent, surveys), is expensive. How can you get the most out of limited dollars? Also, one of the mistakes some organizations make is asking too much — bothering (even pestering) their best customers for information that they could have gathered more efficiently in a planned, coordinated manner.

Thus, your marketing team needs to develop an asking schedule, one which coordinates the surveys, focus groups, and informal asking. It needs to reflect the market priorities established in the plan, as well as the budget realities that constrain you.

Remember to get information back to the people who need it most — direct providers of services.

● **FOR EXAMPLE:** A preschool for inner-city disadvantaged children had instituted a program where all staff (teachers, administrators, cafeteria staff, and receptionists) would constantly be asking people where they heard of the school and how they felt about the services and the education provided. In doing an assessment of their marketing efforts, I reviewed the data gathered by survey, focus group, and informal asking. I noted that there was substantial and valuable information gathered by the surveys, the focus groups, and the interviews conducted by the administrators, but very little if any data from teachers or cafeteria staff. I asked the teachers whether they were doing the regular informal asking, and they said yes, and that they were taking parent suggestions and implementing them whenever they could. I asked if they were getting any complaints or suggestions about other parts of the organization. They said yes, but hadn't passed them on, since they assumed that the same information was gathered by the administration.

The same scenario was being played out by the receptionist and the food service staff. They were asking and dealing with ideas, suggestions, or complaints in their work area. Each assumed that any problems brought up regarding other parts of the organization were being heard there as well. The information never was passed on. It was critical that it should have been. Some serious concerns and some significant opportunities were missed because the information flow was not completed.

Make sure when you ask that the information gets to where it should go. This probably means that a copy of any and all information gathered should come to the marketing team. You may be able to design a routing system that gets the ideas and concerns where they need to be. But, in any event, make sure that the persons who can act on the information are getting the information that you are paying for!

Now let me show you an example of an asking schedule that incorporates the key elements: who you are asking, when, how often, and in what manner. The example below is for a church that has extensive outreach, singles, and youth programs, which are their target markets.

METHOD	MARKET	CYCLE	Deadline for this year
Survey			
	Youth	Every 18 months	One, in February
	New Members	6 months after joining	As needed
	Singles	Every 18 months	One, in June
	General Congregation	Every two years	None
Focus Group			
	Youth	Annual	One, after survey
	Youth Parents	Annual	One, after survey of youth
	New Members	Annual	Two per year
Interview (formal)			None this year
Interview (informal)	*All*	Ongoing	Ongoing

As you can see from the example, the church has decided to focus this year's work on youth and singles, with a second priority on new members. Even though the survey cycle for the general membership is two years, it won't even be done in the next 12 months.

☞ **HANDS-ON:** As I noted in Chapter 9, one of the advantages of asking regularly is that you can measure trends. But how often is often enough? There is a balance between surveying all the time and surveying once a millennium. My general guidelines are these:

• *Staff Surveys: Every 18 months — which gives you enough time to implement appropriate suggestions and have them take effect.*

• *Consumer Surveys: Some people survey annually, some every six months. It will depend on your type of services. A school might formally survey the parents and students semi-annually, while a symphony might ask its patrons only once in a strategic planning cycle. Generally, I would say annually.*

• **Funders:** *Annually, or at the end of each funding cycle.*

• **Donors:** *Every two years, or at the point of the analysis of a large capital campaign.*

• **Referrers:** *Every six months.*

☞ **HANDS-ON:** When you develop asking materials and reports (such as a report of a survey), put right on the cover of the report the date that it was administered *and the date of the next surveying.* For example, if I surveyed staff to ascertain job satisfaction, I might put down that the survey was completed in June 1999, with an update of the survey due in two years, or June of 2001. By putting the deadline of the update on the report, you are more likely to remember to do the survey again. Putting the date on the report lets you quickly see how current it is.

An asking schedule will do much to take out unneeded duplication and unnecessary harassment of the people you should value most: your key markets.

C. TARGETING YOUR MARKETING EFFORT

Throughout this book, I have urged you to target many of your marketing efforts on your most crucial markets. We have reviewed the 80/20 Rule a number of times and its application for your organization. But now you are going to put a plan together, one where you commit your limited resources to try to do everything for everyone. Some of your marketing team (and your board) will want you to interview everyone, or do focus groups on many market segments, or develop promotional material for every tiny niche. Everyone will have their pet idea, their personal priority. How can you do all of this with only so much time and only so much money?

You can't. You need to prioritize and target the most crucial markets and the big-ticket items to get the most for your money and time. Let's look first at what I mean by a crucial market and then we'll look at the important and expensive "big-ticket" items.

1. Your Most Crucial Markets.

Let's make sure that we are on the same wavelength about your most important markets. In Chapter 7 we talked about focusing on the target markets and how the 80/20 method and linkage to the strategic plan are both important. We will review and add a political consideration for your marketing team to evaluate.

- *80/20 Rule, Based on Current Income:* To review, the 80/20 Rule states that 80 percent of your income comes from 20 percent of your customers. Thus, it makes excellent empirical sense to focus your marketing efforts on your biggest customers. This not only applies to income, but also to your services: 80 percent of your client/student/patient/member/parishioner encounters almost certainly come from just 20 percent of those market groups. So make sure some of your focus goes to that twenty percent.

- *Crucial Future Markets:* Many readers may feel that they are too dependent on one group, often government, for their ongoing financial well-being. You may be among them, and intent upon reducing the percentage of your total income from this one group. To do that, you should not shrink overall, but increase the income from other groups, groups of customers that may not currently be in your "20 percent" club. That means that you should focus a portion of your marketing efforts outside the twenty percent. Where you focus should be dictated by your strategic plan. Where do you see opportunities to serve? If you find them outside of your 20 percent, fine! Just remember to allocate your marketing budget accordingly.

- *Markets That Identify with You:* For most not-for-profit organizations, there are customer groups that are a crucial part of their identity. Most parochial schools, for example, take non-Catholic students, but even as the percentage of non-Catholics in the student body grows, the staff would be naive not to continue to market the educational opportunities that the school affords within the Catholic community. Are there markets that truly identify with your organization? Even if they are small markets, can you afford not to market to them?

2. Big-Ticket Marketing Items.

These are the items that use up the most time or the most money. These are the ones that you cannot realistically apply to each and every market evenly.

- *Surveys:* Surveys, while they do not have to be exorbitantly expensive, do cost money and take a lot of time. The cost will be greater for the first cycle of surveying, as you learn to ask the questions in the correct manner and order. If you are surveying regularly (and I hope that you are), repeat cycles should take much less time, but not much less money.

• *Focus Groups:* These are flat-out expensive, costing between $2,000 and $10,000 each, depending on your facilitator, the setting, and the size of the group. This is why most organizations survey first and then hone in on only the most crucial issues in their focus groups.

• *Personal Contact:* Time, time, time is the cost here. If you follow the ideas that I gave you in Chapter 9, you will see how much of your week this can absorb. Even though you will be spreading the personal contact part of marketing throughout the entire Marketing Team, this is still a time-costly part of the mix.

• *Marketing Material:* I hope that I made my point in Chapter 10 that marketing materials do not have to be inordinately expensive. But they do cost something, and it probably does not make sense to have specialty items for the smallest market (unless you expect that segment to grow). But do not just develop a single general-interest piece. Have different material for your different target markets.

As you go about the development of your marketing plan, remember to focus, focus, focus. You and the rest of the team will want to do everything for everyone. You can't, so learn the discipline of focusing.

The marketing plan itself is our next subject.

D. A MARKETING PLAN OUTLINE

I want to provide you with an outline of a marketing plan that you can use tomorrow as you begin the development of your marketing plan. However, I have seen a lot of plans, and I have seen too many that share some common faults. Therefore, before we get into the actual plan contents, I am compelled to provide you with some planning definitions and my suggestions on what the best marketing plan cycle is. Then I'll show you my suggested outline.

1. Definitions.

If you have been in management more than about two hours, you have probably been to a planning workshop or seen an article on planning. That's good. What's *not* good is the many different definitions that people seem to use for the four core components of a plan: goals, objectives, action steps, and outcome measures. Here are my definitions of these important terms.

• *Goal:* A goal is a statement of an intended long-term outcome. The goal may or may not be quantified. It may or may not have a deadline. The adjective "long-term" is the most crucial part of the description.

> **GOAL EXAMPLE: *The Carter County Ballet will regularly revise its marketing material to demonstrate its ability to meet the wants of its target markets.***

• *Objective:* A statement of a shorter-term outcome that supports the goal, has a deadline, has a measurable outcome, and has a person assigned the responsibility for that outcome.

> **OBJECTIVE EXAMPLE: *The director of marketing will review, revise and refresh all printed and electronic marketing material every two years, completing the initial review no later than September 30, 1999.***

• *Action Step:* A short statement of work to be accomplished with a measurable outcome, deadline, and responsible person listed. Must support an objective. These statements are most likely to show up in one-year plans. To most readers they would sound like work plan statements.

> **ACTION STEP EXAMPLE: *In June 1999, the director of marketing will review the target markets and compare the array of marketing material to assure that all target markets have material specialized for their wants and needs.***

• *Outcome Measure:* A measurable statement of *real* outcome. Both objectives and action steps need them, but far too many "outcome" measures that I see in plans are really process measures. An example of a process measure as opposed to an outcome measure would be: "Meet with 40 potential donors each month" as opposed to "Secure two donations of at least $1,000 each month." The first measures activity, and while that activity may eventually lead to donations, it doesn't mandate it. It is a process measure. The second statement mandates a real outcome. Don't get caught in the process trap. It will deflate the value of your plan immediately.

These definitions are what I have in mind when I consider a plan. The need for deadlines should be obvious: work expands to fill the time allowed for it. If you don't have a deadline, it will take forever. The need for a person to be assigned responsibility is also crucial to a plan that will be actually implemented. If you name a person (as opposed to a committee, or even no one), and if that person has had a chance to review the plan before it is finalized, you have, in essence, a contract that the objective or action step will be achieved. And, the person you name can (and definitely should) be held accountable for the implementation of the objective or action step.

2. The Planning Cycle.

One question that is sure to come up with your marketing team as you begin the planning process is this: how long a horizon should the plan have? In other words, what time frame should the plan be written for? There are a lot of different opinions on this, and let me review the advantages and disadvantages of the most common choices organizations make.

• *A Five-Year Plan Written Every Five Years:* I think that five years is far too long to wait to rewrite a marketing plan that is responsive to changing conditions of the market and competition. Too much changes. I agree with a five-year horizon for a strategic plan, however, because I have found that forcing people to think out five years for their goals tears them away from the temptation of the immediate crisis. But for a marketing plan, five years is long.

• *A Three-Year Plan Written Every Three Years.* About right on both the horizon and the re-write, but may not be detailed enough to give staff and board members guidance week-to-week or month-to-month.

• *A One-Year Plan.* We already have work plans. We need a longer-term vision.

• *A Three-Year Plan Written Every Three Years with One-Year Components Done Annually*: Now we're talking. This has the best of both the three-year plan (the long-term view) and the one-year plan(the immediacy of the work). Additionally, by writing the annual portion every twelve months, you can keep up with rapidly changing trends while still being guided by a longer-term view.

Remember that you should always coordinate your marketing plan with your organization's strategic plan. If your strategic planning cycle is five years, you may have a challenge getting on a three-year cycle for marketing. But overall, I think that the three-year period for marketing is best.

3. A Marketing Plan Outline.

The following outline is intended to give you guidance as your marketing team attacks the planning process. It should ensure that you include all the important parts of a comprehensive marketing plan. The sections noted are in the order that I think is the most effective, but if you feel the need to switch or combine some, fine.

a. Mission Statement.

Lead with the mission. It reminds both you and your reader who you are and what you are all about. We are talking, after all, about Mission-Based Marketing. If your organization's board of directors has not reviewed your mission statement in the past few years, now is a good time to make sure that it is up-to-date and still relevant to the services you provide and the markets that you serve.

b. Executive Summary.

This section (which goes first, but should be written last) should *summarize,* not simply repeat the remainder of the plan. Included here should be a *short* description of your organization's markets, services, target markets, a *brief* listing of the core wants of your markets, and a reiteration of at least the goals, and perhaps even the objectives of the plan. No more. A summary should be just that, a summary.

c. Introduction: Purpose of the Plan.

Tell the reader why this plan was written, who its intended audience is, how the plan is to be used, what group developed it, and when your board adopted it.

d. Description of Markets.

Who is it you serve? Where are they? Are they growing or shrinking? What changes are there in your markets? What trends? What is happening in the macroeconomy, on a state or national level, that will affect your markets? Who is your competition? What do they do better or worse than you do? Put your information in text, tables, charts, or graphs — however you feel you can best communicate your situation.

e. Description of Services.

What services do you provide now? To what market segments? How many clients/students/customers do you have in each segment as opposed to five or ten years ago? What growth do you project? What new services are you planning to initiate during the term of the plan?

f. Analysis of Market Wants.
First and foremost, demonstrate that you asked people what they wanted. Did you survey, interview, run focus groups, or ask informally? Then tell the reader what you did and what you learned. Finally, discuss how you plan to meet the wants that you identified.

g. Target Markets and Rationales.
From all the markets you described in the description of markets you have to focus on a few target markets. Tell the reader what those markets are and provide the rationales for why you chose those markets as opposed to others.

h. Marketing Goals and Objectives.
Goals and objectives should be included in a three-year plan. For the one-year plan, you need to get down to the action step level.

i. Appendices.
Whatever "dense" data you feel that you need to support your rationales goes here, as should copies of your marketing surveys and other items that don't need to be in the body of the document. Don't make this part of the plan the thickness of the Los Angeles telephone directory, however. Be reasonable. The vast majority of the people who will read this plan either work for you or are on your board. Thus, if one or two of them want a copy of a survey, focus group report, marketing piece, or market analysis, they can ask for it. Don't burden every reader with all the arcane documentation you can think of. People don't measure the value of the plan by its weight. If it is too big, they may not read it at all.

4. Examples of Goals and Objectives.
The following goals and objectives are actual ones from a rehabilitation center that works with individuals with disabilities in the Midwest. The goal comes from their strategic plan, and it was the core of their eventual marketing plan. What you see below is just part of the plan, and they did an excellent job.

You can see the flow of activity from goal to objective to action step. You can see an assigned agent, a deadline, and a measurable outcome. Use these to compare to your draft goals and objectives. Do they measure up?

GOAL 4: Become a market-driven organization.

Objective 4-1: Identify and quantify 10 key markets that The Center serves by 10/1/9_ (Director of Communications and Marketing).

> *Action Step 4-1-1:* Develop a list of key markets and determine the top 10 markets (4/17/9_ - 6/30/9_; Director of Communications and Marketing).
>
> *Action Step 4-1-2:* Research each of the 10 markets to determine how large each market is in our primary service area, how many we serve, and how many need services (1/2/9_ - 3/29/9_; Director of C&M).

Objective 4-2: Investigate systematically the needs, wants, and preferences of our markets with initial assessment completed no later than June 199_. (Director of Communications and Marketing).

> *Action Step 4-2-1:* Spend time finding out as much about each of our market's needs, wants, and preferences by conducting focus groups, looking at previously gathered information, talking with individuals, sending question-naires, and using any other forms of information gathering that we can afford or tap into. This will be done on the following schedule:
>
> 1) Adult Consumers — April & May 199_
> 2) Vocational Rehabilitation Counselors & VA Referrers — June & July 199_
> 3) Parents — August & September 199_
> 4) Employers — October & November 199_
> 5) Schools — December 199_, January 199_
> 6) Doctors — February & March 199_
> 7) Other rehab. providers - April & May 199_
> 8) Case Managers/Health Care Networks — June & July 199_
> 9) Influencers/Advocates — August & September 199_
> 10) Persons with Barriers to Employment — October & November 199_, Director of C&M, Marketing Manager).

Objective 4-3: Identify 10 key competitors and assess their strengths and weaknesses (1/2/9_ - 3/29/9_; Director of C&M, Marketing Manager, President, Vice President, Vocational & Children's Programs Coordinators).

Action Step 4-3-1: The Center staff make a list of 10 key competitors and what we think are their strengths & weaknesses (1/2/9_ - 1/22/9_; staff named above in objective).

Action Step 4-3-2: Question consumers, referrers, community leaders, board members, and any other appropriate sources to receive their opinions about specific competitors (1/22/9_ - 2/29/9_; Director of C&M, Marketing Manager).

Action Step 4-3-3: Compile information gathered in above two steps in a report which will provide a comprehensive look at The Center's competition which can be used in future marketing decisions (3/1/9_ - 3/22/9_ ;Director of C&M).

As you write your plan, keep in mind the need for outcomes, deadlines, and assigned responsibility. When the goals and objectives are in draft stage, circulate the work and let people comment. Then, complete the entire plan (using the outline provided above), and get the entire board to review, comment, and adopt it.

RECAP

In this chapter you have learned how to transform marketing ideas into reality: by developing a marketing plan. This plan will be the tool you use to assure that your organization truly utilizes all the new marketing skills that you have obtained by reading this book. Without the plan, you may or may not.

First, we went over how to assemble your marketing team, including who should be on the team and what their responsibilities should be. I even gave you a list of the things that the team should accomplish in the first six months. You need to set your goals high so that you accomplish more than the minimum.

Then we turned to the development of an asking schedule, and I provided you with a sample template as well as some general guidelines for how often to ask groups such as staff, funders, customers, and referral sources. Next I showed you how to apply the skill that I have repeatedly discussed: focusing on your target markets. This is crucial now that you are about to develop your marketing plan, and I gave you three criteria — the 80/20 Rule, your strategic plan, and markets that identify with you — on which to base your prioritization.

196

Finally, we got to the plan itself. I provided you with definitions of goals, objectives, action plans, and outcomes, as well as an annotated outline that you can use in your planning efforts.

You have learned a great deal in reading this book. Now is the time to put that knowledge into action in a coordinated, effective manner. Develop your team and write your plan. It is a lot of work, but the rewards for your organization and for the people you serve will be great. Don't skip the planning. You will regret it if you do.

☞☞ **HANDS-ON REVIEW:**
    • **How often to ask**
    • **Dating your materials**

DISCUSSION QUESTIONS FOR CHAPTER 12:

1. Do we have the right people on our marketing team? Should we add or delete anyone?

2. How can we develop an asking schedule? Should we survey and do focus groups? How can we train staff to ask, ask, ask?

3. What about an information loop? How do we assure that what the staff hears gets to where it needs to be?

4. Should we develop (update) our marketing plan? By when? Who should be responsible for this?

Final Words

You are ready to move ahead. You have the tools, the motivation, the capability to make the journey to becoming a market-driven and, of course, still mission-based organization. While the outcome is not assured, the need to make this journey is unarguable. And, a great number of people are depending on you to take the lead.

As you go through the process, you will meet barriers, and I have tried to give you the ways to avoid, and if unavoidable, surmount them. You will tire, you will be frustrated and unsure at times. That is completely natural and, I am sure, part of your daily and weekly work cycle now. I hope that this book has given you not just the tools but also the motivation to stick with it. That was my goal in writing it.

The next ten years will bring unimaginable change to every part of our economy. Our little corner, the not-for-profit world, will be no exception. The not-for-profit players in your community will change drastically year after year as new organizations spring up and some of the oldest and most tradition-bound fall by the wayside or into mission-impotence from their stubborn refusal to see what the community wants and then respond to it. "We've always done things this way" will be the cry of the doomed organization, even when what they have done is good, well-intentioned, and charitable.

The people your organization serve depend on you to be there to provide those services to them. You need to depend on them to guide you with their wants, to show you where the opportunities to serve are, and together, to move your organization, your mission, and your community to new heights of effectiveness, well-being, and success.

Our country will always need our not-for-profits. It depends on the special kind of people who work and volunteer for such organizations to be the philanthropic cement in our society — the positive role models, the keepers of the faith, the hope, and the charity that have made us a great nation. In ten years, however, we won't need not-for-profits that look just like the ones we count on today. We will need organizations that respond to what we will be then. Your organization can be such a not-for-profit if you ask, listen, and respond. In doing so, you will do much to ensure your ability to continue doing your mission. Best of luck on your journey. A lot of people are depending on you to make it a successful one.

APPENDIX A:
SWOT ANALYSIS

SWOT stands for Strengths, Weaknesses, Opportunities, and Threats, and it is a standard and very successful business organizational assessment. It allows the staff and board of your organization to look at your not-for-profit and focus on the things that are its core competencies (its strengths), the things that need improvement (its weaknesses), the areas of the organization and the market where growth may be possible (its opportunities), and the places where it may be vulnerable, both inside and outside of the organization (its threats). Such an analysis can be carried out by a group in a brainstorming session, or can be done by individuals who each fill out a SWOT analysis and then discuss their results with the group.

Let's look at each area of a SWOT analysis individually, defining what that area is, and providing you with some examples.

STRENGTH

Definition: A positive *internal* aspect of your not-for-profit that you can control.

Examples:

> *A distinctive area of competence*
> *Highly-qualified staff*
> *Excellent reputation among funders, service recipients*
> *A strong board*

Very innovative organization
Strong financials
Excellent physical plant
Strong staff training program
Culture of asking
Risk-taking encouraged
Excellent customer service

WEAKNESS

Definition: A negative *internal* aspect of your not-for-profit that you can control, and plan to improve.

Examples:

Obsolete or poorly maintained facilities
No plan or organizational direction or priorities
Weak board
Weak staff
Lack of managerial strength, training, or depth
Rigid, inflexible organization
Weak financials
Poor reputation with funders, service recipients, the public
Poor marketing material
Poor marketing skills on staff
No organizational "asking"
High administrative cost component

OPPORTUNITY

Definition: A positive *external* condition that your not-for-profit does not control, but of which you can take advantage.

Examples:

New markets to serve
New payor models to provide (managed care)
Mergers, consolidations, and collaborations with other not-for-profits
Outside businesses to partner with
Increasing competition for service recipients and funders

THREAT

Definition: A negative external condition your not-for-profit cannot control, but that you can perhaps lessen.

Examples:

Mergers, consolidations, and collaborations with other not-for-profits
New payor models to provide (managed care)
Increasing competition for service recipients and funders
Slower payment by main funders
More need for technology
Slow business cycle locally

APPENDIX B:
SURVEY SAMPLE

This is a survey that was used by an East Coast rehabilitation center to assess the satisfaction of their clients with services. It was administered by interview in the client's home, so they could get away with having it longer than usual.

Note that the numbers to the left of each question's answers are there to facilitate data entry. This was essentially a closed-choice survey. As you read it you will see that in some cases there is a mixed choice for identifying the respondents. This is because in some cases the person with the disability was the respondent and, in some cases, it was the person's advocate.

Also note that this survey does not have (nor does it need) instructions in the beginning and at the end of the survey. The reason for this is that the survey was administered by interview. If you send out surveys by mail, you *need* the instructions.

Date _____

Client name _____

Parent/guardian name _____

Client's age ____

1. Who is responding to this questionnaire? (Please circle the number.)
4   Consumer
3   Family member
2   Guardian
1   Advocate

0   Other: _____
2. Sex of respondent:
2   Female
1   Male

3. Indicate this person's primary disability.
5   Mental retardation
4   Cerebral palsy
3   Epilepsy
2   Autism
1   Other: _____
0   Don't know.

4. Where does this person live?
6   Residential facility   Please describe:_____
5   Parent's home
4   Guardian's home
3   Conservator's home
2   On his/her own (with residential support)
1   On his/her own (no support)
0   Other

5. Do you know what The Center is?
2   Yes
1   No
0   Not sure

**6. When did you/_____ (insert name of client)
first come in contact with The Center?**
5   Less than 6 months
4   6 months to 2 years
3   2 to 5 years
2   5 to 10 years
1   More than 10 years
0   Don't know.

7. Do you know your client program coordinator's name?
2   Yes
1   No
0   Don't know.

8. How well did your coordinator explain your/ _____'s rights and the services available to you?
4   Explained very well
3   Explained somewhat
2   Not well explained
1   Not explained at all
0   Don't know.

9. How satisfied are you with the assessment and the services that were recommended for you/ _____ ?
5   Very satisfied
4   Somewhat satisfied

10. Do you feel your coordinator is acting on your/_____'s behalf in obtaining services for you?
4   Yes, very much
3   Yes, somewhat
2   No, not very much
1   No, not at all
0   Not sure

11. What services are you/is _____ receiving as a result of The Center's assessment and referrals?

_____

_____

12. What providers are currently bringing these services to you/ _____?

_____

_____

13. Does The Center contact you regularly to discuss your/ _____'s progress?
3   Yes
2   No
1   Sometimes
0   Don't know.

14. Have you contacted The Center about any questions or problems you have had?
2   Yes
1   No
0   Don't know/Don't remember.

15. If YES, how helpful was the coordinator in solving your problems?
5   Very helpful
4   Somewhat helpful
3   Not very helpful
2   Not helpful at all
1   I have not contacted The Center concerning a problem.
0   Don't know/Don't remember.

16. When you call The Center with a problem or question, how soon does the client program coordinator respond?
5   Within 24 hours
4   Within 1 week -
3   Within 2 weeks
2   More than 2 weeks
1   I have not contacted The Center concerning a problem.
0   Don't know.

17. Did you feel this action was fast enough to address your situation?
3   No
2   Yes
1   I have not contacted The Center concerning a problem.
0   Don't know.

18. Are you satisfied with the amount of time your case manager spends with you/_____?
5   Very satisfied
4   Somewhat satisfied
3   Neutral/It's OK.
2   Somewhat dissatisfied
1   Very dissatisfied
0   Not sure

19. Have you/has _____ received the assistance you hoped for since you/he/she began working with The Center?

4   Yes, definitely
3   Probably
2   Probably not
1   Definitely not
0   Not sure

20. Would you refer another person with a disability to The Center?

2   Yes
1   No
0   Don't know

21. What 3 things do you think The Center does best?

_____

_____

_____

22. What 3 things do you think The Center could do better?

_____

_____

_____

APPENDIX C: FOCUS GROUP QUESTIONS

This set of focus group questions was used by a midwest rehabilitation organization to assess a potential product that it was planning to manufacture in its sheltered workshop to employ people with disabilities. The people in the focus group were furniture buyers from major stores within a 100-mile radius of the workshop. Included in this focus group was a product demonstration.

Note how the questions are open-ended, and how they move from one subject to the next. Also note that the executive director of the organization was present — which is unusual for most focus groups. He was needed to demonstrate the product and, as he was intimately involved in the product development, to hear ideas from buyers.

1. **Introduction**
   Purpose of this session
   Thank attendees
   Introduce participants
   Introduce Executive Director
   Introduce facilitator

2. **Futon Demonstration and Observation**

3. **Questions - THE PRODUCT**
   a. What is your overall impression of the product? Will it sell against the competition if competitively priced?

b. What would you change in this product? How does it compare to others you have seen?

c. What additional products or accessories might go well with the product?

d. How important are the following product features to gain competitive advantage?

FEATURE	HIGH	MED	LOW
*Quality/species of wood	___	___	___
*Quality, strength, durability of construction	___	___	___
*Fit and finish, appearance	___	___	___
*Ease of assembly and disassembly	___	___	___
*Easy folding mechanism	___	___	___
*Choice of styles	___	___	___
*Choice of stain/color/finish	___	___	___
*Price	___	___	___
*Warranty	___	___	___
*Other _____	___	___	___
*Other _____	___	___	___

4. Questions — THE MARKET
a. What are the trends in your market area over the past 18-24 months?

*Sales levels of futon products?
*Futon styles?
*Number of suppliers?
*Price?
*Quality levels?
*Choices for the consumer?
*Price?
*Types of consumers?
*Changes in distribution methods?

b. Do you have current suppliers of futons?

c. Are you happy with their service, quality, and product options?

ANY OTHER SUGGESTIONS?

WOULD YOU CONSIDER CARRYING THIS PRODUCT?

THANK YOU FOR COMING!

Index

A

Advertisements, louder, brighter, 69–70
America West, 90
Appearance of marketing materials, 160–161
Art organizations, marketing by, 3
Asking, in determining wants, 13
Asking schedule, developing, 184–187
Associations, marketing by, 3
AT&T, 28–29
Attention span, length of, 68–69

B

Benchmarks, developing baseline, 184
Bidding, in not-for-profit world, 3–4
Bid services, 125
Big-ticket marketing items, 188–189
Board meetings, using mission statement in, 48–49
Board members
 as internal market, 113
 marketing materials for, 161
 as members of marketing team, 182
 motivation of, 27–33
 as referral source, 123–124
 as source of competitive information, 124

C

CEO as member of marketing team, 181–182
Chaddock Methodist Boys School, 48

Change(s)
 as group effort, 66
 inevitability of, 64–65
 making small, 67
 pace of, in competitive environment, 67–72
 patience in making, 67
 showing mission outcome of, 65
 stretching, by making regular/ small, 63
 talking about outside, 66
Change agent, being, 65–67
Child welfare agency, mission and values of state, 49–50
Chrysler, 144
Churches
 marketing by, 3, 19–20
 researching new, 23–24
Cohort analysis, 131
Cohorts, 134
Colleges/universities, market segments in, 57
Committee approach to marketing materials, 160
Committee meetings, using mission statement in, 48–49
Competencies, evaluating core, 127
Competition
 avoiding fear of, 12
 being better than, 17–20
 evaluating, 126–127
 pace of change in, 67–72
 reality of, 30–31
 talking about, 66

Competitiveness
  in fund-raising, 4
  in not-for-profit world, 2–4, 10–25
Competitors
  desires of, 124–126
  identifying, 111–120
  and marketing cycle, 87–92
  needed knowledge on, 121–122
  researching, 122–124
Complaints, listening to, 167
Computer software, upgrading, 63
Continuous Quality Improvement
  (CQI), 56
Core values
  focusing on, 126–127
  holding on to, 49–52
Creaming, 88
Criticism
  expectations in, 143–144
  of past, 67
Currentness of marketing materials,
  160
Customers
  bathrooms for, 170
  crises of, 170–174
  founder, 108–109
  greeting, 170
  happiness of, 168
  as income source, 16
  internal, 107–108
  meeting wants of, 12–15
  parking for, 169
  payer, 108–109
  as referral source, 123
  rightness of, 15, 166–168
  risking loss of historically loyal,
    36
  safety for, 169
  service, 109
  solving problems of, 155–156,
    168–170
  treating all markets like, 106–109
  treating everyone like, 11, 15–16
  turning, into referral sources,
    176–177
Customer service
  barriers to, 107
  core rules in, 166–167

  establishing customer contact in,
    174–176
  handing customer crises in
  providing incredible, 164–179
  rightness of customer in, 166–168
  solving problems of customers in,
    168–170
Customer surveys, 186–187

D
Data
  analysis of, 145
  objective, 131
  trend, 135–136
Director of services as member of
  marketing team, 182
Direct service ideas, 125–126
Donors, 99, 124–125
  marketing materials for, 161
  as payer market, 115

E
Edifice complex, 61
80/20 rule, 94, 105, 126, 130, 175,
  187–188
Environment organizations
  making changes in, 64
  marketing by, 3

F
Facilitators for focus groups, 139
Facilities, cleanliness of, 169–170
Federal Express, 81
Fees, user, 100, 115
Financial crisis, 37
Financial flexibility, retaining, 61–62
501(c)(3) organizations, 99
Flexibility, 54–74
  need for, 55–60
  and pace of change in competitive
    environment, 67–72
  retaining capacity for, 60–65
Focus groups, 131, 138–141, 168, 189
  analyzing results between,
    140–141
  compensation for, 140
  facilitator for, 139
  focusing questions for, 139–140

homogeneity of, 140
potential uses for, 138
sample questions for, 206–208
suggestions for improving,
    139–141
time limits with, 140
Focus in marketing materials, 159
Foundations, 98
    marketing materials for, 161
    as payer market, 114
Founder customers, 108–109
Fund-raising, competitiveness in, 4

G
Gore, Al, 79
Government
    marketing materials for, 161
    outsourcing by, 3, 4
    as payer market, 97, 114
Gucci, 81

H
Health care, impact of managed care
    on, 46–47
History lesson in marketing materials,
    159
Hotel industry, market segments in,
    57–58
Human service organizations,
    marketing by, 3

I
Identifiers, limiting, in surveys,
    134–135
Income, sources of, 16
Informal asking, 141–143
Informal interaction, 131
Information
    board members as source of
        competitive, 124
    incorporating, into marketing
        plans, 146–147
    marketing material as source of,
        158
    staff members as source of
        competitive, 124
Innovations, importance of making,
    12

Insurers, 99–100
    as payer market, 115
Internal customers, 107–108
Internal markets, 96
    of not-for-profit organizations, 95
    susceptibility to competition, 112

J
Jargon, avoiding, in marketing
    materials, 158–159

K
Key funders, relationship with, 35

L
Lands' End, 173
Letterhead, changing, 63
Listening
    to complaints, 167
    in determining wants, 13–14
    importance of, 144
    in meeting customer needs, 12

M
Managed care, 56
    impact of, on health care, 46–47
Management meetings, using mission
    statement in, 48–49
Market-driven organization
    characteristics of, 11–12
    community image of, 33
    financial stability of, 34
    moving from monopoly to, 26–40
    results of becoming, 33–35
Marketing
    as competitive edge, 10–25
    defining/redefining, 88–89
    versus public relations, 154–155
    targeting efforts in, 187–189
    as team effort, 20–24
Marketing cycle
    and competitors, 87–92
    as never-ending, 37–38
    for not-for-profit organization,
        75–93
Marketing director as member of
    marketing team, 182
Marketing disability, 151–152

of most not-for-profit
organizations, 86–87
Marketing materials, 149–163
appearance of, 157
asking for money in, 159
avoiding inappropriate
photographs, 159
avoiding jargon in, 158–159
boring, 160
brevity of, 157
components of, 157–158
connecting problems and
solutions in, 157
developing different for different
markets, 160–162
focus of, 157
history lesson in, 159
as information source, 158
lack of focus in, 159
mission in, 157
out-of-date, 160
problems with most not-for-profit,
150–155
references in, 157–158
Marketing planning, 180–197
asking schedule in, 184–187
developing marketing team in,
181–184
develop rough draft in, 184
incorporating information into,
146–147
outline in, 189–195
analysis of marketing wants
in, 193
appendices in, 193
definitions in, 189–191
executive summary in, 192
goals and objectives in,
193–195
introduction in, 192
market description in, 192
marketing goals and
objectives in, 193
mission statement in, 192
planning cycle in, 191–192
service description in,
192–194

target markets and rationales
in, 193
targeting marketing effort in,
187–189
Marketing team
developing, 181–184
members of, 12, 181–182
outcomes for, 183–184
responsibilities of, 182–183
Market orientation, need for, in
not-for-profit world, 4–5
Markets
accommodating wants of, 146
conflict between mission and,
42–45
defining/redefining, 77–78
developing different materials for
different, 160–162
flexibility in changing with,
54–74
focusing on target, 104–106
identifying, 11, 94–110
internal, 96
moving with, and maintaining
mission, 45–48
payer, 96–100
retaining current, 34
reviewing, 126
service, 100–102
treating all, like customers,
106–109
using mission statements in
decisions about, 49
wants and needs of, 78–79, 89,
130–148
Market segmenting, 102–104
Marriott Corporation, 57, 173
McDonald's, 89
Media, louder, brighter, 69–70
Meeting schedules, rethinking, 64
Membership
marketing materials for, 161
of not-for-profit organization,
97–98
as payer market, 114
Mission
conflict between markets and,
42–45

maintaining, and moving with the markets, 45–48
talking about, 31
Mission-based and market-driven organizations, 41–53
Mission statement, using, 48–49
Mistakes, avoiding, 143–144
Monopoly, moving from, to market-driven organization, 26–40
Motel 6, 57
Motivation of board and staff, 27–33

N
National Public Radio's Mission and Values Statement, 50–51
Needs, difference between wants and, 12–15
Notes, keeping excellent, 168
Not-for-profit organizations
    adjusting in, 71
    bidding in, 3–4
    characteristics of market-driven, 11–12
    competitiveness in, 2–4, 10–25
    geographic names for, 2–3
    internal markets for, 95, 96
    marketing cycle for, 75–93
    marketing disability of most, 86–87
    market restrictions for, 3
    markets of, 95–102
    meeting customer wants in, 12–15
    need for market orientation in, 4–5
    payer markets for, 95, 96–100
    problems with marketing materials for, 150–155
    referral sources for, 95, 101–102
    service markets for, 95, 100–102

O
Objective data, 131
Offices, making changes in, 64
Organizational flexibility, 55–56
Outdated services, risk in providing, 35
Outside experts as member of marketing team, 182

Outsourcing, 3
    by government, 3, 4

P
Patience, in making changes, 67
Payer customers, 108–109
Payer markets, 96–100
    of not-for-profit organizations, 95
Photos, avoiding inappropriate, in marketing materials, 159
Poverty-chic, 72
Price, setting sensible, 80–82, 90
Privatizing, 3
Product cycle
    end of annual, 70–71
    length of, 70
Products
    distribution of, 83, 91–92
    evaluation of, 83–86
    promoting, 82–83, 90–91
    shaping/reshaping, 79–80, 89–90
Promises, keeping, 167
Promotion
    focusing on, 149
    of products and services, 82–83
Public relations
    focusing on, 149
    versus marketing, 154–155

R
Redecorating, 63
Reference, using customers as, 177
Referral sources, 101–102
    marketing materials for, 161
    of not-for-profit organizations, 95
    turning customers into, 176–177
Reinventing Government, 79
Research organizations, marketing by, 3
Revenue sources, developing new, 34
Risk-taking, as flexibility tool, 62–63
Ritz-Carlton Hotels, 57, 81, 173

S
Saks, 81
Segmenting, market, 102–104
Service customers, 109

Service-driven organization, results of staying, 35–37
Service markets, 100–102
  of not-for-profit organizations, 95
  using 80/20 rule for, 105
Service recipients, marketing materials for, 161
Services
  distribution of, 83, 91–92
  evaluation of, 83–86
  promoting, 82–83, 90–91
  shaping/reshaping, 79–80, 89–90
  using mission statements in decisions about, 49
Showbiz Pizza, 89
Social entrepreneurship, 62
Stability, case for, 71
Staff members
  as internal market, 113
  marketing materials for, 161
  as member of marketing team, 182
  motivation of, 27–33
  as referral source, 123–124
  as source of competitive information, 124
  surveys of, 186
Strategic plan method, 105–106
Surveys, 130, 131–138
  administration of, 137–138
  benefits of, 131–132
  brevity of, 133
  customer, 186–187
  definition of, 132
  focus of, 133
  frequency of, 133
  limiting identifiers in, 134–135
  need for professional help in developing, 137–138
  pilot-testing, 137
  providing instructions in, 132–133, 136
  question development for, 137
  questions on, 133–134
  sample in, 138, 201–205
    selection of, 137

  staff, 186
  suggestions for improving, 132–138
  thanking participants, 136
SWOT analysis, 127, 198–200
  opportunity in, 199
  strength in, 198–199
  threat in, 200
  weakness in, 199

T
Table of organization, reorganizing, 64
Target markets
  assigning team members for, 184
  concerning wants of different, 162
  contacts for, 183–184
  focusing on, 104–106
  identifying, 183
Team effort, marketing as, 20–24
Titles, making changes in, 64
Traditions, 152–153
Trend analysis, 131
Trend data, consistency in, 135–136

U
United Way, 3, 57, 98–99
  as payer market, 115
User fees, 100
  as payer market, 115
Utilities, 39

V
Values, organization, 51–52
Volunteers, 125
  as referral source, 123–124

W
Wants, difference between needs and, 12–15

X
Xerox Corporation, 47

Y
YMCA, 47, 78, 91